2.10

Series 2 / Summer 2021

Editorial collective
Claudia Aradau
Brenna Bhandar
Victoria Browne
David Cunningham
Peter Hallward
Stewart Martin
Lucie Mercier
Daniel Nemenyi
Hannah Proctor
Rahul Rao
Martina Tazzioli
Chris Wilbert

Engineers
Daniel Nemenyi
Alex Sassmanshausen

Cover image
Yafabiel, *Piedra del Peñol*, 2019

Creative Commons BY-NC-ND
Radical Philosophy, Summer 2021

ISSN 0300-211X
ISBN 978-1-9999793-9-3

Covid-19 and rebordering the world

Claudia Aradau and Martina Tazzioli

In April 2021, dozens of asylum seekers were moved back to the Napier Barracks in the UK, after the barracks had been emptied a month earlier following protests and media reports on its unsuitable conditions. Migrant support groups and NGOs denounced the 'terrible conditions of the substandard accommodation and the effects it is having on its residents'.[1] Asylum seekers organised many protests against the unliveable conditions and several started hunger strikes. In the wake of this mobilisation, the Independent Inspector of Migration, Border and Asylum also reported inadequate resources and that the 'environment at both sites [Penally Camp and Napier Barracks], especially Napier, was impoverished, run-down and unsuitable for long-term accommodation'.[2] Finally, public outcry after a Covid-19 outbreak at the barracks led the Home Office to transfer the asylum seekers to hotels where they were to wait to be transferred to an accommodation centre or a flat, according to the 'dispersal policy' that has been enforced in the UK since 1999. At about the same time, the UK government introduced hotel quarantine for travellers crossing borders from a number of countries deemed a risk for bringing 'mutant' Covid-19 variants to the UK. Notably, this continuum of hybrid forms of confinement has been enforced in the name of both migrants' and citizens' protection.

Anthropologist Didier Fassin has compared the treatment of undocumented asylum seekers and prisoners in France, observing that the latter received more attention than the former during the pandemic. While undocumented migrants were forcibly contained and confined, thus exposing them to the increased risk of Covid-19 infection, the French government simultaneously took measures to reduce the carceral population.[3] Fassin analyses these contrasting measures as indicative of moral hierarchies, which place migrants at the bottom of a scale of humanity, and the resulting politics of indifference towards migrant lives. Indeed, Covid-19 has made visible many of the hierarchies of life, while obscuring others. Yet, Fassin's distinction between incarcerated and undocumented populations leaves out the extensive use of bordering as a technique of governing in the pandemic. Responses to Covid-19 have been characterised by a *confinement continuum*. The proliferation of languages of lockdown, quarantine or self-isolation and the numerous measures taken at borders, 'vaccine nationalism' or the geopolitics of travel restrictions illustrate the heterogeneous forms of bordering and rebordering enforced by states to respond to the pandemic.

In this piece we investigate the multiplication of heterogenous bordering mechanisms during the Covid-19 pandemic and question the misleading opposition between freedom of movement and claims for equal access to public health that have followed from this. Covid-19 has not only become coterminous with borders and bordering, but it has entrenched their acceptability as techniques of governing. We argue that we need to challenge bordering mechanisms at large and that collective struggles for health cannot be divorced from collective struggles against borders and bordering mechanisms. The multiplication of borders during Covid-19 has intensified social-economic inequalities and hierarchies of vulnerability, as migrants' confinement during the pandemic highlights. Yet, with the exception of mobilisation against migrants' confinement in barracks, borders have tended to be seen as primarily a means of protection against the virus, both in public debate and on the left. A case in point is the debate within the UK Labour Party, where those who endorsed the so-called 'Zero Covid strategy', building on Australia and New Zealand as examples, advocated for border closures in the name of citizens' protection against the virus.[4]

Covid-19 has triggered a spatial crisis on multiple

levels: during the lockdown, class, gender and racial inequalities intersected and became newly visible in terms of the space that people could or were forced to live in. Cramped spaces and spatial deprivation have been among the main factors which intensified the highly unequal impact of the pandemic. As feminist abolitionist scholar Ruth Gilmore has stressed, the state's organised violence and organised abandonment have become blatant during the pandemic.[5] Yet, together with such a spatial crisis, we suggest, Covid-19 has also been a crisis of borders. Indeed, in March 2020, in the space of a few weeks, states introduced multiple border restrictions and people's movements were suddenly distinguished between 'essential' and 'non-essential'.[6] In February 2021, the UK strengthened border controls by imposing two mandatory expensive Covid tests to everyone who enters the country and a hotel quarantine system for travellers coming from countries on a 'red list'. At the same time, a travel ban has been imposed on people who exit the country 'without a reasonable excuse'. The 'reasonable excuses' to leave the UK include carrying out 'activities related to buying, selling, letting or renting a residential property'.[7]

During the pandemic, borders have not simply multiplied. Most border restrictions have been conditionally or de facto unequally enforced. The borders of Covid-19 encapsulate what Balibar has defined as the function of differentiating individuals.[8] By speaking of rebordering the world we do not, then, refer only to the re-establishment of many restrictions to freedom of movement. We use bordering here to refer to the practices of constructing, maintaining and reproducing borders and boundaries.[9] In fact, rebordering is not only about more borders: it also concerns the enactment of class-based and racialised access to mobility. Even during the moments of strictest lockdown, mobility has never been fully stopped; rather, it has been an object of deep asymmetries and inequalities – in terms of who is allowed to travel and who can actually do it, due to the costs of mandatory tests, forced quarantines and diverted routes. These asymmetries have also concerned those who continued to be forcibly moved, as deportation flights have continued throughout Europe.

Visible borders: geopolitical rebordering

Historically, pandemics and epidemics have been moments of deep economic and geopolitical restructuring. As Alison Bashford has pointed out, 'infectious disease has been central to the political, legal and commercial history of nationalism, colonialism and internationalism, as well as to the twentieth century of a newly imagined space called "the world"'.[10] In fact, the bordering mechanisms that infectious diseases have historically triggered have been not only spatial and physical frontiers, but also racialising boundaries. For instance, during the yellow fever at the end of the nineteenth century, immunity in New Orleans functioned as a criterion for redefining and strengthening modes of exploitation, exclusion and commodification of slaves.[11]

In fact, as Foucault has retraced, the responses to diseases reveal specific regimes of power and of power transformations – leprosy: sovereign power; plague: disciplinary power; smallpox: biopower and security dispositifs.[12] The ongoing rebordering of the world should be situated within this history of contagion, health and borders and, at the same time, grasped in its specificity. Yet, Covid-19 is the first pandemic that has triggered a global lockdown. Fassin has pointed out that the current health crisis 'is not unprecedented because of the pandemic, but because of the response to the pandemic. We have had worse pandemics in the past, but we have never had one for which confinement has been imposed on a global level'.[13]

The question of how to respond to the virus has largely been framed in terms of the binaries of confinement/travel, borders/freedom of movement, economy/health. Borders become tied to a neoliberal discourse of circulation, while the claims of health have been underpinned by an imaginary of protection, voluntary confinement, rights restrictions and emergency measures. Carlo Caduff asks how such interventions and lockdowns have become so widespread globally and argues that '[t]he locked-country approach seemed to obviate the necessity of justifying a differentiated strategy that might have looked unequal and unfair and that might have intensified social and political conflicts along multiple internal fractures and fault lines'.[14] Caduff's attempt to formulate a transversal critique has been a rare intervention, particularly as many scholars and activists urged against delaying lockdowns and demanded border closures in the UK. Much of the discourse on the left was formulated as demands for more or total restrictions in the name of protection, a call to render borders impermeable (for the virus): the more we close borders and restrict mobility, the argument goes, the more we regain control over the global health threat.

Borders can never be made impermeable, however, and the discourses of stopping movement versus neoliberal circulations obscured the intensification and multiplication of racialised and class-based bordering. More recently, scholars have drawn attention to how responses to Covid-19 'have relied heavily on border management and borders being rapidly reinvigorated as a key strategy to contain the virus'.[15] Borders were not only reactivated or reinforced at the state borders, but also at a whole series of levels, from the household to the city and the region. This happened despite World Health Organisation advice against travel and trade restrictions. In fact, borders have never been completely closed in Europe, even as restrictions on movement have been implemented in the Schengen area and the UK. Rather, different filtering mechanisms were brought to bear upon non-EU populations. In the EU, the initial travel 'ban' applied to non-EU countries and the new category of 'non-essential' travel.

The distinction 'essential'/'non-essential' differentiated not only social behaviour, but also movement across borders. As the 2020 harvest season was about to start, masses of seasonal workers were brought to EU countries. In April and May 2020, about 40,000 seasonal workers, mainly from Romania, were brought to Germany on special charter flights. If the category of 'essential' has applied to different forms of work throughout the pandemic, this was not the case for intimacy. Family and personal relations were subjected to border restrictions and subsequently to different practices of filtering and increased border surveillance. In the Netherlands, for instance, long-distance relationships can become exempted from the travel ban, but only under certain conditions of intensified policing of intimacy:

> You and your partner have been in a relationship for at least 3 months. Before the entry ban came into force due to coronavirus, you saw each other within your relationship at least twice in person. For example, during a stay at a house or a hotel. Or once for a period of at least 4 weeks. You have proof of this, such as airline tickets and hotel reservations.[16]

In the third lockdown in the UK, the language of 'essential travel' was subtly modified by 'reasonable excuse', so that work and study could be supplemented by 'property viewings'.[17] In the Schengen area, property took on another meaning when restrictions applied in practice mostly to those travelling by public transport, but not those driving in private cars.[18]

Different bordering techniques have governed the distribution of bodies in time and space during the pandemic. Spatial separation or segregation, for instance, supplemented delays in visas and asylum applications alongside the slowing down of movement. The other boundary that emerges is between 'governable' and 'non-governable' populations. The governable are those who embrace hygienic citizenship and sanitary borders, while those deemed potentially ungovernable need to be trained into hygienic conduct and responsibility to others or forcibly compelled into the practice of hygiene. As Bashford remarked about the governing of tuberculosis, 'new powers were created for the regulation of those persistently represented as "dangerous" and ungovernable'.[19] These lines that separated the governable from the ungovernable are drawn through 'the complicated play of race, space and power'.[20] The making of non-governable populations during the pandemic should be considered in conjunction with a politics of letting some populations die, as was the case with various vaccine campaigns – for instance, Israel not supplying vaccines to Palestinians.

The pandemic reframed questions of rights and struggles as questions of ungovernability. Those deemed incapable of self-governing became the target of militarised measures, as in the case of the Roma in Romania, Hungary, Italy or Slovakia. Lockdowns of Roma communities were often enforced by police violence and militarised presence. As the European Roma Rights Centre notes, 'Restrictions on freedom of movement made it impossible for Roma who are day labourers or dependent on the casual economy to travel to earn money'.[21] Internal frontiers became the new *cordons sanitaires* of Covid-19, while anti-Roma racism justified violence in these internal borderzones as limited to the ungovernable, the disorderly and the disruptive.[22] In Italy, evictions from Roma camps continued throughout the pandemic.[23] As Caduff noted, the generalised lockdown appeared to avoid the problem of internal fractures and boundaries by presenting the image of an undifferentiated mass – or that of equal citizens able to govern the limits of their freedom. Yet, the lockdown was an archipelago of carcerality, which multiplied borderzones along both internal and external frontiers and fragmented the territorial unity of the nation state through the proliferation of local 'red zones'. The pandemic was made governable through visible technologies of bordering and rebordering.

The 'ungovernability of migration' took centre stage during the global lockdown. In Europe, in April 2020, Italy and Malta closed their ports to migrants' disembarkation by declaring them to be 'unsafe harbours' in Covid times. For the first time, two European states closed their borders to people seeking asylum by arguing that, due to the rate of Covid infections, they were not safe territories for migrants. Even on the mainland, tactics of migration containment have been rife. Hybrid sites of confinement and detention have been used for isolating migrants in the name of their own protection, as well as the protection of citizens. In Greece, asylum seekers have been subjected to protracted forced lockdowns in refugee camps and in hotspots, while migrants who landed in Italy or who were already on the territory and who tested positive have been transferred back to the sea, on board so-called 'quarantine ships'.[24] The quarantine ships do not just isolate migrants – both those who reach Italian shores and even those who are already on the territory. They become sites of filtering and deportation.[25] In Northern Italy, buses have been used for isolating migrants. In fact, throughout the Covid-19 pandemic, humanitarian and security logics have been inflected by the logic of 'confine to protect'.[26]

However, Covid-19 did not stop, nor did it substantially decelerate, migrants' movements. Even if in 2020 there had been an overall decline in migrants' arrivals across the Mediterranean Sea, if we look at statistics in detail, we observe a shift in migrants' routes rather than a sharp drop. Arrivals from the so-called central Mediterranean route (from Libya to Italy) have largely intensified, while those from the so-called Eastern Mediterranean route (via Turkey) have decreased.[27] But the substantial drop in arrivals from Turkey was mainly caused by political tensions between Greece and Turkey, and the

Greek government's policy of border closure along the Northern land frontier. The key point is that the pandemic has impacted significantly on migrants' access to international protection, due to the multiple restrictions, obstacles and temporary suspensions in accessing the asylum procedure. In fact, asylum applications in Europe were down about 31% in 2020, compared to 2019.

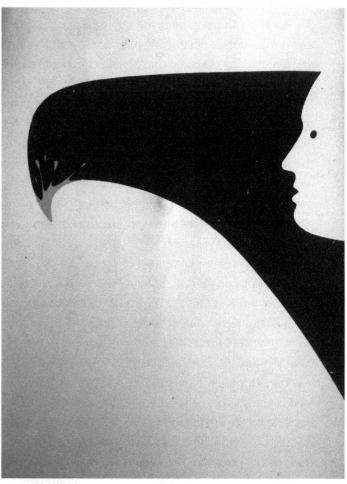

In the UK, deportations continued throughout the pandemic, even as the number of people being deported was inevitably smaller. For instance, while there were hardly any deportations to Afghanistan in 2020, there were hundreds of deportations to Albania in each quarter of 2020. Deportations also continued outside Europe, for instance, to Brazil. Most deportations were to France, under the Dublin Regulations, which were due to end in the UK on 31 December 2021. According to the Dublin Regulations, asylum seekers need to apply for asylum in the first safe country they reach.[28] The UK updated its inadmissibility criteria for asylum claims under the Dublin Regulations and recently extended the criteria to include any country that the government deems to be a 'safe third country' for an asylum seeker. Other countries such as France and Italy had recourse to earlier bilateral agreements to justify pushbacks at their borders. In its overview of 2020 activities, the European Border and Coast Guard Agency (Frontex) reported that it lent its support towards deportations so that 'Member States returned over 12 000 non-EU nationals with the support of the Agency, only 24% fewer than in 2019'.[29]

Covid-19 did not stop movement at large or make borders impermeable: rather, it intensified and multiplied the obstructions that some people face in accessing rights, protection and mobility.

Invisible heterogenous borders

The borders that have been enforced and multiplied during Covid-19 are not only geopolitical borders. One of the distinctive features of Covid-19 has been the heterogeneity of bordering mechanisms that have proliferated at different scales and across multiple sites: urban borders, social boundaries, regional and zonal borders, and hygienic borders. Such heterogeneity of bordering technologies sheds light onto the uneven spatial management of the pandemic. For instance, while in some countries – such as Italy – the lockdown has been implemented on a regional or even urban scale, in other countries it has been enforced in a more homogenous way. Overall, apart from country-by-country specificities, the pandemic has fragmented the space of the nation state, multiplying borders and bordering mechanisms within and across cities and regions.

Urban borders. The space of the city has been crisscrossed by invisible racialised and class-based boundaries. Indeed, the lockdown measures and the injunction to 'stay at home' have strengthened deep social and economic inequalities in the urban context. In London, the rate of infection peaked in the 'Covid triangle'[30] formed by the councils of Barking and Dagenham, Barking and Newham, where a high number of the population are 'essential workers' and, therefore, cannot work from home. The forced hyper-exposure to the virus and the cramped living conditions contributed to rendering that area a Covid hub. In many cities across Europe class-based boundaries have multiplied as a result of housing conditions, and unequal access to 'smart work'.

Regional/zonal borders. In April 2021, the Italian government announced a plan to gradually re-open the country after the lockdown and to loosen mobility restrictions. As part of the plan, the government will introduce a special pass to allow (some) people to move across regions. In fact, to date the mobility across the country is subjected to multiple restrictions that differ from region to region, according to a three-colour emergency system (yellow, orange and red). Such a regional-based Covid management was introduced last year to differentiate restrictions on the basis of infection rate and places available in hospitals. In the space of a few weeks, regional and local borders have fragmented and interrupted people's mobility – even if never fully stopping it.

Hygienic borders. During his New Year's message, last year Boris Johnson argued that 'for the first time, politicians taught citizens how and how often they should wash their hands'. Overall, the pandemic has enhanced another shift: bordering mechanisms and modes of governing have been structured around a hygienic-sanitary rationale.[31] That is, many border enforcement measures and restrictions to freedom of movement have been enacted and justified on the basis of hygienic reasons. In fact, public health claims have been conflated with and superseded by hygienic-sanitary norms which consist in a series of gestures: wash your hands, wear masks, maintain 'social' distance from each other. As Robert Castel highlighted in his genealogy of the hygienic-sanitary rationale, the latter had been mobilised to legitimise the introduction of 'social medicine',[32] meaning by that medicine whose main purpose was to control 'the health and the bodies of the needy classes, to make them more fit for labour and less dangerous to the wealthy classes'.[33] Hygienic-sanitary borders are nowadays accepted in the name of the fight against a 'global health threat'. In fact, it could be argued that hygienic borders consist in the disciplining and enjoining of certain gestures that people are expected to repeat during the day. By hygienic-sanitary borders we refer to bordering mechanisms which introduce or multiply exclusionary processes grounded on hygienic rules that individuals are expected to follow. Indeed, hygienic borders are enforced on an individual basis – since everyone is expected to act responsibly – and, at once, they influence and alter social relationships. That is, hygienic borders often also become borders among individuals insofar as, first, they essentially consist in keeping a distance between individuals and, second, because they generate asymmetries when some do comply with them and others do not.

Social bordering: the simultaneity of mobility restrictions, hygienic borders and unequal urban boundaries has multiplied mechanisms of social bordering, strengthening some already in place and also enacting some along new lines. In some contexts the restrictions on sociality and movement imposed by state authorities have been internalised by citizens to the point that their compliance has been guaranteed by the widespread practices of peer-to-peer surveillance. By peer-to-peer surveillance we refer to the daily practices of control and monitoring exercised by citizens over other citizens. The 'active engagement of individuals in their own surveillance' has been key to the acceptability of borders and control.[34] For instance, during the first lockdown in Italy, people have been reported to the police or filmed by their neighbours while they were infringing the Covid-19 restrictions by walking in the street 'for no essential reason'. Peer-to-peer surveillance has progressively consolidated into a social bordering practice.

A common denominator of these heterogeneous borders and bordering mechanisms is that they have been enacted and justified in the name of the 'common good'; that is, in the name of the common fight against a global health threat. Yet we would question the widespread acceptance of these multiple rebordering processes and the binary opposition between rights to mobility, on the one side, and struggles for common good, on the other. To put it in Foucault's terms, upon which conditions has this configuration of power turned out to be acceptable?[35] Moreover, how can we disrupt such widespread acceptability of bordering technologies? Caduff highlights how difficult, or even impossible, critique has become in countries like Brazil, the UK or the US, where such critical diagnosis is seen 'as playing into the hands of Trump, Johnson, and Bolsonaro, political figures who seem unconcerned with public health and staggering inequalities that afflict our world'.[36]

This is partly due to how freedoms and struggles have been isolated, and how the loss of rights has been rendered as temporary and limited to a present to be superseded by an imaginary future of health and rights. The separation between a present of lack of rights and a future of regained freedoms has also been reiterated

geopolitically. A prominent voice in the Covid-19 debates in the UK stated that 'Once richer countries such as the UK have handled and controlled their domestic problem, they must support less well-off countries in their efforts to vaccinate their populations'.[37] The relegation to the future – rather than past – of the majority of world populations obscures their exclusions from the common struggles over the present.

Holding together in the present: health and border struggles

The mobilisations of the global feminist movement *Ni Una Menos* have been characterised by a focus on the connections between different forms of violence: gender violence, border violence and state violence. During the first lockdown in 2020, *Ni Una Menos* Italy (*Non una di Meno*) insisted on the mutual connections between social reproduction, unequal access to health and border violence. Freedom of movement, they contended, should be at the core of any discussion about social reproduction, and Covid-19 has exposed the extent to which 'food distribution is dependent on migrant workers'. They argue that 'the same border regime which kills women and men confronts us with the constitutive nexus between freedom of movement and conditions of social reproduction'. The pandemic makes clear that 'freedom of movement should be at the centre of our struggles for an equal access to welfare, rights and income'.[38]

A year later, during the global feminist strike on 8 March 2021, the connections between struggles for the right to healthcare and struggles against borders have been reiterated further by *Non Una di Meno* as key claims in Covid times. In so doing, *Non Una di Meno* draws attention to the multiple bordering mechanisms which have been strengthened during the pandemic, while positing claims for freedom of movement and for equal access to health as struggles to be carried out jointly. Importantly, *Non Una di Meno* has foregrounded how racialised border restrictions regulate the conditions for social reproduction and, at the same time, make (some) people die, for instance by forcing migrants to travel along unsafe routes and by exposing some to unsafe environments during the pandemic.

As we have shown, the binary opposition between freedom of movement and health has underpinned the debate about border restrictions and has been one of the reasons for the absence of critique directed towards the rebordering of the world. Such an ethical and political impasse has, however, been unsettled by the abolitionist movement which makes claims for freedom of movement as a part of struggles for racial justice and against mass incarceration.[39] Feminist abolitionist scholars have drawn attention to the unequal and racialised access to health systems and, at the same time, have highlighted the multiplication of confinement and detention practices, often justified in the name of protection. As Angela Davis has notably stressed, an abolitionist perspective frames struggles for freedom as the overarching umbrella for different kinds of struggles – including gender struggles, anti-detention struggles and antiracist mobilisations.[40] Mobilising abolitionism as a method enables, we contend, elaborating struggles for freedom of movement outside of a liberal framework. This latter ultimately replicates individualist claims – 'I want back my unrestricted freedom of movement' – and does not question either the global inequalities in the right to mobility nor the links between 'the mobility of capital and the mobility of labour'.[41]

The current geopolitical struggle over vaccines and the rise of 'vaccine nationalisms' further complicate the discussion over freedom of movement in pandemic times. Indeed, the sheer asymmetries in vaccine distribution which happen in conjunction with the multiplication of borders foreground the importance of not disjoining struggles for freedom of movement and claims for an equal access to public health. In fact, the pandemic should be seized as an opportunity for radically rethinking health, care and the public health system, as well as patents and intellectual property which have become key to the vaccine's unequal borders. Mobility restrictions and bordering mechanisms have been justified on the basis of a blackmailing principle that posits mobility and health as in opposition to each other: if people do move, the argument goes, and in particular if they move for 'non-essential reasons', this would be detrimental to public health. Hence, a critique of Covid-19's borders, we suggest, could take as a starting point the need to hold together struggles for freedom of movement and social justice claims.

If Covid-19 has been a moment of rebordering of the world and in which racial and class inequalities have blatantly emerged or re-appeared through spatial deprivation, the possibility for critique in Covid-19 times is connected with the undoing of racialised bordering technologies. The struggle over the borders of Covid-19 is not only a spatial one. In fact, the tacit acceptance of bordering mechanisms is reinforced by the argument that giving up on freedom of movement might be necessary to ensure citizens' safety in the pandemic. Following that argument, restrictions to mobility should come first, as anytime in the future could be too late for fighting the pandemic. Against this logic, struggles against spatial confinement need to be intertwined with a radical questioning of the temporality of 'incompatible priorities' between freedom of movement and health. Freedoms relegated to an indefinite future only reinforce a present of inequality and injustice.

Claudia Aradau and Martina Tazzioli are members of the Radical Philosophy *editorial collective*

Notes

1. Care4Calais, 'Home Office to Continue Using Napier Barracks to House Asylum Seekers', 5 April 2021, https://care4cal-ais.org/news/home-office-to-continue-using-napier-barracks-to-house-asylum-seekers/.
2. Independent Chief Inspector of Borders and Immigration, 'An Inspection of the Use of Contingency Asylum Accommodation', 8 April 2021, https://www.gov.uk/government/news/an-inspection-of-the-use-of-contingency-asylum-accommodation-key-findings-from-site-visits-to-penally-camp-and-napier-barracks.
3. Didier Fassin, 'Hazardous Confinement During the Covid-19 Pandemic: The Fate of Migrants Detained yet Nondeportable', *Journal of Human Rights* 19:5 (2020), 613–623.
4. Richard Seymour, 'Give Them Freedom or Give Them Covid-19', *The New Statesman* (3 June 2020).
5. Ruth Gilmore, 'Ruth Gilmore on Covid-19, Decarceration and Abolition', Haymarket Books Public discussion, 17 April 2020, https://www.haymarketbooks.org/blogs/128-ruth-wilson-gilmore-on-covid-19-decarceration-and-abolition.
6. Elspeth Guild, 'Covid-19 Using Border Controls to Fight a Pandemic? Reflections From the European Union', *Frontiers in Human Dynamics* 2 (2020), 1–6.
7. UK Government, 'Coronavirus (COVID-19) Travel Guidance', https://www.gov.uk/guidance/coronavirus-covid-19-declaration-form-for-international-travel.
8. Étienne Balibar, *Politics and the Other Scene* (London: Verso, 2002).
9. Nira Yuval-Davis, Georgie Wemyss and Kathryn Cassidy, *Bordering* (Cambridge: Polity, 2019).
10. Alison Bashford, '"The age of universal contagion": history,

disease and globalization', in *Medicine at the Border*, ed. Alison Bashford (Basingstoke: Palgrave Macmillan, 2007), 4.

11. Kathryne Olivarius, 'The Dangerous History of Immunoprivilege', *New York Times* (12 April 2020).

12. Michel Foucault, 'Territory', *Security, Population: Lectures at the Collège de France 1977–1978* (Basingstoke: Palgrave MacMillan, 2007).

13. Fassin, 'An Unprecedented Health Crisis: Didier Fassin on the Global Response to the Covid Pandemic', 2020, https://www.ias.edu/ideas/fassin-covid-global-response.

14. Carlo Caduff, 'What Went Wrong: Corona and the World after the Full Stop', *Medical Anthropology Quarterly* 34:4 (2020), 467–87.

15. Steven M. Radil, Jaume Castan Pinos, and Thomas Ptak, 'Borders Resurgent: Towards a Post-Covid-19 Global Border Regime?', *Space and Polity* (2020), 1–9.

16. Government of the Netherlands, 'EU Ban and Exceptions', https://www.ias.edu/ideas/fassin-covid-global-response.

17. Free Movement, 'Coronavirus and the Immigration System', 18 May 2021, https://www.freemovement.org.uk/coronavirus/.

18. Home Office, 'Supplementary Written Evidence submitted by the Home Office (CHA0054)', UK Parliament. For up to date information on inadmissibility, see https://righttoremain.org.uk/the-new-asylum-inadmissibility-rules/.

19. Alison Bashford, *Imperial Hygiene: A Critical History of Colonialism, Nationalism and Public Health.* (Basingstoke: Palgrave Macmillan: 2003), 80.

20. Bashford, *Imperial Hygiene*, 92.

21. European Roma Rights Centre, *Roma Rights in Times of Covid*, September 2020, http://www.errc.org/uploads/upload_en/file/5265_file1_roma-rights-in-the-time-of-covid..pdf.

22. In Romania, the National Centre for Roma Culture Romano-Kher condemned the media coverage, which criminalised the Roma for not respecting the Covid-19 restrictions, 26 March 2020, https://romania.europalibera.org/a/reprezentan%C8%9Bii-romilor-condamna-asocierea-cu-stiri-negative-privind-coronavirusul/30510810.html.

23. European Roma Rights Centre, *Roma Rights in Times of Covid*.

24. Layli Foroudi and Federica Marsi, 'Tunisians risking their lives to escape Italy's quarantine boats', 15 April 2021, https://www.aljazeera.com/features/2021/4/15/the-tunisians-risking-their-lives-to-escape-quarantine-boats.

25. Anticra, 'Les bateaux quarantaine ou comment l'Italie enferme en haute mer' ['Quarantine Ships or How Italy Confines in the High Seas'], 22 April 2021, https://abaslescra.noblogs.org/les-bateaux-quarantaine-ou-comment-litalie-enferme-en-haute-mer/.

26. Martina Tazzioli and Maurice Stierl, 'Europe's unsafe environment: migrant confinement under Covid-19', *Critical Studies on Security* (2021), 1–5.

27. See EASO, 'Latest asylum trends 2021'; UNHCR Italy, 'Italy Weekly Snapshot', 10 January 2021, https://data2.unhcr.org/en/documents/details/84146.

28. UK Government, last update 25 February 2021, https://www.gov.uk/government/statistical-data-sets/returns-and-detention-datasets.

29. Frontex, *2020 in Brief* , 2021, https://frontex.europa.eu/assets/Publications/General/In_Brief_2020/20.0147_in-brief_2020_11th_web_fixed4.pdf, 30.

30. Raval Anjli, 'Inside the "Covid Triangle": A Catastrophe Years in the Making', *Financial Times* (5 March 2021).

31. Martina Tazzioli, 'Stay Safe, Stay Away and Put Face Masks On: The Hygienic-Sanitary Borders of Covid-19', 21 September 2020, https://www.perc.org.uk/project_posts/stay-safe-stay-away-and-put-face-masks-on-the-hygienic-sanitary-borders-of-covid-19/.

32. Robert Castel, *L'ordre psychiatrique. L'âge d'or de l'aliénisme* (Paris: Éditions de Minuit, 1976).

33. Michel Foucault, 'The birth of social medicine', in *Power: Essential Works 1954-84*, ed. James D. Faubion (New York: The New Press, 2000), 155.

34. Didier Bigo, Elspeth Guild and Elif Mendos Kuskonmaz, 'Obedience in Times of COVID-19 Pandemics: A Renewed Governmentality of Unease?' *Global Discourse: An interdisciplinary journal of current affairs* 11:1-2 (2021).

35. Foucault, *The Will to Knowledge: The History of Sexuality*, Vol. I (London: Penguin, 1998).

36. Caduff, 'What Went Wrong'.

37. Devi Sridhar, 'How the Covid Pandemic Could End – and What Will Make it Happen Faster', *The Guardian* (15 February 2021).

38. Non Una Di Meno, 'La vita oltre la pandemia' ['Life beyond the Pandemic'], 29 April 2020, https://www.dinamopress.it/news/la-vita-oltre-la-pandemia/.

39. Meera Santhanam, 'Covid-19 and the Case for Prison Abolition', 29 July 2020, https://www.chicagomaroon.com/article/2020/7/29/covid-19-case-prison-abolition/.

40. Angela Davis, *Freedom Is a Constant Struggle: Ferguson, Palestine, and the Foundations of a Movement* (Haymarket Books, 2016).

41. Sandro Mezzadra, 'MLC 2015 Keynote: What's at Stake in the Mobility of Labour? Borders, Migration, Contemporary Capitalism', *Migration, Mobility, & Displacement* 2:1 (2016).

Wounds of Democracy

Adorno's *Aspects of the New Right-Wing Extremism* and the German antisemitism debate

Jonathon Catlin

Scholars of European history and critical theory observing American politics in recent years have often found themselves experiencing déjà vu. History, the truism goes, does not repeat itself, but last summer, with calls for 'law and order' and armed right-wing militias clashing with anti-racist protestors across America, many asked, what more are you waiting for?[1] Then came the Capitol riot of 6 January 2021. The historian of fascism Robert Paxton declared that while he had until then hesitated to call Trump a fascist, the failed insurrection pushed him to do so.[2] Other historians demurred, emphasising major differences between contemporary America and interwar Europe (war, economic ruin, untested democracies): 'You can't win the political battles of the present if you're always stuck in the past', declared Richard Evans.[3] While Trump 'performed' fascism or 'aspired' to it, he did so out of weakness, not strength.[4]

The riot nevertheless bore out Sinclair Lewis's quip that when fascism comes to America it will be wrapped in the American flag and carrying a cross – or wrapped in a Confederate flag with the cross being used as a battering ram. Paxton, in fact, suggested years ago that the Ku Klux Klan could be considered the first fascist movement.[5] More recent analysis by Sarah Churchwell and Alberto Toscano confirms what many Black Marxist intellectuals have said for decades: 'American fascism: It has happened here'.[6]

The fascism analogy is not without its critics. Peter E. Gordon stressed the logical and moral necessity of analogies in all historical thinking, but cautioned that analogies can stymie analysis as much as inform it.[7] Samuel Moyn and Daniel Bessner have consistently argued that

the fascist label conveniently 'Trump-washes' recent history of deeper currents of racism and inequality of which Trump is more a symptom than a cause, and thus enabled the quietist narrative of a 'return to normal' once the aberrant Trump was removed from office, playing into the hands of America's neoliberal and imperialist 'never Trump' centre.[8] In a particularly egregious analogy, Timothy Snyder compared the 'rapid deployment teams' Trump sent to cities like Portland to the *Einsatzgruppen* or 'taskforces' that perpetrated the Holocaust by bullets.[9]

More circumspect historians like Christopher Browning argued that if there is an analogy to be made with the rise of Nazism, it is not one of a dramatic seizure of power but of conservative elites like senate majority leader Mitch McConnell selling out democracy to a would-be strongman.[10] David Bell likewise argued that Trump is not a fascist but a run-of-the-mill 'racist demagogue' and 'charismatic authoritarian'.[11] This hardly offers reassurance. As Steven Levitsky and Daniel Ziblatt have shown, there are countless ways besides fascism for a democracy to die.[12] But defeated at the polls and in the courts, Trump did ultimately leave office on 20 January. Beleaguered as it undoubtedly is, America passed Joseph Schumpeter's elegant, if reductive test of a democracy, a political system in which the people choose their own leaders. Alexandria Ocasio-Cortez memorably told her Instagram followers, 'there's no going back to brunch'. Conspiracy theories, racism, transphobia, and voter suppression continue to drive mainstream Republican politics and inspire many a gun-toting American.

Fascism within democracy

Analysing the nature of imminent right-wing threats to democracy was the *raison d'etre* of the Institute for Social Research upon its founding in Frankfurt in 1923. The *New Yorker*'s Alex Ross proclaimed shortly after Trump's election that 'The Frankfurt School Knew Trump Was Coming',[13] and the more recent publication of one of Adorno's postwar lectures attests to the ongoing relevance of critical social theory that similarly grappled with historical analogies and precedents. On April 6 1967, at the invitation of the Austrian Socialist Students' Association at the University of Vienna, Adorno gave a lecture entitled '*Aspekte des neuen Rechtsradikalismus*' (translator Wieland Hoban updates the original term, 'radicalism', with 'extremism').* Adorno spoke against the backdrop of the rise of the German National Democratic Party (NDP), a successor to the far-right Deutsche Reichspartei, which held five seats in West Germany's first Bundestag, and the Socialist Reich Party, which was declared unconstitutional and disbanded in 1952. The NDP formed in 1964 and by 1968 had gained seats in seven state parliaments, only to be defeated in the 1969 federal election by falling short of the five percent threshold required for representation in the Bundestag.

The NPD wore the clothing of a legitimate democratic party (just compare its name to some of its far-right predecessors) but underneath, Adorno said, lay 'a sadism cloaked in legal ideas' (35). For Adorno, the NPD's rise exemplified a broader problem for post-fascist democracies: 'Openly anti-democratic aspects are removed' from party platforms, while right-wing movements 'constantly invoke true democracy and accuse the others of being anti-democratic' (24) – thus restricting 'the real people', as Jan-Werner Müller has argued of populism generally, to its own adherents.[14] The historian Walter Laqueur determined that the NPD was not a 'strict conservative' party, as its leaders claimed, but also not a genuine neo-Nazi party, in which case it would have been banned.[15] While the NPD tapped into apologetics for the Nazi regime and resentment towards foreigners, it was sufficiently restrained by Germany's 'militant

democracy' that it never developed into the dynamic 'cultural synthesis' of interwar fascism.[16] Adorno analysed this resurgence primarily through the lens of the psychosocial needs it fulfilled. More often contrasting than conflating this new right-wing extremism with the 'old' fascism of the Nazis, Adorno sought to illuminate how a far-right movement could still garner popular support twenty years after the Nazis had led the country to ruin.

Adorno begins by observing that the grim thesis he made some years earlier in his influential 1959 radio address 'The Meaning of Working through the Past' had become only more evident: 'I consider the survival of National Socialism *within* democracy to be potentially more menacing than the survival of fascistic tendencies *against* democracy'.[17] In 1959 he reflected that he 'did not wish to go into the question of neo-Nazi organizations', so palpable were the legacies of Nazism itself, including the prominence of leading officials in the Federal Republic with Nazi pedigrees. However, the latent fascistic potential that 'was not yet truly visible' in 1959 had, by 1967, risen to the surface at the polls (1). Socially, if not politically, Adorno argues, the widespread potential for fascism continued to exist – just as Adorno and his colleagues had argued about America in their influential empirical study *The Authoritarian Personality* first published in 1950 and reissued by Verso last year with a new introduction by Adorno scholar Peter E. Gordon.

It has long been fashionable to chide Adorno as an apolitical 'mandarin' who, as he claimed in his last interview, was 'not at all afraid of the term ivory tower'.[18] Yet the principal reason Adorno gave for the continued possibility of fascism was hardly out of step with the view of his radical '68er students: 'the still prevailing tendency towards concentration of capital' (2). Resulting 'immiseration', he argued, put continual pressure on the petit bourgeoisie, who in turn 'want to cling to, and possibly reinforce, their privileges and social status' (9, 2). But this group lays blame for their decline not on the capitalist social order but on the spectre of 'socialism'. Since 1966, Germany's Social Democratic Party under the leadership of Willy Brandt had compromised itself in a governing coalition with the conservative CDU. Together they accounted for over ninety per cent of the Bundestag,

---

* Theodor W. Adorno, *Aspects of the New Right-Wing Extremism*, trans. Wieland Hoban (Cambridge: Polity, 2020). Subsequent references given as page numbers in the text. A recording of the original lecture can be listened to on Österreichischer Mediathek's website, https://www.mediathek.at/oesterreich-am-wort/suche/treffer/atom/014EEA8D-336-0005D-00000D5C-014E5066/pool/BWEB

creating openings for extremism on both sides of the political spectrum. The leftist student radicals of the era pursued 'extra-parliamentary opposition' to disturb political consensus and complacency. On the right, the NPD mobilised disaffected voters with slogans such as 'Now one can choose again' (27).

Above all else, Adorno says, far-right movements speak to 'the feeling of social catastrophe', which he understands as 'a distortion of Marx's theory of collapse' (9–10). Such movements 'want the catastrophe, they feed off apocalyptic fantasies' by exploiting an 'appeal to the unconscious desire for disaster, for catastrophe' (10). It has been argued that an analogous kind of despair – 'a hope gap' – led many voters to Trump in 2016; this reached a high point in Trump's 'American Carnage' inauguration speech authored by Steve Bannon.[19] While Adorno diagnosed present crises as symptoms of what Walter Benjamin called the 'permanent catastrophe' of capitalist modernity, he resisted a Spenglerian capitulation to decline that would make 'common cause with the catastrophe'.

Adorno's insights into right-wing subjectivity derive from Freudian psychoanalysis but go beyond pathologising individuals. He argues that psychological susceptibilities grow in the poisoned soil of objective powerlessness: 'the spectre of technological unemployment continues to haunt society to such a degree that in the age of automation ... even the people who stand within the production process already feel potentially superfluous ... potentially unemployed' (3). The economic troubles of the 1967-69 recession, he argues, funnelled discontent into the NPD. Insofar as its followers felt powerless to change their own fates or transform their society, they yearned instead for 'the demise of all' (11). As Volker Weiss updates this view in his afterword, 'The experience of being interchangeable as an employee can ... lead to the rightist phantasm of a "great replacement" between ethnic groups' (54).

Such trends continue to stoke xenophobic anxieties today. We still observe 'an increasing discrepancy between provincial and urban areas' when it comes to voting (6). And 'of course there are old Nazi cadres', Adorno says, but also the younger 'new right', drawn in by the idea that 'Germany has to be on top again' (7–8). In the summer of 2020, thousands of maskless, self-proclaimed 'anti-corona' protestors marched on the German capital decrying 'corona dictatorship'. As Quinn Slobodian and William Callison have shown about 'Querdenker', many such conspiracy theorists purportedly vote for a smattering of parties and reject xenophobia and Holocaust denial, yet make affirming nods to QAnon, which enjoys surprising popularity in Germany.[20] Adorno rejects the idea that such people should be dismissed as 'eternally incorrigible' or 'a lunatic fringe', for 'there is a certain quietist bourgeois comfort in reciting that to oneself' (8). Blaming a distinct group of 'deplorables' or 'fascists' lets progressives off too easily from doing the actual work of politics: building new coalitions.

By 1967, the official antifascism of the Allied occupation had long since given way to the anticommunism of the Cold War. 'Fear of the East' – of actually existing communism – manifested in the popular 'feeling of a foreign threat' (3–4). The new nationalism, Adorno says, was a compensation for Germans' 'perpetual fear for their national identity' (12). The 'unity complex' that had haunted them for centuries once again became acute under partition (12). Nationalism generally grows from a contradictory desire, the 'attempt to assert oneself in the midst of an integration' into an imagined collective (25). Adorno deems nationalism 'pathic' to the extent that it is a psychic response to defeat and has an 'aspect of selling something to people in which they themselves do not entirely believe' (5). Of course, the 'famous Hitlerian technique of the bare-faced lie' is hardly foreign to us today, either (31). Yet we learned from Trump not to mistake far-right leaders' 'low intellectual level and lack of theory' for weakness (12): on the contrary, Adorno considers 'the ideological component entirely secondary to the political will to have one's turn' (25). For, as scholarship has borne out, 'there was never a truly, fully developed theory in fascism', but rather open-ended *movements* set into motion by charismatic leaders (28). As Rahel Jaeggi has remarked of far-right voters, 'even though their real interests are not satisfied, their *ressentiment* is'.[21]

Adorno saw right-wing reliance on propaganda as the flipside of the 'blindness, indeed abstruseness of the aims they pursue' (13). What he called the 'culture industry', centred on profit and 'mass distraction' rather than truth, and continues to fuel our fake news economy today. Propaganda's combination of 'rational means and irrational ends', Adorno argues, 'corresponds to the overall tendency of civilization' that he and Max Horkheimer diagnosed in their 1947 *Dialectic of Enlightenment* (13). Thus 'real interests' are exchanged for 'fraudulent aims' peddled by agitators until 'propaganda actually constitutes the substance of politics' (13). Without a concrete basis, right-wing movements 'are somewhat akin to the ghost of a ghost', reduced to 'manipulation and coercion' (15). To be sure, when Adorno calls such movements ideologically hollow and 'essentially no more than techniques of power', his analysis suffers from the one-sidedness of the 'totalitarianism' hypothesis in his time, which over-emphasised the top-down, 'administered' power of agitators and underestimated genuine popular support (21). But today the outsize power of right-wing media to churn up resentments generate powerful feedback loops; it is not for nothing that Verso has just re-released Norbert Guterman and Leo Löwenthal's (his Frankfurt colleagues) 1949 work *Prophets of Deceit: A Study of the Techniques of the American Agitator*. Ideologically vacuous right-wing agitation continues to fuel a deluded and grandiose 'politics of catastrophe'.

Rumours and conspiracies

Adorno remarked during his American exile from Nazi Germany that antisemitism was 'the rumour about the Jews'.[22] It is also among the most stable elements of modern right-wing ideology. As Adorno wrote in 1967, 'Obviously, in spite of everything, antisemitism continues to be a "plank in the platform". It outlived the Jews, one might say, and that is the source of its own ghostly nature' (22). Officially taboo in the postwar Federal Republic, what Adorno and his colleagues called 'crypto-antisemitism' was instead conjured with a wink and a nudge: 'We're not allowed to say it, but we understand each other. We all know what we mean' (23). Adorno investigated such veiled prejudice and apologism for the Nazi regime upon returning to Germany in 1949 in his study of 'non-public opinion' *Guilt and Defense: On the Legacies of National Socialism in Postwar Germany*. Recall for a moment Trump's final campaign ad in 2016, which showed menacing images of prominent Jewish people accompanied by the following conspiratorial voice-overs: George Soros, 'those who control the levers of power in Washington'; Janet Yellen, 'global special interests'; Lloyd Blankfein, 'put money into the pockets of a handful of large corporations'.

According to Adorno and Horkheimer's theory of 'pathic projection', antisemitic prejudice is rooted in the ego-weakness of the individuals who fall prey to it. Their internal anxiety is projected onto groups who are vulnerable in a given social context. In the postwar era, Adorno writes, 'as long as one cannot be openly anti-semitic' after the Holocaust, this prejudice is veiled as anti-intellectualism, anti-cosmopolitanism, and hatred of migrant workers (21). In *The Dialectic of Enlightenment*, Adorno and Horkheimer went so far as to write that 'the blindness of antisemitism, its lack of intention' means that to a certain extent its 'victims are interchangeable: vagrants, Negroes, Mexican wrestling clubs, Jews, Protestants, Catholics' etc.; they thus conclude that 'there is no authentic antisemitism, and certainly no born antisemite'.[23] As Weiss argues in his afterword, in some respects the spectre of the Jewish threat has shifted to Islamist jihad today, suggesting that progressives would be remiss to abandon that complex subject to the xenophobic and Islamophobic far right (55).

The rise of authoritarian populism around the globe has come with a spike in antisemitic attacks from the far right, who account for a vast majority of antisemitic attacks in both Europe and the United States.[24] But this violence should not be confused with the discourse of the so-called 'new antisemitism', a dubious notion that conflates violent far-right antisemitism with legitimate criticism of Israeli policy, plays upon fears about rising Muslim and refugee populations in Europe who are assumed to be de-facto antisemitic, and mischaracterises the nature of the Boycott, Divestment, Sanction (BDS) movement.[25]

Such times lead to strange bedfellows. Yair Netanyahu, son of former Israeli Prime Minister Benjamin Netanyahu, has become a poster boy for the far-right Alternative für Deutschland (AfD) due to his condemnations of open borders, cosmopolitanism and the EU, which he has called 'evil'.[26] In the U.S., the alliance of the alt-right and evangelical Christian leaders close to Trump taught us that antisemitic Zionism is not a contradiction but a real product of resurgent ethnonationalism. Antisemitic far-right European leaders like Victor Orbán received warm welcomes in Israel by Netanyahu. This all represents a new turn. In its time the NPD exaggerated and campaigned against German reparations to Israel, which had been paid since 1952, and such antisemitic stances discredited their legitimacy. These days the AfD outdoes all other parties in its philosemitism, yet some of its leaders have also decried Berlin's Holocaust memorial as a 'monument of shame' and declared it time to end the 'cult of guilt' about the Holocaust (58).[27] Some on the far right have even characterised themselves as 'the new Jews' because they are vilified by much of German society.

This context has converged with a renewed campaign of 'anti-antisemitism' that traces back to the Antideutsche, an offshoot of German antifa defined by their concern about antisemitism and support for Israel.[28] As the lecture's translator (a progressive activist in his own right) Wieland Hoban notes, this stance has grown into an official 'antisemitism industry, in which certain theoretical models are used to endlessly repeat the same theorems, often referring to the work of Theodor W. Adorno'.[29] In April 2020, a politician from the German liberal party and then Germany's anti-antisemitism commissioner Felix Klein called for the prominent Cameroonian postcolonial scholar Achille Mbembe to be disinvited from giving the keynote at a German literary festival because of his alleged antisemitism, support for BDS, and the vague charge of 'relativising the Holocaust'. The ensuing debate continues to roil the German intellectual scene. Wielded against Mbembe was his essay, 'The society of enmity', published in *Radical Philosophy* in 2016 (RP 200), in which he writes that 'the Israeli occupation of Palestinian territories can be seen to serve as a laboratory for a number of techniques of control, surveillance and separation, which today are being increasingly implemented in other places on the planet'.[30] Mbembe also wrote the foreword to the 2015 book *Apartheid Israel*, in which he called the occupation of Palestine 'the biggest moral scandal of our times' and claims, 'To be sure, it is not apartheid, South African style. It is far more lethal. It looks like high-tech Jim Crow-cum-apartheid'.[31] Mbembe's *parrhesia* ran roughshod over German sensibilities, most prominently one codified by the International Holocaust Remembrance Alliance's controversial definition of antisemitism, which, as Aleida Assmann has noted, in its surreptitiously abridged form widely adopted in Germany conflates criticism of Israel with antisemitism.[32] Mbembe responded to the charges of the hostile German commentariat: 'I respect the German taboos, but they are not the taboos of everyone else in the world'.[33]

In a series of open letters, hundreds of academics voiced their outrage at Mbembe's racist treatment and demanded the resignation of Felix Klein. Michael Rothberg, the 1939 Society Samuel Goetz Chair in Holocaust Studies at UCLA, debunked hostile misreadings of Mbembe's work. Rothberg noted that many of Mbembe's critics assumed the framework of 'competitive memory' that his own 2009 book *Multidirectional Memory: Remembering the Holocaust in the Age of Decolonisation* had long since challenged, arguing that 'memory does not obey the logic of the zero-sum game. Rather, all memory cultures develop dialogically – through borrowing, appropriation, juxtaposition, and echoing of other histories and other traditions of memory' – notably between the Holocaust, colonial violence, and other genocides.[34] When Rothberg's book was subsequently translated into German in 2021, a 'second historians' debate' revealed even more clearly what Dan Stone calls the 'provincialisation of German memory culture which isolates the Holocaust from world history, preferring to "keep" it to themselves as a purely German phenomenon'.[35] In contrast to the ritualistic, redemptive philosemitism Dirk Moses has pejoratively called 'the German catechism',[36] Rothberg aptly reprised the counsel of the German-Jewish survivor Jean Améry that the proper attitude of Germans to the Holocaust is not one of 'mastering' the past but one of 'self-mistrust'. Rothberg's call, with the historian of Africa Jürgen Zimmerer, to 'abolish the taboo on comparison!' is emphatic in its call to *expand* German responsibility for past atrocities to include the crimes of colonialism, not to diminish it.[37]

The Mbembe affair should be understood as the first major test of a May 2019 resolution passed by the Bundestag that condemned BDS as antisemitic and called for states and municipalities to cut off organisations supporting it from public funding. An alternative resolution proposed by the philo/antisemitic and pro-Isreal AfD would have banned BDS outright! The resolution was so vaguely worded that it was broadly interpreted and overapplied to blacklist anyone with the slightest association with criticising Israel, leading to 'an expansive culture of fear and inquisition'.[38] Aleida Assmann declared that 'a spectre is haunting Europe: the accusation of antisemitism'.[39] Shortly after the resolution was passed, in June 2019, the Jewish Museum Berlin tweeted an article about a petition by 240 Jewish studies scholars opposing the resolution in the name of academic freedom. As a result, its non-Jewish director (a foremost contemporary scholar of Judaism) Peter Schäfer was forced to resign. In response, one of the museum's minority of Jewish staff, Yossi Bartal, publicly resigned 'in protest against the crass political intervention by the German government and the State of Israel in the work of the museum.'[40] Broadly, however, the passing of the resolution has been followed by self-censorship and an informal '*Berufsverbot*' (professional ban) against those with links to BDS. Hence one of the authors in a forum on the affair in the *Journal of Genocide Research* published their piece anonymously.[41]

Time and again, voices of progressive Jews, Palestinians, Muslims and people of colour have been silenced in Germany in the name of anti-antisemitism.[42] The American-born German public intellectual Susan Neiman has even doubted whether progressive, German Jews like a Hannah Arendt or an Albert Einstein, who criticised racist tendencies in Israeli politics in their time, would be allowed to speak in Germany today; the initiative for 'world-openness' endorsed by Neiman and dozens of German cultural institutions condemned the Bundestag resolution as a 'counter-boycott' to BDS that had had a chilling effect on the 'diversity of views' permissible in the German public sphere.[43] A feature in *Haaretz* illustrated how a paradoxical result of anti-antisemitic legislation is the silencing of progressive Jews, such as when an anti-Zionist university reading group run by an Israeli student in Berlin was shut down and classified as an antisemitic event alongside far-right attacks like that in Halle in 2019.[44] (And in the case of Halle, when an armed neo-Nazi was blocked from entering a synagogue, few seemed to notice that he instead shot up a nearby Turkish kebab shop and then rammed a Somali man with his car – leading Hoban to describe the incident as 'a textbook illustration of intersectional hatred: a neo-Nazi targeted the Jewish, Turkish and black communities'.[45]) When Judith Butler – a Jewish supporter of BDS who wrote about 'Israel/Palestine and the paradoxes of academic freedom' in *RP* 135[46] – was awarded the Adorno Prize by the city of Frankfurt in 2012 (the acceptance speech was published in *RP* 176), they were met with protestors proclaiming 'No Adorno Prize for antisemites!' and 'No hate for Israel in Adorno's name![47] But the issue is not limited to 'Butler Trouble'.[48] As Neiman reflected on increased concern about antisemitism

following the latest Israeli onslaught on Gaza, 'Caught in the shame of being descendants of the Nazis, some Germans find it easier to curse universalistic Jews as antisemites than to realize how many Jewish positions there are'.[49] Mbembe said in defence of his work: 'I think the time is fast coming when we will have to ask why does Germany appear to have become a laboratory for a powerful offensive against certain traditions of critical thought and progressive politics? Why is this offensive taking as its prime targets the minority voices in Europe and voices of the formerly colonised worlds? Who gains the most if indeed these voices are reduced to silence?'[50] Certainly not Europe's Jews.

Ruth Klüger, who survived Auschwitz and who passed away last year, was right to have her doubts about the alleged assurances of official Holocaust memory: 'To be sure, a remembered massacre may serve as a deterrent, but it may also serve as a model for the next massacre'.[51] Klüger later taught in Germany and bridled at the complacency she found among her students, a sense of cultural superiority for having 'mastered' their past. I recall sitting in Berlin's Haus der Kulturen der Welt in the summer of 2017 to hear Wendy Brown deliver a lecture entitled 'Democracy under Attack: Apocalyptic Populism'.[52] As she attempted to explain to a foreign audience the economic inequality, racial resentments and wounded masculinity that had made Trump's election possible, she drew upon a slew of disturbing polls indicating that America had become far more accepting of blatantly authoritarian and anti-democratic agendas, including, for example, 'the number of Americans who think it would be a good idea for the army to rule has doubled over the past two decades'. Members of the audience laughed. Amused at the seemingly unique stupidity of Trump supporters, they remained oblivious to the possibility of a similar movement amassing support in their own country. Brown's analysis held that insofar as neoliberalism was behind the rise of right-wing populism, its spread was going to be global. In the discussion, one of Brown's German interlocutors said he wasn't convinced by her analysis: It might apply to Hungary or Poland, he said, but that's an *eastern* problem. In the federal election three months later, the AfD won 12.6 per cent of the vote, making it the first far-right party to enter the Bundestag since the downfall of the Third Reich.

The myopia of some reaches of Holocaust studies

to this new political landscape is striking. Commenting on the U.S. Capitol riot, the American historian Deborah Lipstadt – the author of *Denying the Holocaust*, the basis of the film *Denial* – tweeted, captioning a photo of a neo-Nazi who had stormed the Capitol: 'Note the t-shirt: Camp Auschwitz. There is antisemitism on the left, for sure, but it[s] there on the right too'. When a leading authority on Holocaust denial and antisemitism is so consumed with searching for antisemitism on the left that she is *surprised* to see antisemitism among literal Nazis, something has gone very wrong indeed.

Contrary to Antideutsch interpretations of his work, Adorno's stance on 'relativising the Holocaust' and the interrelation of antisemitism and other racisms is clear: While he saw Auschwitz as a world-historic, even metaphysical rupture in history, he also said in a 1965 lecture that his fixation on it should be taken to refer to 'not only Auschwitz but the world of torture which has continued to exist after Auschwitz and of which we are receiving the most horrifying reports from Vietnam'.[53] The historical possibility of Auschwitz and the use of the atomic bomb, in Adorno's view of history as progress toward catastrophe, 'form a kind of coherence, a hellish unity'. In his 1967 lecture Adorno notes that some of

the same figures on the German right drawn into Nazism had earlier been complicit in 'gruesome' violence in the colonisation of Africa, and then later pivoted to Cold War anticommunism (19). For this time of racial reckoning, when streets in the German capital will finally be stripped of their racist and colonial names (my own Neukölln street was named after 'colonial hero' Hermann von Wissmann), Adorno reminds us that antisemitism most often comes together with other forms of racism. As the recently authored Jerusalem Declaration on Antisemitism, an alternative to the IHRA definition signed by over two hundred scholars, rightly claims, 'What is true of racism in general is true of antisemitism in particular'.[54] Both are still spearheaded by actual Nazis. We don't need to look far for the source of a 'new antisemitism'. It's old, and it's right under our noses.

Historicising the Frankfurt School

Adorno's lecture was a surprise bestseller in Germany when it appeared in 2019. Its prestigious publisher Suhrkamp called this handy edition a 'message in a bottle to the future', emphasising its timeliness. The volume's reception sparked a fruitful debate in German feuilletons

about how the Frankfurt School should be historicised. As Pola Gross observed, reviewers saw 'astonishing parallels' between right-wing radicalism in the 1960s and 'current developments', calling Adorno's analysis of the NPD 'frighteningly valid' when applied to the far right today.[55] *Der Spiegel* went so far as to title its review: 'What Adorno already knew about the New Right in 1967'.[56] Weiss's afterword notes that more than half a century later, 'one is struck by the continued validity of his analysis, which reads in parts like a commentary on current developments' (42). Weiss warns his reader against creating any 'simplistic equivalence' and claims that a critic must 'distinguish between context-dependent and fundamental aspects' (44). Yet he goes on to apply Adorno's words directly to both contemporary movements and to National Socialism with little contextualisation, for example, when he writes that current right-wing discourse about 'cultural Marxism ... has meanwhile taken over from the Nazi propaganda phrase "cultural Bolshevism"' (57). In 1967 the notion of 'communism' was an 'imago' or 'bugbear' – an 'elastic concept' ripe for distortion and projection (20); and indeed recent work has shown how Nazi paranoia about 'Judeo-Bolshevism' evolved into Cold War anticommunism.[57] Undoubtedly, such resonances and historical links are there for the taking. But, to return to our initial question, are we justified in employing them in what are ultimately rather sweeping analogies?

Weiss concludes with the striking claim that amidst a resurgent right-wing, 'there is no reason to historicize critical theory' as so many elements of Adorno's analysis 'can be directly transferred to offers of discussion today' (63, 61). By contrast, Magnus Klaue's cutting review in the *FAZ* reminds us, with its sardonic title, that 'Adorno was not in the Antifa'.[58] He rightly notes that Adorno criticised many of the same aspects of his era's right as its new left, with which he notoriously clashed: crude anti-Americanism and anti-intellectualism, the persecution fantasy of being silenced by the media, and the priority of political activity devoid of conceptual orientation. Adorno emphasises crucial differences between his time and the rise of Nazism in the Weimar period in order to 'avoid thinking in schematic analogies' the way both '68ers and conservatives often did through crude moral equivalences between the Holocaust and American imperialism or the Soviet gulags (16). Critical theory, he and Horkheimer stressed, is nothing without its 'temporal core'.[59] And as Klaue closes his review: 'A way of thinking is only alive if it doesn't apply to every era'.

Adorno concludes his lecture by addressing the old question of what is to be done to combat right-wing extremism. 'Aside from the political struggle by purely political means', he says, 'one must confront it on its very own turf' (39). Despite their propagandistic and ideological substance, right-wing movements can only be counteracted with the 'penetrating power of reason, with the genuinely unideological truth' (40). Lies cannot be fought with lies, but only with reflective enlightenment. In his still-untranslated 1962 lecture 'Combating Anti-semitism Today', Adorno arrived at a similar, remarkably Freudian conclusion: only 'militant Enlightenment' can break the 'spell' of prejudice by bringing its unconscious mechanisms to the light of reason, reflection and public debate. 'One should not shrink from anti-intellectual arguments', he says, but must rather speak as if to a world in which the term *intellectual* applied not to an exclusive and maligned class but to all members of humanity, for 'basically all people can be and actually should be what is generally reserved for intellectuals'.[60]

One might object, with Adorno in 1967, 'The fact that people do not fully believe in the cause does not make things any better' (15). Far-right voters, however strong their cognitive dissonance, may still vote for the far right. But in each contradiction, Adorno believed, lurks the potential resistance of reason. Strategically, Adorno says, 'the only thing that really strikes me as effective is to warn potential followers of right-wing extremism about its own consequences, to convey to them that this politics will inevitably lead its followers to their own doom too' (17). Hence, 'if one is serious about opposing these things, one must refer to the central interests of those who are targeted by the propaganda', especially youth (17).

But how effective is reason at combatting right-wing movements built on reaction and resentment? As Adorno notes in his 1954 short essay 'Ideology', 'the critique of ideology, as the confrontation of ideology with its own truth, is only possible insofar as the ideology contains a rational element with which the critique can deal', for example in the cases of liberalism or individualism. This fails in the case of movements like National Socialism that have no rational core: 'Where ideologies are replaced by approved views decreed from above, the critique of ideology must be replaced by *cui bono* – in whose interest?'[61] For our time of extreme inequality, dark money in politics, and the alliance of the conservative establishment with authoritarian demagogues, this suggests that the critique of ideology may be less important than the direct critique of power and its interests. Adorno recalls that in his study on the authoritarian personality, enemies of FDR would suddenly behave 'relatively rationally' when the subject changed to New Deal programs that benefitted them (37). This 'split in people's consciousness' remains a starting point for forming new coalitions (37).

Of course, self-reflection and criticism are not enough. Yet 'by making this a problem', by clearly articulating the contradictions at play, 'a certain naivety in the social climate has been eliminated and a certain detoxification has taken place' (39). It was this conviction that led Adorno the public intellectual to return to Germany in 1949 to critically mould the next generation through teaching and delivering over 300 public lectures and radio addresses on pressing topics, twenty more of which were recently published in a new volume from Suhrkamp.[62] In perhaps the most influential of these, his 1966 'Education after Auschwitz', Adorno also stresses the importance of cultivating love and warmth in parenting to overcome the cold, instrumental, and authoritarian forces that characterise bourgeois society.[63]

Adorno leaves us with some cause for hope: 'It is very often the case that convictions and ideologies take on their demonic, their genuinely destructive character precisely when the objective situation has deprived them of substance' (5). If Nancy Fraser is right that we find ourselves in a Gramscian 'interregnum' after the collapse of neoliberal hegemony, the winds of resentment that have filled the sails of right-wing populism in recent years may yet shift course.[64] If they do so, revealing such movements to have been vacuous all along, the opportunity arises for the left to step into its place and deliver more than empty words. In this spirit, Adorno's lecture is surprisingly emphatic about what genuine social democracy would have to entail: 'I have already told you that one should appeal to real interests instead of moralizing; I can only repeat it once more' (37). With its 'socio-economic content' still unrealised amidst widespread precarity and inequality, 'democracy has not yet become truly and fully concrete anywhere but is still

formal' – and, of course, not always even that (8). 'In that sense', Adorno says, 'one might refer to the fascist movements as the wounds, the scars of a democracy that, to this day, has not yet lived up to its own concept' (9). In the cruel shadow of right-wing reaction nursing its wounded attachments, Adorno sees democracy's promise waiting to be fulfilled by material social transformation.

Jonathon Catlin is a PhD Candidate in the Department of History and the Interdisciplinary Doctoral Program in the Humanities at Princeton University. From 2019–2020 he was a Fulbright Scholar based at Berlin's Leibniz-Zentrum für Literatur- und Kulturforschung.

Notes

1. Dylan Riley's influential piece 'What Is Trump?' emphasised the (then missing) essential ingredient of paramilitary violence to interwar European fascism, *NLR* 114 (Nov/Dec 2018).
2. Robert Paxton, *The Anatomy of Fascism* (New York: Knopf, 2004), 49; and 'I've Hesitated to Call Donald Trump a Fascist. Until Now', *Newsweek* (11 January 2021).
3. Richard J. Evans, 'Why Trump isn't a fascist', *New Statesman* (13 January 2021).
4. Masha Gessen, 'Donald Trump's Fascist Performance', *New Yorker* (3 June 2020); William E. Connolly, *Aspirational Fascism* (Minneapolis: University of Minnesota Press, 2017).
5. Robert Paxton, *The Anatomy of Fascism* (NY: Knopf, 2004), 49.
6. Sarah Churchwell, 'American Fascism: It Has Happened Here', *NY Review of Books* (22 June 2020); Alberto Toscano, 'The Long Shadow of Racial Fascism', *Boston Review* (28 October 2020).
7. Peter E. Gordon, 'Why Historical Analogy Matters', *New York Review of Books* (7 January 2020).
8. See Daniel Bessner and Udi Greenberg, 'The Weimar Analogy', *Jacobin* (17 December 2016); Samuel Moyn interviewed by Len Gutkin, 'The Fascism Question', *Chronicle of Higher Education* (11 January 2021); and Samuel Moyn, 'The Trouble with Comparisons', *New York Review of Books* (19 May 2020).
9. Timothy Snyder, 'Him', *Slate* (18 November 2016) and 'Take it from a historian', *The Guardian* (23 July 2020).
10. Christopher R. Browning, 'The Suffocation of Democracy', *New York Review of Books* (25 October 2018).
11. David A. Bell, 'Trump is a racist demagogue. But he's not a fascist', *The Washington Post* (26 August 2020).
12. Steven Levitsky and Daniel Ziblatt, *How Democracies Die* (New York: Crown, 2018).
13. Alex Ross, 'The Frankfurt School Knew Trump Was Coming', *The New Yorker* (5 December 2016).
14. Jan-Werner Müller, *What Is Populism?* (Philadelphia: University of Pennsylvania Press, 2016).
15. Walter Laqueur, *Fascism: Past, Present, Future* (Oxford: Oxford University Press, 1996), 113.
16. Anson Rabinbach, 'Unclaimed Heritage: Ernst Bloch's Heritage of Our Times and the Theory of Fascism', *New German*

Critique 11 (Spring 1977), 5–21.

17. Adorno, 'The Meaning of Working through the Past', *Critical Models*, trans. Henry W. Pickford (NY: Columbia, 1998), 89–103.

18. Theodor Adorno, 'Who's Afraid of the Ivory Tower?', *Monatshefte* 94:1 (Spring 2002), 10–23.

19. Andrew McGill, 'Hope Is What Separates Trump Voters From Clinton Voters', *The Atlantic* (19 August 2016).

20. William Callison and Quinn Slobodian, 'Coronapolitics from the Reichstag to the Capitol', *Boston Review* (12 January 2021).

21. Rahel Jaeggi and Nancy Fraser, *Capitalism: A Conversation in Critical Theory* (Cambridge: Polity, 2018), 218.

22. Adorno, *Minima Moralia*, (NY: Verso, 1974), 110.

23. Adorno & Horkheimer, *Dialectic of Enlightenment* (Stanford: Stanford University, 2002), 140, 272.

24. Joel Swanson, 'The ADL's data proves it: The right owns anti-Semitism in America', *Forward* (13 May 2020).

25. Brian Klug, 'The Myth of the New Anti-Semitism', *The Nation* (15 January 2004); Esra Özyürek, 'German Muslims' "Shocking' Response to the Holocaust", *Haaretz* (1 February 2021).

26. 'Netanyahu's Son Becomes Star of German Nationalist Party After Calling EU "Evil" ', *Haaretz* (8 May 2020). See also Susan Neiman, 'Ignoranz aus Scham', *Die Zeit* (26 May 2021).

27. See Petr Bystron, 'The two pariahs, Israel and AfD, should work together', *Arutz Sheva* (18 Sept. 2019).

28. Sarah E. James, 'Anti-Anti-Semitism or the "Alt-Right"?' *Art Monthly* 440 (October 2020). For a philosophical critique of anti-antisemitism, see Elad Lapidot, 'A Critique of Anti-Antisemitism', *Tablet* (19 May 2021).

29. Wieland Hoban, ' "They're also accusing Jewish people of antisemitism"', *TheLeftBerlin* (14 March 2021).

30. Achille Mbembe, 'The society of enmity', *Radical Philosophy* 200 (Nov/Dec 2016).

31. Achille Mbembe, Foreword to *Apartheid Israel: The Politics of an Analogy* (Chicago: Haymarket Books, 2015), viii.

32. Aleida Assmann, 'A Spectre is Haunting Germany: The Mbembe Debate and the New Antisemitism', *Journal of Genocide Research* (4 December 2020).

33. Sonja Zekri, 'Ich respektiere die deutschen Tabus', *Süddeutsche Zeitung* (14 May 2020).

34. Michael Rothberg, 'The Specters of Comparison', *Goethe Institute/ Latitude* (15 May 2020).

35. Dan Stone, 'In Germany, Coming To Terms With Its Past Is An Ongoing Struggle', *Rantt Media* (27 April 2021).

36. A. Dirk Moses, 'The German Catechism', *Geschichte der Gegenwart* (23 May 2021).

37. Michael Rothberg and Jürgen Zimmerer, 'Enttabuisiert den Vergleich!', *Die Zeit* (30 March 2021).

38. Emily Dische-Becker, Sami Khatib and Jumana Manna, 'Palestine, Antisemitism, and Germany's "Peaceful Crusade"', *Protocols* 8 (December 2020).

39. Aleida Assmann, 'A Spectre is Haunting Germany: The Mbembe Debate and the New Antisemitism', *Journal of Genocide Research* (4 December 2020).

40. Yossi Bartal, 'Why I Resigned From Berlin's Jewish Museum', *Haaretz*, 22 June 2019.

41. Anon., 'Palestine Between German Memory Politics and (De-)Colonial Thought', *Journal of Genocide Research* (2020).

42. Irit Dekel and Esra Özyürek, 'Perfides Ablenkungsmanöver', *Die Zeit* (2020); 'What Do We Talk About When We Talk about Antisemitism in Germany?', *Journal of Genocide Research* (2020).

43. Susan Neiman, 'Hannah Arendt dürfte heute hier nicht sprechen', *Deutschlandfunk* (2020); 'Antisemitism, Anti-Racism, and the Holocaust in Germany: Discussion between Susan Neiman & Anna-Esther Younes', *Journal of Genocide Research* (2021).

44. Itay Mashiach, 'In Germany, a Witch Hunt Is Raging Against Critics of Israel', *Haaretz* (10 Dec. 2020).

45. Wieland Hoban, 'Germans on Israel: Undermining Anti-Racist Solidarity', *TheBattleground.eu* (5 November 2020).

46. Judith Butler, 'Israel/Palestine and the paradoxes of academic freedom', *Radical Philosophy*, 135 (Jan/Feb 2006).

47. Barbara Goldberg, 'Protest gegen Adorno-Preis für Judith Butler', *Jüdische Allgemeine* (11 September 2012).

48. Shaul Magid, 'Butler Trouble: Zionism, Excommunication, and the Reception of Judith Butler's Work in Israel/Palestine', *Studies in American Jewish Literature*, 33:2 (2014), 237–259.

49. Susan Neiman, "'Von den Deutschen lernen": Ignoranz aus Scham', *Die Zeit* (26 May 2021).

50. René Aguigah, 'The conviction and conscience of Achille Mbembe', *New Frame* (23 April 2020).

51. Ruth Klüger, 'The Future of Holocaust Literature', *German Studies Review* 37:2 (May 2014), 391–403, 392.

52. Wendy Brown, 'Democracy under Attack: Apocalyptic Populism', lecture at Berlin's Haus der Kulturen der Welt (2017)

53. Adorno, *Metaphysics: Concepts and Problems*, trans. Edmund Jephcott (Stanford: Stanford University, 2001), 101–104.

54. 'The Jerusalem Declaration on Antisemitism', https://jerusalemdeclaration.org.

55. Pola Groß, 'Stilisierung zum Kuschel-Philosophen. Zur Rezeption von Adornos "Aspekte Des Neuen Rechtsradikalismus" ', ZfL-Berlin Blog (27 January 2020).

56. Benjamin Moldenhauer, 'Was Adorno 1967 schon über die Neue Rechte wusste', *Der Spiegel* (6 August 2019).

57. Paul Hanebrink, *A Specter Haunting Europe: The Myth of Judeo-Bolshevism* (Cambridge: Harvard University Press, 2018).

58. Magnus Klaue, 'Adorno war nicht in der Antifa', *Frankfurter Allgemeine Zeitung* (30 August 2019).

59. Theodor W. Adorno and Max Horkheimer, *Dialectic of Enlightenment* (Stanford: Stanford University, 2002), xi.

60. Theodor W. Adorno, 'Zur Bekämpfung des Antisemitismus Heute', *Vermischte Schriften I* (Frankfurt: Suhrkamp, 1986), 382.

61. Thanks to Johannes von Moltke for the reference. Adorno, 'Ideology', *Aspects of Sociology* (London: Heinemann, 1973), 190.

62. Adorno, *Nachgelassene Schriften. Abteilung V*, ed. Michael Schwarz (Berlin: Suhrkamp, 2019). On Adorno as a public intellectual, see Michael Schwarz, ' "Er redet leicht, schreibt schwer": Theodor W. Adorno am Mikrophon", *Zeithistorische Forschungen* 8:2 (2011), 286–294; and Harry F. Dahms, 'Adorno's Critique of the New Right-Wing Extremism: How (Not) to Face the Past, Present, and Future', *disClosure* 29 (2020).

63. Adorno, 'Education after Auschwitz', *Critical Models* (NY: Columbia University, 1998), 191–204.

64. Nancy Fraser, *The Old is Dying and the New Cannot be Born* (NY: Verso, 2019).

Counter-violence, a 'Hegelian' myth

Minor variations on the master-slave dialectic

Matthieu Renault

Beyond a doubt Hegel knew about real slaves and their revolutionary struggles. In perhaps the most political expression of his career, he used the sensational events of Haiti as the linchpin in his argument in *The Phenomenology of Spirit*. The actual and successful revolution of Caribbean slaves against their masters is the moment when the dialectical logic of recognition becomes visible as the thematics of world history, the story of the universal realisation of freedom.[1]

These sentences are taken from Susan Buck-Morss' essay 'Hegel and Haiti', first published in 2000. The main thesis of Buck-Morss' essay can be succinctly summarised: Hegel, one of the major figures of German Idealism, had drawn inspiration from the Haitian Revolution – the struggle to the death of the slaves of Saint-Domingue against their white masters – when composing the famous dialectic of mastery and servitude [*Herrschaft und Knechtschaft*] in *The Phenomenology of Spirit*, which was published in 1807, just three years after Haiti's independence. As is well known, this phenomenological sequence seeks to give an account of the passage from consciousness (of something) to self-consciousness as one that entails the encounter, confrontation and conflict with another consciousness. A struggle for recognition ensues between these two consciousnesses, one that from the outset takes the form of a battle to the death. And yet, Buck-Morss argues, while 'bringing into his text the present, historical realities that surrounded it like invisible ink', Hegel concealed his abolitionist Caribbean source.[2] The reality of the self-emancipation of the plantation slaves, accomplished in the wake and in the shadow of the French Revolution, was implanted in the text, if only to better philosophically nullify the potentially subversive effects of this reality, to better suppress it.

By way of proof, Buck-Morss emphasises that Hegel had attentively followed the events of Saint-Domingo from the autumn of 1804 to the end of 1805 as they were recounted in the journal *Minerva*, which had 'informed its readers not only of the final struggle for independence of this French colony – under the banner of Liberty or Death! – but of events over the previous 10 years as well.'[3] That 'freedom cannot be granted to the slaves from above', that the 'self-liberation of the slave is required through a "*trial by death*"', this had been demonstrated in the act of the Haitian Revolution. It is this 'trial by death' endured to the end by the Haitian slaves that Hegel would have had in mind when writing: 'The individual, who has not staked his life, may, no doubt, be recognized as a Person' – in the legal sense, 'the agenda of the abolitionists!', remarks Buck-Morss – 'but he has not attained the truth of this recognition as an independent self-consciousness'.[4] And so Buck-Morss concludes:

> Given the facility with which this dialectic of lordship and bondage lends itself to such a reading one wonders why the topic Hegel and Haiti has for so long been ignored. Not only have Hegel scholars failed to answer this question; they have failed, for the past two hundred years, even to ask it.[5]

Even if we put to one side the dispute over this failure by Hegel scholars – which pitted Buck-Morss against the Cape Verdean philosopher Pierre-Franklin Tavares, who had published an article in 1992 entitled '*Hegel et Haïti, ou le silence de Hegel sur Saint-Domingue*' [Hegel and Haiti, or Hegel's silence on Saint-Domingue][6] – it should still be noted that as early as 1975, in the appendix to the second volume of his monumental history of slavery, *The Problem of Slavery in the Age of Revolu-*

tion, David Brion Davis initiated a dialogue between the master-slave dialectic and the Haitian Revolution by depicting a 'partly imaginary' struggle to the death between Napoleon and Toussaint Louverture. Although this 'elemental struggle' culminated in Toussaint's capitulation and surrender, the Haitian Revolution was nonetheless the proof of the truth of the 'message' bequeathed by Hegel, namely, that 'man's true emancipation, whether physical or spiritual, must always depend on those who have endured and overcome some form of slavery.'[7] This comparison re-emerged a decade later when the Haitian sociologist Laënnec Hurbon maintained that, although '*The Phenomenology of Spirit* ignores Toussaint Louverture ... [h]istory seems to prove Hegel right.'[8] The Hegelian completion of the experience of Western consciousness in the Napoleonic State-Empire was being replayed, in parallel, mirrored, and accelerated so to speak, on another stage, with the creation of the state of Haiti, soon followed by the coronation of Jean-Jacques Dessalines as Emperor.

Deborah Jenson has recently evoked the figure of Dessalines in order to push Buck-Morss' thesis further still. Jenson stresses that the journal *Minerva* did more than narrate the events at Saint-Domingue in the third person. It also published Dessalines' texts and speeches, including extracts from his military field journal and the declaration of independence signed by himself. In Dessaline's acceptance of his imperial nomination, he used the following words:

> Citizens, if anything to my eyes justifies this august title your trust has bestowed upon me, it is without a doubt my zeal to ensure the salvation of the empire and my will to consolidate our enterprise, an enterprise that will give the nations who are least friendly to freedom the image of us not as a passel of slaves, but as men who cherish their independence even in the knowledge that the major powers never grant it to people who, like us, are the artisans of their own liberty, men who have no occasion to beg for foreign assistance to break the idol to which we were sacrificed.[9]

According to Jenson, this and other declarations by Dessalines prefigured the Hegelian *leitmotif* of a freedom that can never be given but must be conquered in the heat of struggle. Insofar as there would be, not only 'something of Haiti', but also 'a lot of Dessalines' in Hegel, it becomes necessary to listen for the 'proto-

Hegelian resonance of [Dessalines'] proclamations.'[10] Jenson thereby portrays a Hegel who had ventriloquised Dessalines: what is silently expressed in the very texture of *The Phenomenology of Spirit* – this story of European modernity's painful birth, described by Hegel as a 'voyage of discovery' – would be nothing other than its darker side, and the *voice* of the black slave who risked his life and won his emancipation.

Since its publication, Buck-Morss' essay has received both praise and criticism. The latter essentially falls into two categories. For some, as Buck-Morss herself remarks, 'the very suggestion of resurrecting the project of universal history from the ashes of modern metaphysics appeared to collude with Western imperialism'.[11] In a well-known move, the history of non-European peoples found itself placed under the yoke of European thought. For others, it is the empirical-historical corollary of Hegel's 'Mastery and Servitude' that is the problem – that is, whether such a corollary, in the singular, can be identified at all. Andrew Cole, for example, holds that the German term *Knecht*, as used by Hegel, refers much more immediately to the serf of still feudal Germany at the turn of the nineteenth century than to the plantation slaves, for whom Hegel elsewhere uses the term *Sklave*.[12]

It is nevertheless surprising that amongst the readers of Buck-Morss, her critics included, few have remarked upon the fact that Hegel's 'Mastery and Servitude' does not actually concern a struggle to the death of slave against master. As Hegel narrates it, the struggle to the death is that founding struggle which gives shape to the figures of master and of slave-servant. Equality, or at least equivalence, is the starting point, inequality or domination is the result. The reversibility of this process is untraceable in Hegel's account. If, in this chapter, the Hegelian slave is already proceeding along the path of his emancipation, it is only through his servile work, carried out under the influence of the fear of death instilled in him by the master, through which he starts to gain his autonomy, laboriously achieving his own self-consciousness. Moreover, this emancipation is fundamentally incomplete and the master-slave dialectic quickly gives way to stoicism (chapter 4b), to scepticism and finally to the 'unhappy consciousness' divided within and against itself. Nowhere in these passages does a struggle to the death destroy slavery. Since the master-slave relation is nevertheless considered as a transhistorical concrete universal, it is only thanks to an interpretative forcing that the passages which Hegel devoted to the French Revolution and its aftermath, the Terror, could be re-interpreted as the definitive abolition of the relation of mastery and servitude depicted several hundred pages before. We will flush out the party 'guilty' for this in what follows.

Buck-Morss certainly hints at having recognised as much, when in echo of the last lines of 'Mastery and Servitude', she declares: 'Hegel's text becomes obscure and falls silent at this point of realization. But given the historical events that provided the context for *The Phenomenology of Spirit*, the inference is clear.' And this inference is the following: 'Those who once acquiesced to slavery' after a first struggle till death, 'demonstrate their humanity when they are willing to risk death rather than remain subjugated.' Fearing the philosophical-political consequences of this inevitable conclusion, Hegel would have balked at 'taking the next step to revolutionary practice', the second struggle to the death, for emancipation. Well before the European proletarians, 'Hegel knew' that the slaves of Saint-Domingue were 'taking this step for him.'[13] Regardless of whether this inference is judged to be legitimate or not, it ultimately places the burden of proof on the meaning given to an absence, a silence. It is up to us to fill in this gap, which remains by its very definition, open to multiple and competing interpretations.

However novel Buck-Morss' thesis may be, it has none of the 'facility' its author attributes to it. Rather, it presupposes a set of mediations that provide its conditions of possibility. The thesis, as will become clear, is the fruit of Hegelianism's long intellectual and political history in the twentieth century, a history marked by an inversion, or at the very least by a split, of the phenomenological stage of the trial by death, such that the latter came to be conceived not only as what *produces* relations of mastery and servitude, but also and indissolubly as what one must pass through in order to undo them. Not only did the idea of emancipatory violence thereby come to the fore, but so did the idea that this final violence, ultimate in every sense of the word, sounds the death knell for a first and founding violence, albeit through endlessly repeating and re-enacting this violence within oppressive structures. In other words, the violence of the oppressed, of the slave, was destined to be defined

as counter-violence. The formation of this 'Hegelian' paradigm of counter-violence is what we propose to re-trace step by step, by restoring, if not its entire history, then at least the main scansions within it.

Future perfect: Frederick Douglass in Hegelian (Davis, Gilroy)

The year is 1969. Angela Davis is hired to teach philosophy at the University of California. She will soon be fired for her communist affinities, then charged in the Soledad Brothers affair. After several weeks on the run, she will be arrested and ultimately acquitted of all charges. In the autumn of 1969, for her first-term course, she proposes to study the 'recurrent philosophical themes in black literature', the first of which is a re-examination – in light of this literature – of a classical concept of European philosophy: freedom. From the outset, Davis notes that such a re-examination necessarily implies rethinking the relation between the theory and the practice of freedom, defying their systematic disassociation in Western history – the presence of slavery in the age of Enlightenment being the most striking proof of this.[14] In her first lectures, Davis takes as her object the autobiography of Frederick Douglass, the former slave and a prominent figure of the abolitionist struggle in the U.S. The first edition of this work was published in 1845 and, in conjunction with the rediscovery of slave narratives from the nineteenth century, it has fuelled an abundant critical literature both within and beyond the field of black studies since the 1960s.[15]

Although we must wait until the end of the second lesson to see Davis make explicit reference to *The Phenomenology of Spirit*, one need not be a Hegel scholar to discern that her reading – centred on the mutations of the slave's (self-)consciousness and revealing the progressive inversion of the relation of dependence between the slave and his master – is deeply marked by the Hegelian thematisation of the mastery and servitude relation. For Davis, it is not so much a question of applying the Hegelian thematisation to a supposedly particular instance – 'black' in this case – as it is of testing it against Douglass' lived experience. Within Douglass' narrative, Davis first of all discovers, or rediscovers, the idea that 'the first condition of freedom is the open act of resistance – physical resistance, violent resistance.' '[V]iolent retaliation' here not only indicates that the slave refuses to be physically enslaved, but first and foremost that he refuses the 'definitions of the slave-master', that is, the image of himself that the slave-owner once furnished, such that the 'journey from slavery to freedom' undertaken by Douglass was indissolubly 'physical' and 'spiritual'.[16]

This is demonstrated in what Davis judges to be 'the most crucial passage' of Douglass' autobiography.[17] The scene unfolds when an already recalcitrant Douglass is consigned to the 'slave-breaker' Covey, who is charged with the task of returning Douglass to the straight and narrow by crushing any trace of resistance in him, by destroying any form of conscience or desire. Douglass suffers Covey's violence until one day, on the brink of annihilation and about to be whipped once more, he decides to defend himself:

> [B]ut at this moment – from whence came the spirit I don't know – I resolved to fight; and, suiting my action to the resolution, I seized Covey hard by the throat; and as I did so, I rose ... My resistance was so entirely unexpected, that Covey seemed taken all aback. He trembled like a leaf. This gave me assurance, and I held him uneasy, causing the blood to run where I touched him with the ends of my fingers ... We were at it for nearly two hours. Covey at length let me go, puffing and blowing at

a great rate, saying that if I had not resisted, he would not have whipped me half so much. The truth was, that he had not whipped me at all ... The whole six months afterwards, that I spent with Mr. Covey, he never laid the weight of his finger upon me in anger. This battle with Mr. Covey was the turning-point in my career as a slave. It rekindled the few expiring embers of freedom, and revived within me a sense of my own manhood. It recalled the departed self-confidence, and inspired me again with a determination to be free.[18]

Initially, Davis is concerned with the consequence of this struggle for the master himself. Covey, she emphasises, is certainly physically strong enough to overpower Douglass, who is only 16 at the time, in hand-to-hand combat. Rather, he proves himself incapable of responding to the slave's unexpected resistance. At that exact moment, Covey comes to realise that he is dependent on the slave, not only for his subsistence, but also for the definition of his own identity as master. What he discovers in the struggle is that 'he is no longer the recognised master, the slave no longer recognises himself as slave.'[19] And it is precisely this rupture in the unilateral, vertical relation of recognition of the slave towards the master which, so to speak, meant that, for Covey, the battle had been lost before it had even begun.

At the end of her second lesson, Davis announced that during her next session, she would discuss the effects of the struggle from the slave's point of view.[20] Unfortunately, Davis' 'Lectures on Liberation', such as they were published, end there. There is little doubt, however, that Davis considered this scene of the struggle to the death with the master as the pivotal moment, if not the final stage, of Douglass' liberation. Little doubt, in other words, that she conceived of the slave's counter-violence, his 'eye for an eye, tooth for a tooth' response to the master's violence, as representing for Douglass the supreme form of resistance to slavery. For reasons that are easily understood, in light of the extreme exploitation founding plantation slavery, the master-slave dialectic here finds itself amputated from Hegel's central thesis concerning the nature, at once alienating, formative and partly liberating, of servile work. Davis puts in its place the motif of the slave's struggle to the death for his emancipation, which, it bears noting once more, is absent in Hegel.[21]

Whether consciously or not, it fell to Paul Gilroy to resume where Davis left off. Like Davis, Gilroy accords supreme importance to the battle between Douglass and

Covey, paying specific attention in his *The Black Atlantic* (1993) to the passage that follows immediately on from our previous citation.

> The gratification afforded by the triumph was a full compensation for whatever else might follow, even death itself. He only can understand the deep satisfaction which I experienced, who has himself repelled by force the bloody arm of slavery. ... It was a glorious resurrection, from the tomb of slavery, to the heaven of freedom. ... I now resolved that, however long I might remain a slave in form, the day had passed forever when I could be a slave in fact. I did not hesitate to let it be known of me, that the white man who expected to succeed in whipping, must also succeed in killing me.[22]

In the Hegelian narrative of mastery and servitude, the slave is he who, in the course of an originary struggle, has refused to risk his life and has given in to the fear of death, choosing life over the freedom of consciousness. In doing so, the slave 'voluntarily' submits to his adversary, the latter thereby becoming his master. Gilroy observes that: 'Douglass's version is quite different. For him, the slave actively prefers the possibility of death to the continuing condition of inhumanity on which plantation slavery depends.'[23] He prefers dying to a continued life lived in slavery, that is, to survival. In this manner, Douglass' narrative can be read, in Gilroy's words, as an 'alternative', a 'supplement if not exactly a trans-coding' of the Hegelian master-slave dialectic. The radical inversion of the relation to death in the slave, but also in the master – since, if Covey was defeated, it was first of all because he feared for his life – signals the translation of 'Hegel's meta-narrative of power' (from the standpoint of the oppressor) into 'a meta-narrative of emancipation' (the standpoint of the oppressed).[24] Inextricably, it signals the transformation of enslaving violence into liberating counter-violence.

Since Davis' and Gilroy's seminal readings, there has been a proliferation of more or less successfully interlaced analyses of Hegel's chapter on 'Mastery and Servitude' and Douglass' narrative, some of which have been carried out in order to question the legitimacy of such a connection.[25] What is surprising in these interpretations, Gilroy's included, is that they suggest that Douglass would have situated himself in relation to Hegel, either with and/or against him. Even if we were to put to one side the fact that in the middle of the nineteenth cen-

tury *The Phenomenology of Spirit* was, in comparison with *The Science of Logic*, only a marginal work in the Hegelian corpus, and that no one had accorded a pre-eminent position or even specific status to the section on 'Mastery and Servitude', not even Marx as we will see, there can be no doubt that at the moment when he was drafting the first version of his autobiography, Douglass had no knowledge of Hegel's writings. Certainly, he was later granted privileged access to Germanic culture though his relationship with the militant feminist and abolitionist Ottilie Assing, a German immigrant in America. In 1871, the same Assing wrote a letter to the then almost 80-year old 'young Hegelian' Ludwig Feuerbach, singing the praises of his *opus magnum*, *The Essence of Christianity*, by stating that it had provoked in Douglass, 'one of the most famous men in America', a 'total reversal of his attitudes' on religion and the church, making possible his conversion to atheism.[26] Eight years later, she further encouraged Douglass to recount in a new version of his autobiography how the 'helping hand' of Feuerbach had allowed him to '[break] the chains of a second bondage': slavery to God.[27] But this relation to a 'Left Hegelian' like Feuerbach only makes it more obvious that, for Assing and even more so for Douglass himself, there was never a question of referring his 'first' or actual enslavement to Hegel's philosophy. If we wish to grasp what has authorised the invention of a posthumous dialogue between Douglass and Hegel, we must go back in time, before the versions of Gilroy and Davis.

The (second) struggle till death: the work of counter-violence (Fanon)

Return to 1952, the year Frantz Fanon's *Black Skin, White Masks* was published. If, throughout his book, Fanon confronts Hegel's master-slave dialectic head-on, and compares it to the reality of colonial racism, this confrontation culminates in the seventh and final chapter, 'The Black Man and Recognition', specifically in its second section, 'The Black Man and Hegel.' Fanon's thesis is well known by now. He argues that the black man, or at least the black man of the French colonies, the Caribbean ones in particular – in his terms the 'Black Frenchman' (*le Noir français*) – remains a slave, be that a slave with no master, but rather an 'imaginary' master, since the black man has never risked his life in a struggle to the death for recognition: 'There is no open conflict between White and Black'; '[o]ne day the white master recognized without a struggle the black slave.'[28] Fanon may not say so explicitly but no doubt he is thinking here of the abolition of slavery, which would have conferred upon the black man only a false sense of recognition and a troubled self-consciousness, since, quite simply, this recognition was bestowed upon him by the other and not won for himself.

> Out of slavery the black man burst into the lists where his masters stood. ... The black man did not become a master. When there are no more slaves, there are no masters. The black man is a slave who was allowed to assume a master's attitude. The white man is a master who allowed his slaves to eat at his table.[29]

It was the white man who decided to 'promote some men-machine-beasts to the supreme rank of *men*', it was not the black man himself who raised himself to humanity. 'The upheaval reached the black man from the outside. The black man was acted upon ... [He] does not know the price of freedom because he has never fought for it.'[30]

Historically, abolition resulted in the petrification of the dialectical process of the slave's (self-)emancipation. Fanon thematises this anti-dialectic, which after the abolition of slavery, at least in the context of the French colonial empire, governs relations between whites and blacks. In the United States of America, where racism is at its height and where whites do not even bother to pretend to recognise blacks as equals, the latter are engaged in the true process of liberation: 'There are battles, there are defeats, truces, victories.'[31] In contrast, where open conflict is, or at least seems to be, impossible, the black man comes to interiorise the image of the master, to identify with him: he hides his black skin behind a white mask; a split which could be reinterpreted in terms of the Hegelian figure of unhappy consciousness, as has been the case with W.E.B. Du Bois' motif of double consciousness.[32] That, however, would be another chapter in the story of Hegelian or counter-Hegelian re-readings of black radical thought, underway now for half a century.

In order to support the idea that a struggle to the death against the master is absolutely necessary, Fanon cites those same passages of *The Phenomenology of Spirit* to which Buck-Morss will refer: 'The individual, who has not staked his life, may, no doubt, be recognised as a Person; but he has not attained the truth of this recognition as an independent self-consciousness.'[33] And as Buck-Morss will, Fanon extracts this from the phenomenological context of Hegel's text, where the struggle constitutes, rather than destitutes, the figures of master and of slave. Indeed, Buck-Morss' hypothesis implicitly rests on a Fanonian reading of Hegel. However, she also turns this reading against itself. Whereas Fanon maintains that the struggle to the death between the slaves and their masters never took place, Buck-Morss declares that, at least in one instance, it gloriously did, and furthermore that this struggle provided Hegel with an archetype of all other such struggles.[34]

One such Hegelian substratum still feeds the famous theory of violence set out in *The Wretched of the Earth*. For Fanon, the Algerian War of Independence was in many regards the realisation of this struggle to the death against the master that the black Caribbean was incapable, still, of engaging in. And there is a reason why anti-colonial violence is defined, at least in the initial phase of the struggle, as counter-violence: 'The violence of the colonial regime and the counter-violence of the colonized balance each other and respond to each other in an extraordinary reciprocal homogeneity ... Violence among the colonized will spread in proportion to the violence exerted by the colonial regime.'[35] Initially at least, the violence of the colonised is nothing more than colonialism's extreme, everyday violence turned against itself. It is an 'ironic return of things': a backlash.[36] This struggle to the death is, in fact, the necessary, if not sufficient, condition for the abolition of colonialism's founding violence: it is the reverse of colonial conquest, committed as this was to the erasure of history.[37]

In *Black Skin, White Masks*, Fanon asserted that unlike the Hegelian slave, who 'loses himself in the object and finds the source of his liberation in his work', the black man 'abandons the object' in the desire to be 'like his master.'[38] In the context of slavery and colonialism, it is problematic, to say the least, to invest work with emancipatory virtue. However, in *The Wretched of the Earth* Fanon does appeal to a form of work: 'for the colonized this violence is invested with positive, formative features because it constitutes their only work.'[39] Undoubtedly, this is a reference to the formative – in the sense of the term *Bildung* – function that work, for Hegel, takes on for the self-consciousness of the slave. Except that for

Fanon, there is no other work than the work of a struggle to the death; no work that is not the work of violence.

From this perspective there is one major difference between the Fanon of *Black Skin, White Masks* and the Fanon of *The Wretched of the Earth*. The former perceives the dilemmas of a recognition *as man* that means recognition *as white*, and yet he continues to conceive of the struggle to the death as a struggle for recognition, and as a point of departure for a process of reconciliation: 'I can already see a white man and a black man *hand in hand.*'[40] The latter declares instead a prohibition on seeking the recognition of the coloniser as a preliminary condition for the emancipation of the colonised; in place of colonialism's relentless enforcing of 'divide and rule', there must be, before all else, a mutual recognition between the colonised/slaves, a learning to recognise one another.[41] This 'horizontal' self-recognition unfolds in battle, a battle that seeks the abolition, not only of the figure of the master/coloniser, but also of the conditions of (neocolonial/endogenous) reproduction of (colonial/exogenous) forms of 'vertical' recognition. 'Horizontal' recognition implies that the turn to violence that defines the beginning of the anti-colonial struggle is succeeded by a transformation of violence, inextricable from the reinvention of work itself, in its anthropological, economic and political sense: the task of decolonising bodies and minds, extending well beyond the struggle for political-national independence.

It is clear that the Fanonian appropriation of Hegel has played, and continues to play, a determinate role in subsequent anti-racist reconfigurations of the master-slave dialectic. However, Fanon neither introduced nor invented the dominant motif of the second struggle to the death, the struggle of the slave for his emancipation, which, as has been emphasised here, from an exegetical perspective, is nowhere to be found within Hegel. Fanon took this moment for granted. That is, he inherited it. But from whom? A final step backwards is required in order to answer this question.

At the origins of the myth: Hegelian variations (Marcuse, Kojève)

The pivotal year is 1932, the year Marx's *1844 Manuscripts* are finally published. The young Herbert Marcuse immediately produces an extended analysis of them,

discovering a clear filiation between Hegel's chapter on 'Mastery and Servitude' and the Marxist conception of alienated labour under capitalism – in other words, a filiation between Hegel's slave-servant and Marx's labourer-worker, and, furthermore, between the master-slave dialectic and the schema of class struggle, such that the latter would be the translation of the former from a Marxist perspective.[42] As a *topos* of critical philosophy, this idea still persists today, although Chris Arthur has long since shown it to be nothing more than a 'myth of Marxology'.[43] However, as is often the case with the history of ideas, the 'truth' here has little weight when faced with the formidable productivity of this Hegelian-Marxist matrix, which for decades has been a veritable machine for the production of an apparently inexhaustible variety of discourses on oppression and emancipation, extending well beyond the remit of the Marxist sphere *stricto sensu*. If this is a 'myth', it should not be understood (only) in a negative sense, as we will soon see.

This Marx-Hegel connection is fundamental to the invention of that 'supplement' to the master-slave dialectic that is the struggle to the death for liberation. Think only of Engels' *Anti-Dühring*, a Marxist catechism for a whole generation of communists and still a point of reference, albeit critically, for Fanon in *The Wretched of the Earth*. If violence is first of all that of a founding and then conserving (bourgeois) state power, Engels equally conceives of the inversion of the 'internal state power' into an emancipatory and revolutionary counter-violence, carried out by the very forces engendered by capitalism itself: 'violence [*Gewalt*], however, plays yet another role in history, a revolutionary role; ... in the words of Marx, it is the midwife of every old society pregnant with a new one.'[44] Violence is, to cite the concluding paragraphs of the *Communist Manifesto,* the conduit for the 'overthrow of all existing social conditions.'[45]

It is significant in this regard that in 1970, Davis – a student and friend of Marcuse, then a Jewish immigrant in the States – sent him a letter from prison, asking if he would agree to write a preface for the publication of her *Lectures on Liberation*. Confessing that he was ill at ease with discussing a work on 'a world to which I am still an outsider', Marcuse nevertheless praised Davis' effort to 'translate' the philosophical concept of 'human freedom' into the language of the struggle of black people and of 'the oppressed everywhere'; and for having deftly demonstrated, in the act, the Hegelian thesis of the reversal of the relationship of dependence between master and slave which they had studied together in his seminar: 'In your lecture … Hegel's philosophical analysis comes to life in the struggle in which the black slave establishes his own identity and thereby destroys the violent power of the master.'[46]

The principal character responsible for the invention of the Hegelian Marxist master-slave dialectic was however not Marcuse, but another philosopher, the Franco-Russian Alexandre Kojève, who from 1933 to 1939 gave what would become a legendary seminar at the EPHE (*École pratique des hautes études*). It was above all Kojève who, in a Heideggerian-inspired crypto-Marxist vein, isolated the Hegelian narrative of mastery and servitude in order to reconstitute it as an autonomous dialectic. Whereas to Hegel it was but a 'moment' in a process from which it could not be extricated, Kojève instead made it the dynamic principle within spirit's whole procession traced in *The Phenomenology of Spirit*, both its origin and end. Kojève identified this procession with the 'anthropogenetic' history of humanity; a history that began with the formation of a master-slave relation and which ended, or which would end, with its definitive abolition.

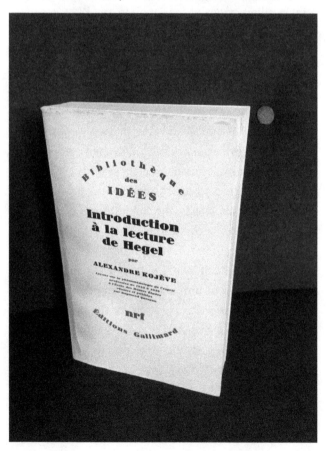

For Kojève, the liberation of the slave-worker entails that he makes the master's warrior principle – the principle of risk to life – his own, and consequently the 'murder' of the other, or at least its possibility, generates a synthesis of the 'servile element of work' and the 'element of the Struggle over life and death', a synthesis of the master and the slave which Hegel names the 'citizen', warrior and worker, labourer in arms, of the Napoleonic State.[47] After having 'gratuitously' projected the grammar of mastery and servitude onto Hegel's reflections on the French Revolution, Kojève could easily 'demonstrate' that the master-slave dialectic culminated in a second great struggle to the death, which devastated the figures of master and slave, and which was nothing other than the repetition by inversion of the original struggle to the death for 'pure prestige' that had first led to their creation. It was then Kojève who, in a true *tour de force*, introduced the 'Hegelian' motif of revolutionary counter-violence.

It should be noted, moreover, that for Kojève the revolutionary moment proper had not been 1789, since the already crumbling monarchy had died a natural death, albeit a death lightly precipitated by Enlightenment propaganda. Rather, it was 1793, the Terror. He assures us that for a long while there had been only 'slaves without masters' of flesh and blood, slaves of God or of capital, nothing but the rich or poor bourgeois – hardly an orthodox Marxist assertion. Under these conditions, the risk to life could no longer take the form of a 'class [struggle] properly [speaking], a war between the Masters and the Slaves.'[48] The 'slave' could only free himself definitively through a 'bloody struggle for recognition.'[49] '[T]he working Bourgeois, turned Revolutionary' for this reason had to create 'the situation that introduce[d] into him the element of death.'[50] He had to stake his life, and that of others, for nothing; let blood flow without reason or, at least, without an apparent reason. The French Revolution thus simply expressed the law of all revolutions – which Kojève seems to have problematically extracted from the Russian Soviet experience, including that of Stalinism – namely, their division into two moments: 'A great revolution is always bloodless at its outset; no trace of struggle. The old regime succumbs to an illness.'[51] But this initial phase must be followed by a 'second stage', the stage of a 'violent collective death' marked by a 'fury of annihilation.'[52] 'Liberation without a bloody Struggle, therefore, is metaphysically impossible'[53] because it is 'the murderous war [that] guarantees historical freedom and the free historicity of man.'[54]

If those who come to inherit this rewriting of the Hegelian narrative of mastery and servitude remain largely unconcerned by such an apology for the Terror, the fact still remains that subsequent appropriations of the master-slave dialectic will be nourished by Kojève's attribution of an intrinsic value to revolutionary violence as a deliberately assumed 'trial by death', not only as a means or instrument of social transformation, but also as what drives real psychological revolution, a mutation in the consciousness of the slave. Foremost among these, without doubt, is Fanon. As Sartre observed, Fanon identified the logic of terror functioning at the very heart of the (anti) colonial war: 'Terror, counter-terror, violence, counterviolence. This is what observers bitterly report when describing the circle of hatred which is so manifest and so tenacious in Algeria.'[55]

Although this is not the place for a genuine demonstration, I am nevertheless convinced that Kojève should be (re)read less as a historian of philosophy and more as the creator of a myth (or a variant of the multifaceted Western myth of modernity) conceived of not merely as a conventional fiction, but in a properly anthropological sense. This is a myth that has permeated and informed critical thought all the more profoundly in that it did so anonymously. Kojève was meticulous in obscuring the true nature of his intervention and the distortion of Hegel's text it involved. Like the Lévi-Straussian myth, the Kojèvian narrative operates through a proliferation of fixed and opposed terminological pairs, and tends to reintroduce a binary logic into the heart of the Hegelian (ternary) dialectical logic, in a sense de-dialectisising the dialectic, divesting it of its essential fluidity. Such a (re)binarisation of the Hegelian dialectic has its roots in Kojève's 'ontological dualism' (mind *versus* nature, man *versus* animal), which, as Judith Butler notes, is fundamentally alien to Hegelian thought.[56] Anthropogenesis, the becoming human of man, is in effect defined by Kojève as the process through which man, throughout the whole of history, extricates himself from his animal condition, sublating (at once suppressing and conserving) nature within him and around him. Thus, it seems that the old theme of the opposition between nature and culture, and in particular the passage from the first to the second, is (re)played here – this passage being, for Lévi-

Strauss, at the foundation of all myth. Moreover, the teleological schema so commonly attributed to Hegel is here rendered more complex by a 'mythical', circular conception of history, which ends with a brutal return to the animal condition, albeit in a fully humanised, that is, technological world. More importantly, Kojève puts forward a cyclical conception of absolute knowledge that, despite his own endeavour to dichotomise science and myth (especially the myth of faith), performs a loop back to primitive 'mythological' and 'magical' reason.'[57]

In a letter written in late 1948 to Tran Duc Thao, Kojève blithely confided in the latter, writing that his reading of Hegel 'was intended as a striking piece of propaganda', continuing: 'For this reason I deliberately bolstered the role of the master-slave dialectic and, in a general manner, schematised the content of the phenomenology.'[58] However, this form of schematisation must be understood not only in the standard sense of simplification or vulgarisation – although it was certainly that and deliberately so – but also as an attempt to formalise the dynamic relations of mastery and servitude. What Kojève develops could be characterised as a combinatorics of so-called constitutive elements of human existence – first and foremost, 'struggle' and 'work', as activated and modulated by the relation to 'death' – thereby authorising a game of substitution, permutation, inversion and reconfiguration of terms, characters, functions and relations, which enabled everyone to rewrite their own variation of the myth, according to their lived experience and standpoint. More precisely put, it enabled the oppressed to don the garb of the Hegelian slave in order to rethink the very forms and conditions of their self-emancipation. Kojève was certainly the first to emphasise that *as a dynamic* the Hegelian relation of mastery and servitude could only be articulated from within the slave's situated perspective, and that, whereas mastery had revealed itself to be an 'existential impasse',[59] being therefore without history, servitude presented itself as the source of all becoming, human history being nothing but the long and painful process of the slave's liberation: 'If idle Mastery is an impasse, laborious Servitude, in contrast, is the source of all human, social, historical progress. History is the history of the working slave.'[60]

It is from this perspective that we should reconsider the multiple minoritarian appropriations that were forged from the master-slave dialectic (feminist, anti-racist and, in part, Marxist), minor appropriations in a Deleuzo-Guattarian sense that extend far beyond the names cited here, and that persist well after the 'death sentence' pronounced by professional French philosophers on a Hegelian myth, Deleuze himself leading the charge. These re-engagements, moments of dis-engagement here included, should be analysed as theoretical-political translations, or, to pastiche Lévi-Strauss' *Mythologies,* as musical variations on a theme.[61] There is no doubt that the motif of the emancipatory struggle to the death or revolutionary counter-violence has played a decisive role in these minor transformations of the master-slave dialectic. From this viewpoint, even Buck-Morss' and other contemporary attempts to excavate the true historical sources of the Hegelian scheme of mastery and servitude appear as nothing but new mythical variations. Beginning (presumed) and end (provisional) coincide: exegesis proves to be part of myth-making.

Let us conclude by anticipating a potential objection. Lévi-Strauss makes clear that the choice of a myth or one of its variations is always arbitrary, at least 'ontologically', if not methodologically or 'strategically'.[62] That is to say, any other variant could justifiably fulfil this function. There is no such thing as an 'authentic or primitive' or 'true version'.[63] Expanding on this, Eduardo Viveiros de Castro remarks in *Cannibal Metaphysics* that, to the extent that any original theme disappears, there are strictly speaking only variations, processes of reciprocal translation and permanent displacements.[64] Surely, as we have shown, Hegel's *Phenomenology of Spirit* should not be considered as an origin in this sense, but at most, and *ex post*, as itself a variant, whose undeniable privilege relies not on the fact that it was the so-called 'first version', but rather that the philosopher and the text are an integral part of the very myth as it also describes the genesis of absolute knowledge, which means its own creation. Still, by retracing a genealogy of the 'Hegelian' motif of counter-violence, we did indeed set out to find the origins of the myth, which we in the end localised on the old continent, with Kojève. There is no denying that a tension or perhaps a contradiction between the historical (genealogical) and the mythological perspectives persists within this interpretation, but here I would like to adopt Lévi-Strauss's remarks in relation to his own analyses of myths, namely that, in the final instance,

they were new variations on these very myths.[65] This is a statement already made in 'The Structural Study of Myth' with regard to the Freudian interpretation of the Oedipal myth.[66] As such, what we have produced is a myth of the origins of the 'Hegelian' myth of mastery and servitude: a meta-myth, as it were, that unlike the Lévi-Straussian analysis does not even claim to make 'explicit' what the other variants only 'embodied'. In other words, the structure of the myth has not been 'revealed to itself' here, nor its transformations suspended.[67] This meta-myth is then conceived of as nothing more than a new chapter in the history it tells, certainly not its conclusion.[68]

Translated by Olivia Fairweather and Marie Louise Krogh

Matthieu Renault is Reader in Philosophy at the University of Paris 8 Vincennes-Saint-Denis, and a member of the Laboratory of Studies and Research on Contemporary Logics of Philosophy (LLCP). Recent publications include L'empire de la révolution. Lénine et les musulmans de Russie *(2017).*

Notes

1. Susan Buck-Morss, 'Hegel and Haiti', *Critical Inquiry* 26:4 (Summer 2000), 852. The following article is a revised version of a paper presented under the title 'La contre-violence, un mythe "hégélien" (Fanon, Douglass, Toussaint Louverture)' at the symposium 'Focus sur les révoltes anticoloniales (Martinique – Guadeloupe – Réunion)'. The latter took place on 3 October 2018 at the Fondation Maison des Sciences de l'Homme and was organised by the members of the Caribbean worlds and transatlantic movements research group (Linda Boukhris, Christine Chivallon, Didier Nativel) and by Elsa Dorlin.
2. Buck-Morss, 'Hegel and Haiti', 846.
3. Buck-Morss, 'Hegel and Haiti', 835.
4. Hegel quoted in Buck-Morss, 'Hegel and Haiti', 849.
5. Buck-Morss, 'Hegel and Haiti', 849.
6. Pierre-Franklin Tavares, 'Hegel et Haïti ou le silence de Hegel sur Saint-Domingue' [Hegel and Haiti, or the Silence on Saint Domingue], *Chemins critiques* 2 (May 1992), 113–31. In this regard, see the letter from Tavares to Jean Ristat published in *L'Humanité* 2 Decembre 2006, accessed 3 February 2020, https://www.humanite.fr/node/361462. Note that in her essay, Buck-Morss mentions Tavares' work but confides that she has not had the opportunity to read the article in detail and the thesis in question. See Buck-Morss, 'Hegel and Haiti', 843–4n72.
7. David Brion Davis, *The Problem of Slavery in the Age of Emancipation, 1770-1823* (Chicago: Chicago University Press, 1999), 12, 558–60, 564.
8. Laënnec Hurbon, *Comprendre Haïti. Essai sur l'État, la nation et la culture* (Paris: Karthala, 1987), 63. Les Classiques des Sciences Sociales, accessed 26 May 2021, http://classiques.uqac.ca/-

contemporains/hurbon_laennec/comprendre_haiti/comprendre_haiti.pdf

9. Jean-Jacques Dessalines, 'Acte d'acceptation par le gouverneur-général de sa nomination à la dignité impériale', 15 février 1804 ['Acceptance of his Imperial nomination by the Governer-General', 15 February 1804], reprinted in Louis Boisrond-Tonnerre, *Mémoires pour servir à l'histoire d'Haiti* (Paris: France Libraire, 1851), 9. [Translator's note: Partial translations of this paragraph can be found in Deborah Jenson, *Beyond the Slave Narrative. Politics, Sex and Manuscripts in the Haitian Revolution* (Liverpool: Liverpool University Press, 2011), 97 and 142.]

10. Deborah Jenson, *Beyond the Slave Narrative*, 97–98; Deborah Jenson, 'Hegel and Dessalines. Philosophy and the African diaspora', *New West Indian Guide*, 84:3-4 (2010), 269–75.

11. Susan Buck-Morss, *Hegel, Haiti and Universal History* (Pittsburgh: University of Pittsburgh Press, 2009), ix.

12. Andrew Cole, *The Birth of Theory* (Chicago and London: Chicago University Press, 2014), 65. See also Alain Badiou, 'Hegel's Master and Slave', trans. Frank Ruda, *Crisis and Critique* 4:1 (March 2017), 34–47. Much ink has been spilled, and not only in French, over the translations of Hegel's *Knecht* ('valet', 'servant', 'serf' or even 'slave'), and, to a lesser extent, of *Herr* ('lord' or 'master'), a translation conundrum that we have only barely touched upon here. The fact however remains that these translation issues are intimately linked with the problematic of the variations of the 'master-slave' dialectic which will emerge at the conclusion of the present analysis.

13. Buck-Morss, 'Hegel and Haiti', 848–9. On this point, see also Sibylle Fischer, *Modernity Disavowed: Haiti and the Culture of Slavery in the Age of Revolution* (Durham, NC: Duke University Press, 2004), 27–8.

14. Angela Davis, 'Lectures on Liberation', in *Narrative of the Life of Frederick Douglass, An American Slave, Written by Himself* (San Francisco: Open Media Series/City Light Books, 2010) 45–7.

15. Davis makes use of the third edition of Douglass' autobiography, *Life and Times of Frederick Douglass* (1881, revised in 1892). As regards this article, references are to the first version as it has been translated into French. This poses no great consequence in terms of the content, since the later editions are essentially augmented and extended versions of the first, including the later parts of Douglass' life.

16. Davis, 'Lectures on Liberation', 49, 52.

17. Davis, 'Lectures on Liberation', 81.

18. *Narrative of the life of Frederick Douglass, an American slave, written by himself* (Cambridge, MA: The Belknap Press of Harvard University Press, 2009), 77–8.

19. Davis, 'Lectures on Liberation', 79, 82–3.

20. Angela Davis, *Lectures on Liberation* (Los Angeles: National United Committee to Free Angela Davis, 1971), 24. This last paragraph does not appear in the recent reprint of Davis' lectures.

21. In her introduction to the new edition of Douglass' narrative, Davis, emphasising the use she could have made in her lectures on the Hegelian master-slave dialectic, admits that she regrets having ignored the meaning of manhood in Douglass' account, nowhere more explicit that in the physical confrontation with Covey: 'In fact, today I find it simultaneously somewhat embarrassing to realise that my UCLA lectures on Douglass rely on an implicitly masculinist notion of freedom, and exciting to realise how much we have matured with respect to feminist analysis since that period.' (Davis, 'Introduction', in *Narrative of the Life of Frederick Douglass*, 28). Nevertheless, let us note that as early as 1971, Davis published an essay in *The Black Scholar* on 'The Black Woman's Role in the Community of Slaves', still imbued with Hegelian or Hegelian-Marxist influences, in which work, 'productive activity', has a positive function for the formation of the 'black woman's consciousness', to the extent that, although it was still enslavement, it was nevertheless 'proof of her ability to transform things' and to reveal to her 'the oppressor's utter dependence on her.' Angela Davis, 'The Black Woman's Role in the Community of Slaves', *The Black Scholar* (December 1971), 6.

22. *Narrative of the life of Frederick Douglass*, 78.

23. Paul Gilroy, *The Black Atlantic: Modernity and Double Consciousness* (London and New York: Verso, 1993), 63.

24. Gilroy, *The Black Atlantic*, 60.

25. Particularly notable in this respect is the thesis of Cynthia Willett, who claims that the phenomenology of the Black American consciousness has, historically, developed according to a dialectic that differed significantly to Hegel's, particularly with regard to the 'transformation of the self' and 'social change'. This 'second dialectic' would already be at work in Douglass, whose autobiographical narrative shows that the Western conception of freedom – an ascetic conception based in the supposed contradiction between, on the one hand, natural life and bodily desire, and on the other, freedom and reason – is foreign to the mainstreams of African-American culture. According to Willett, Douglass' violent struggle against Covey is not a risking of death but an affirmation of life. See Cynthia Willett, *Maternal Ethics and Other Slave Moralities* (New York and London: Routledge, 1995), in particular, chapter 5, 'Hegel's Master Narrative of Freedom and the African American Experience', 103–27, and chapter 6, 'A Slave Narrative of Freedom. Frederick Douglass and the Force of Manhood', 129–56. However, one does wonder whether such claims of an 'outside' to Western thought really does something other than restage the binary oppositions that structure it internally.

26. Ottilie Assing, Letter to Ludwig Feuerbach, 15 May 1871, cited in Maria Diedrich, *Love Across Color Lines: Ottilie Assing and Frederick Douglass* (New York: Hill and Wang, 1999), 259–60.

27. Ottilie Assing, Letter to Frederick Douglass, 6 January 1879, in *Radical Passion: Ottilie Assing's Report from America and Letters to Frederick Douglass*, ed. Christoph Lohmann (New York: Peter Lang, 1999), 351.

28. Frantz Fanon, *Black Skin, White Masks*, trans. Richard Philcox (New York: Grove Press, 2007), 191.

29. Fanon, *Black Skin, White Masks*, 194.

30. Fanon, *Black Skin, White Masks*, 194–5. Translation amended.

31. Fanon, *Black Skin, White Masks*, 196. Translation amended.

32. See in particular Shamoon Zamir, *Dark Voices: W. E. B. Du Bois and American Thought, 1888-1903* (Chicago: Chicago University Press, 1995), 143.

33. Fanon, *Black Skin, White Masks*, 194.

34. Why does the Haitian revolution remain in the shadows within Fanon's work? At least two interlacing reasons for such an occlusion can be teased out, one 'positive' and the other 'negative'. First, and this is a *leitmotif* in *Black Skin, White Masks*, Fanon is clearly mindful not to make the *present* emancipation of black people dependent upon the past, however glorious it may have been: 'Whether we like it or not, the past can in no way be my guide in the actual state of things.' (Fanon, *Black Skin, White Masks*, 200. Translation amended.). While one must know how to take on the past, in order to overcome it, this past cannot be exclusively black, rather it is the past of all of humanity: 'I am a man, and I have to rework the world's past from the very beginning. I am not just responsible for the slave revolt in Saint Domingue' (201) – this reference to the Haitian revolution being a hapax in Fanon's oeuvre. Second, while it is known that his library contained an edition of C.L. R. James' *The Black Jacobins: Toussaint L'Ouverture and the San Domingo Revolution* – see: 'Frantz Fanon's library' in Frantz Fanon, *Alienation and Freedom*, eds. Jean Khalfa and Robert J.C Young (London: Bloomsbury, 2018), 738 – Fanon remained reliant upon a white-colonialist-capitalist historiography (one prefix is in this regard as good as another), which had systematically either ignored or denounced as savage those revolts that punctuate the history of slavery and colonisation. In other words, Fanon to a large degree remained dependent upon a representation of non-Europeans that cast them as the passive matter of a world history that so far had been made entirely by the peoples of Western Europe.

35. Frantz Fanon, *The Wretched of the Earth*, trans. Richard Philcox (New York: Grove Press, 2004), 46.

36. Fanon, *The Wretched*, 42. Translation amended.

37. Fanon, *The Wretched*, 42.

38. Fanon, *Black Skin, White Masks*, 195n10.

39. Fanon, *The Wretched*, 50.

40. Fanon, *Black Skin, White Masks*, 194.

41. Fanon, *The Wretched*, 50.

42. Herbert Marcuse, 'The Foundation of Historical Materialism' in *Studies in Critical Philosophy*, trans. Joris de Bres (Boston: Beacon Press, 1973), 1–48.

43. Chris Arthur, 'Hegel's Master-Slave Dialectic and a Myth of Marxology', *New Left Review* 142 (November-December 1983), 67–75.

44. Friedrich Engels, *Anti-Düring*, in *Marx/Engels Collected Works*, vol. 26 (London/Moscow: Lawrence & Wishart/Progress Publishers, 1987), 170–1.

45. Karl Marx and Friedrich Engels, *The Communist Manifesto*, trans. Samuel Moore (London: Penguin Classics, 2002), 258. [Translator's note: The English translations in both cases renders *Gewalt* as 'force'. To accord with the arguments presented here, which in part rests on the French translation of *Gewalt* as 'violence', we have carried that meaning over and modified the English translations to 'violence'.]

46. Herbert Marcuse, Letter to Angela Y. Davis, 18 November 1970, in *The New Left and the 1960s, Collected Papers of Herbert Marcuse*, vol. 3, ed. Douglass Kellner (London and New York: Routledge, 2005), 49–50.

47. Alexandre Kojève, *Introduction to the Reading of Hegel*, trans. James H. Nichols, Jr. (Ithaca: Cornell University Press, 1980),

69. [Translator's note: The English translation of Raymond Queneau's collection of Alexandre Kojève's lectures on Hegel does not cover all of the lectures cited here. Where lectures not included in the English translation are cited, reference is given to the French].

48. Kojève, *Introduction to the Reading of Hegel*, 69.

49. Kojève, *Introduction à la lecture de Hegel* (Paris: Gallimard, 1968), 143.

50. Kojève, *Introduction to the Reading of Hegel*, 69.

51. Kojève, *Introduction à la lecture de Hegel*, 141.

52. Kojève, *Introduction à la lecture de Hegel*, 143, 557.

53. Kojève, *Introduction to the Reading of Hegel*, 56.

54. Kojève, *Introduction à la lecture de Hegel*, 560.

55. Fanon, *The Wretched*, 47; Jean-Paul Sartre, 'Preface', in Fanon, *The Wretched*, lii.

56. Judith Butler, *Subjects of Desire: Hegelian Reflections in Twentieth-Century France* (New York: Columbia University Press, 2012), 81. See also Tran Duc Thao, 'Letter to Alexandre Kojève', 30/X 1948, *Genèses* 2 (December 1990), 136–7.

57. Alexandre Kojève, *Identité et réalité dans le 'Dictionnaire' de Pierre Bayle* [Identity and Reality in the 'Dictionary' of Pierre Bayle] (Paris: Gallimard, 2010), 20.

58. Alexandre Kojève, 'Letter to Tran Duc Thao', 7 October 1948, in Gwendoline Jarczyk and Pierre-Jean Labarrière, 'Alexandre Kojève et Tran Duc Thao. Correspondance inédite' ['Alexandre Kojève and Tran Duc Thao. The Unpublished Correspondence'], *Genèses* 2 (December 1990), 134.

59. Kojève, *Introduction à la lecture de Hegel*, 25, 55, 114, 174.

60. Kojève, *Introduction to the Reading of Hegel*, 20.

61. In particular, see Claude Lévi-Strauss, *Introduction to a Science of Mythology, volume 1: The Raw and the Cooked*, trans. John and Doreen Weightman (New York and Evanston: Harper and Row, 1969).

62. See, for example, Lévi-Strauss, *Introduction to a Science of Mythology: 1. The Raw and the Cooked*, 1; and Claude Lévi-Strauss and Didier Éribon, *De près et de loin* [From Far and Wide], (Paris: Odile Jacob, 1988).

63. Claude Lévi-Strauss, 'The Structural Study of Myth' (1958), in *Structural Anthology*, trans. Claire Jackobson and Brooke Grundfest Schoepf (New York: Basic Books, 1963), 478. Translation modified.

64. Eduardo Viveiros de Castro, *Cannibal Metaphysics*, trans. Peter Skafish (Minneapolis: Univocal, 2014), chapter 13, 'Becomings of Structuralism', 197–219.

65. 'But this philosophic caution, which makes it possible to avoid the pitfalls of reductionist interpretations, is also a strength. It supposes that each suggested new interpretation of a myth – and this means, for a start, my own interpretations - takes its place in sequence after the already known variants of that myth.' (Claude Lévi-Strauss, 'Finale' in *Introduction to a Science of Mythology, volume 4. The Naked Man*, trans. John and Doreen Weightman (New York: Harper & Row, 1981), 628.

66. Lévi-Strauss, 'The Structural Study of Myth', 478.

67. Lévi-Strauss, 'Finale', 628.

68. I would like to thank Christine Chivallon for having drawn my attention to the mythological dimension of my reading and for having thus set the course for this reflexive hypothesis.

Against 'Effective Altruism'

Alice Crary

Effective Altruism (EA) is a programme for rationalising charitable giving, positioning individuals to do the 'most good' per expenditure of money or time. It was first formulated – by two Oxford philosophers just over a decade ago – as an application of the moral theory consequentialism, and from the outset one of its distinctions within the philanthropic world was expansion of the class of charity-recipients to include non-human animals. EA has been the target of a fair bit of grumbling, and even some mockery, from activists and critics on the left, who associate consequentialism with depoliticising tendencies of welfarism. But EA has mostly gotten a pass, with many detractors concluding that, however misguided, its efforts to get bankers, tech entrepreneurs and the like to give away their money cost-effectively does no serious harm.

This stance is no longer tenable. The growth of EA has been explosive, with some affiliated organisations, such as Open Philanthropy, now recommending grants amounting to hundreds of millions of dollars annually. Partly building on congenial trends in development economics, and in tandem with movements like 'impact investing', EA has become a force capable of leaving its imprint on whole fields of public engagement. This is in evidence in the domain of animal advocacy, to which EA has brought substantial new attention and funding. One result of the windfall is that EA-guided ratings groups serve as king-makers, raising up pro-animal organisations deemed 'effective' by EA and denigrating and partly defunding many organisations deemed 'ineffective', while pressuring others to artificially shift their missions in order to conform to operative metrics of 'effectiveness' and secure funding. This has led to objections from animal advocates (often muted due to fear of alienating EA-admiring funders). Yet champions of EA, whether or not concerned with the cause of animals,

for the most part adopt the attitude that they have no serious critics and that sceptics ought to be content with their ongoing attempts to fine-tune their practice.

It is a posture belied by the existence of formidable critical resources both inside and outside the philosophical tradition in which EA originates. In light of the undisputed impact of EA, and its success in attracting idealistic young people, it is important to forcefully make the case that it owes its success primarily not to the – questionable – value of its moral theory but to its compatibility with political and economic institutions responsible for some of the very harms it addresses. The sincere dedication of many individual adherents notwithstanding, reflection on EA reveals a straightforward example of moral corruption.

Anatomy of EA

Consequentialist ideas inform the way EA is implemented by many EA-affiliated groups focusing largely on human outreach, such as Development Media International, GiveWell, and Giving What We Can. Such ideas also inform EA's implementation by groups focusing largely on animals, such as Animal Charity Evaluators and Faunalytics, and by groups like Open Philanthropy that address both humans and nonhuman animals. Consequentialism is a rather big tent, accommodating a variety of EAs. Some advocates argue that it is not necessary for effective altruists to be consequentialists.[1] Others go further, claiming that EA is 'independent of any theoretical commitments'.[2] This last claim is false, reflecting ignorance of competing ethical traditions from which criticism of EA arises. But it is fair to set aside the question of whether one can be an effective altruist without being a consequentialist. The consequentialist stances that have figured in the articulation and institutional actualisation of EA presuppose a distinctive philosophical worldview, and it is possible to move from criticism of this worldview to a thoroughgoing attack on EA's most destructive aspects. The resulting non-consequentialist outlook makes it possible to expose as confused EA-style talk of doing 'most good', delegitimising evaluations of charitable organisations that presuppose such talk's coherence, and thus rendering moot the question of whether such evaluations are invariably consequentialist.

Consequentialism is the view that moral rightness is a matter of the production of the best consequences or best state of affairs. What is 'best' is what has the most value. So consequentialist stances are grounded in prior theories of value. Within this scheme, consequentialists can be very open about what things are assessed as right or wrong.[3] They can talk about the rightness not only of actions but of anything that has consequences, including desires, beliefs, dispositions and sets of actions. While consequentialists can also be fairly open about what counts as values, they make epistemological assumptions that constrain what values can be like.

Effective altruists often demonstrate consequentialist commitments by locating themselves within consequentialism's spaces of alternatives. During EA's brief history, self-avowed effective altruists have tended to take as the objects of moral assessment particular actions, while also taking as their core value the sort of well-being capturable by the metrics of welfare economics. One instrument that some have recommended for assessing actions in terms of well-being is the quality-adjusted-life-year or QALY, an economic metric for health programmes, which integrates measures of the value of extending individuals' lives with measures of the quality of life over the relevant period, with one QALY standing for one year of life in perfect health.[4] Some effective altruists use QALYs to determine which of a set of actions (say, intervening medically to prevent 'ten people from suffering from AIDs [versus intervening to prevent] one hundred people from suffering from severe arthritis') produces more well-being and does more good.[5] The assessments often involve further steps such as randomised control trials to get reliable accounts of interventions' consequences, calculations of interventions' marginal utilities and counterfactual considerations of the value of outcomes that would be produced by different interventions that individuals are positioned to make.

There is a further respect in which effective altruists fly consequentialist colours. Consequentialists sometimes gloss their take on the moral enterprise by saying that moral reflection is undertaken from the 'point of view of the universe', accenting that they conceive such reflection as disengaged and dispassionate.[6] This abstract moral epistemology is one of the marks of a moral radicalism that, although sometimes criticised for the extent of its demands, gets celebrated by consequentialists. The morally radical suggestion is that our ability to act so as to produce value anywhere places the same moral demands on us as our ability to produce value in our immediate circumstances. Consider here a famous case from the prominent philosopher and EA-advocate Peter Singer. If we take well-being as a value, our ability to act so as to address suffering in any spot on earth places the same moral demands on us as does our ability to address the suffering of an unaccompanied toddler drowning in a shallow pond next to the road on which we're walking.[7]

This radical twist on consequentialism's abstract moral epistemology underlies two of effective altruists' signature gestures. First, effective altruists inherit it when they exhort us to be guided by their recommendations in a way that treats as irrelevant the question of who is helped, without following our passions or favouring projects to which we have particular attachments.[8] Second, effective altruists presuppose a radical take on an abstract moral epistemology in urging us to do the 'most good'. Their abstract approach excludes any virtue-oriented view on which the rightness of actions is appropriately engaged responsiveness to circumstances, and this makes it seem more natural to account for rightness by looking to the value of actions' consequences. Consequentialists may hold that there are multiple kinds of valuable things, and there has never been 'a consensus among [them] about the relative weights of any sets of values'.[9] But it is the idea that rightness is a matter of the value of quantifiable consequences, allowing for difficulties of juggling different classes of values, that makes it seem coherent to speak of single judgments about how to do the most good.

EA's god's eye image of moral reflection constrains how we can conceive of ethical thought and practice, leaving no room for views intolerant of the idea that moral reflection proceeds from the standpoint of the universe.

Thereby excluded are views – e.g. some Kantian constructivisms – that combine accounts of moral reflection as essentially perspectival with understandings of theoretical reflection as maximally abstract.[10] Also excluded are views that combine accounts of moral reflection as essentially engaged with understandings of theoretical reflection on which such reflection likewise goes unregulated by an ideal of abstraction. Under the latter heading are various outlooks, some associated with strands of virtue theory, that represent values as woven into the world's fabric, so that we need particular sensitivities to recognise them.

Many effective altruists fail to register this last exclusion as an exclusion. EA's Oxford-trained founders work in a philosophical tradition, indebted to classic empiricism, shaped by the assumption that subjective endowments have an essential tendency to obstruct our access to the world. Thinkers in this tradition often simply take it for granted that any genuine, objective aspects of the world are abstractly accessible. Acquaintance with local history suggests this posture is at least questionable. Twentieth century Oxonian philosophy featured high profile debates about whether subjective propensities internally inform our ability to bring the world into focus. Among the most outspoken participants were members of a set of women philosophers at Oxford during and after World War Two – including G.E.M. Anscombe, Philippa Foot and Iris Murdoch – who distanced themselves from the idea that subjective endowments invariably tend to block our view of things. These philosophers made room for views on which evaluative concepts trace out forms of regularity that, while objective, are only available from non-neutral standpoints.[11] To sideline this part of Anglophone philosophy is to overlook its most notable resources for criticising consequentialism and consequentialism's EA-oriented offshoots.

EA's guiding ideas should be considered alongside the work of groups that implement them. Focusing on animal advocacy, we might take a snapshot of the activity of a prominent EA-affiliated animal charity assessor, Animal Charity Evaluators. Nine pro-animal organisations received either Animal Charity Evaluator's highest ('top') or second highest ('stand out') rating for 2019. Of these at least eight focus on farmed animals. (The one possible exception, Faunalytics, itself uses principles of EA to rate animal charities.) Animal Charity Evaluator's website explains that, for every dog or cat 'euthanised' in a shelter worldwide, 3,400 farm animals are killed, yet spending on organisations that address animals in industrial agriculture is a small fraction of pro-animal giving. Of the eight recommended organisations that deal with farmed animals, six – or 75% – are primarily concerned with welfare improvements within industrial animal agriculture (The Albert Schweitzer Foundation, Animal International, The Humane League, Compassion in World Farming, The Federation of Indian Animal Protection Organisations, Sinergia Animal), with the other two (The Good Food Institute and Sociedade Vegetariana Brasileira) focused more on structural transformation. Animal Charity Evaluator's website explains that it has more confidence in assessments of the short term impact of welfarist interventions than in those of the long term impact of efforts at systems change.

The institutional critique

The most fully elaborated criticism of EA, developed largely by economists and political theorists, is sometimes referred to as the *institutional critique*.[12] This critique attacks effective altruists for operating with a damagingly narrow interpretation of the class of things that are assessable as right or wrong. It targets effective altruists' tendency to focus on single actions and their proximate consequences and, more specifically, on simple interventions that reduce suffering in the short term. Advocates of the institutional critique are on the whole concerned to decry the neglect, on the part of EA, of coordinated sets of actions directed at changing social structures that reliably cause suffering. EA's metrics are best suited to detect the short term impact of particular actions, so its tendency to discount the impact of coordinated actions can be seen as reflecting 'measurability bias'. A leitmotif of the institutional critique of EA is that this bias is politically dangerous because it obscures the structural, political roots of global misery, thereby contributing to its reproduction by weakening existing political mechanisms for positive social change.[13]

The institutional critique of EA can be brought to bear on Animal Charity Evaluator's 2019 ratings. Animal Charity Evaluator's favouring of welfare improvements in the conditions of farmed animals can be taken to reflect forms of ('measurement') bias in its metrics, which

are best suited to detect the outcomes of simpler efforts with clear short term impacts. This orientation speaks for striving to change the methods of meat companies in ways that leave unquestioned the larger political context in which the companies operate. The result is that, despite its sincere pro-animal stance, Animal Charity Evaluator is at risk of strengthening an industrial agricultural system that reproduces horrific animal suffering on a massive scale.

A number of effective altruists have responded to the institutional critique. Responses generally allow that some EA programs have placed undue stress on quantitative tools for capturing short term effects of individual actions and that, in thus overemphasising 'the importance of relying on quantifiable evidence of the kind that [randomized control trials] can provide',[14] they demonstrate measurability bias.[15] The responses also mostly claim that, properly understood, EA calls on us to evaluate anything with relevant consequences, including collective efforts to produce institutional change. This is the

stance of two advocates who argue that EA obliges us to take seriously the role that coordinated actions and other tactics can play 'within and across social movements', where this involves being open to consulting fields such as 'history and social, political and economic theory' for instruments to measure their effects.[16] While replies to the institutional critique bring out that there is room to include collective actions among EA's objects of assessment, and to introduce new tools for capturing effects of such actions, they leave unexamined questions about whether it is confused to insist on causal effects as the standard for evaluating collective attempts to change the normative structure of society. The general idea is that EA can treat the institutional critique as an internal critique that calls for more faithfully realising, not abandoning, its core tenets.[17]

Although this rejoinder to the institutional critique is to some extent valid, it would be wrong to conclude that effective altruists can simply treat the institutional critique as a merely internal one. The institutional critique can and should be given a philosophical twist that transforms it into a direct challenge to EA's main philosophical tenets.

The philosophical critique

The *philosophical critique* is an apt moniker for a cluster of attacks on EA which target the god's eye moral epistemology that makes it seem possible to arrive at single judgments about how to do the most good. These attacks charge that it is morally and philosophically problematic to construe moral reflection as abstract. Critics leveling this charge often present themselves as building on a line of argument that Bernard Williams develops in publications in the 1970s and 1980s, about how efforts in ethics to look at our lives from an Archimedean point oblige us to abstract from even our most valued relationships and practices and accordingly represent a threat to our integrity.[18] Effective altruists who respond to the philosophical critique take Williams to be urging us to protect our integrity even at the cost of doing the wrong thing.[19] They regard this solicitude toward the self as misplaced and self-indulgent, and, because they assume that philosophical critics of EA operate with the same understanding of Williams, they dismiss these critics' gestures as without philosophical interest.

The stance of these effective altruists is understandable. The interpretation of Williams they favour is widely received, and it is difficult to find a philosophical critique of EA that is elaborated precisely enough to make clear that this take on it is inaccurate. At the same time, this is a major missed opportunity for critical reflection. It is not difficult to develop philosophical critics' worries about a god's eye morality so that they rise to the level of a devastating objection. All that is required is to combine worries about point-of-viewless moral reflection with views about values, like those championed by the group of mid twentieth-century women philosophers at Oxford, on which concepts of values determine neutrally unavailable worldly patterns.[20] The point of the philosophical critique is not that EA's abstract moral epistemology imposes integrity-threatening moral demands. The more telling charge is that an Archimedean view deprives us of the resources we need to recognise what matters morally, encouraging us to read into it features of whatever moral position we happen to favour.[21]

It might seem that effective altruists are justified in dismissing the charge. The target is EA's point-of-viewless moral epistemology, and this moral epistemology is at home within a larger philosophical outlook, itself a pivot of contemporary analytic philosophy, on which abstraction is a regulative ideal for all thought about the empirical world. Why should effective altruists take seriously an attack on a philosophical worldview that many of their colleagues take as an unquestioned starting point?

The late twentieth and early twenty-first centuries witnessed significant philosophical assaults on abstract conceptions of reason, and there is a notable philosophical corpus in which the merits of these assaults get debated.[22] Although it is by no means obvious that those who favour abstract views have better arguments, and although their interlocutors raise fundamental questions about these views' tenability, abstract construals of reason have for more than half a century played an organising role in the discipline of philosophy, structuring research programmes in numerous subfields.[23] This suggests that the construals' staying power is at least partly a function of ideological factors independent of their philosophical credentials. That – the fact that these conceptions of reason are manifestly open to contestation – is one reason why effective altruists should attend to a philosophical critique that depends for its force on rejecting abstract images of reason. A second reason for effective altruists to attend to the philosophical critique has to do with the seriousness of the moral charge it levels against them. It alleges nothing less than that their image of the moral enterprise is bankrupt and that moral assessments grounded in this image lack authority.

The philosophical critique brings into question effective altruists' very notion of doing the 'most good' or having the 'greatest impact'. Effective altruists invite us to regard the rightness of a social intervention as a function of its consequences, with the outcome involving the best states of affairs counting as doing most good. This strategy appears morally confused when considered in terms of the ethical stance of the philosophical critique. To adopt this stance is to see the weave of the world as endowed with values that reveal themselves only to a developed sensibility. To see things this way is to make room for an intuitively appealing conception of actions as right insofar as they exhibit just sensitivity to the worldly circumstances in question. This is consistent with allowing that right actions can have the end of promoting others' happiness or flourishing. Here acting rightly includes acting, when circumstances call for it, in ways that aim at the well-being of others, and, with reference to this benevolent pursuit of others' well-being, it makes sense to talk – in a manner that may seem to echo effective altruists – about good states of affairs. But it is important that, as Philippa Foot once put it, 'we have found this end within morality, forming part of it, not standing outside it as a good state of affairs by which moral action in general is to be judged'.[24] Here right action also includes acting, when circumstantially appropriate, in ways that aim at ends – e.g. giving people what they are owed – that can conflict with the end of benevolence. Apt responsiveness to circumstances sometimes requires acting with an eye to others' well-being and sometimes with an eye to other ends. In cases in which it is not right to attend to others' well-being, it is incorrect to say that, because we haven't thus attended, we achieve a morally worse result. Things only seem this way if we allow our understanding to be shaped by what now appears to be a confused understanding of morality. What we should say is that the result we wind up with is morally best. That is what it comes to to say that, within the context of the philosophical critique, there is no room for EA-style talk of 'most good'.[25]

This critique alleges that EA's claim to be doing the most good founders on a misunderstanding of the nature of morality and that the enterprise needs to be either radically reconceived or abandoned altogether. It thus confronts EA with challenges that it cannot meet with mere internal adjustments.

The composite critique

The philosophical critique charges that EA's god's eye moral epistemology disqualifies it from authoritatively trafficking in values, and it thus casts new light on the institutional critique's charge that EA fails to do justice to sets of actions aimed at progressive social change. The resulting *composite critique* presupposes, in line with the philosophical critique, that values are essentially woven into the texture of the social world and that EA's Archimedean take on moral reflection deprives it of resources needed to describe – irreducibly normative –

social circumstances. The upshot of this new line of criticism is an update of the institutional critique, charging that EA cannot give accurate assessments of sets of actions because it forfeits capacities necessary for all social assessment. This means that the tendency of EA-affiliated organisations to wrongly prioritise evaluation of the proximate effects of particular actions is not a fixable methodological flaw. The organisations focus on these evaluations because it is only here that their image of the moral enterprise seems plausible. It is often right to act in ways that aim to improve the welfare of others. But recognising the instances in which this is (or isn't) right requires capacities for engaged social thought that EA disavows. Further, when it comes to evaluating actions coordinated with an eye to social transformation, EA's image of the moral enterprise is patently implausible. Such actions are efforts to restructure the normative organisation of society, and their relevant 'effects', far from obeying merely causal laws, are at home in the unpredictable realm of politics. Attempts to evaluate these efforts in EA's terms are manifestly confused.

This composite critique finds extensive support in philosophical reflection about the social sciences. At the critique's heart is an image of the social world as irretrievably normative such that understanding it requires non-neutral resources. A classic argument for this image within social philosophy centres on a conception of actions as conceptually articulated and constitutively normative. Granted that social concepts are categories for actions (or for character traits, practices and institutions that can themselves only adequately be understood in reference to actions), it follows that these concepts need to be understood as tracing out patterns in an irreducibly normative ground – patterns that only reveal themselves to an evaluatively non-neutral gaze.[26] Further arguments for conceiving social understanding as thus normative can be found in numerous discussions about methods and authority of the social sciences. This includes anti-positivist debates in sociology,[27] disputes in anthropology about the need for ethnographic methods alongside quantitative ones[28] and calls by Frankfurt School theorists to retain an ineluctably normative notion of social analysis.[29] These interrelated literatures supply additional backing for the verdict that EA, with its abstract methods, bars itself from responsibly dealing in social assessments.

Yet further support can be found in contemporary discourses of liberation. Anguish at the violence of being forced to live within 'false universals' is a rallying cry echoing through numerous strands of twentieth and twenty-first century emancipatory thought. What inspires the cry is the experience of being subjected to forms of social life that appear to conform to laudable social ideals (e.g. equality, freedom and non-violence) only when looked at from elite perspectives that are wrongly presented as neutral and universal. Expressions of this experience often go hand in hand with claims about how the route to a just understanding of a set of unjust social circumstances must involve, not a new supposedly neutral stance, but a stance shaped by an appreciation of the suffering of the marginalised. Such claims recur in a wide array of overlapping – feminist, anti-racist, anti-colonial, anti-ableist – liberating theories,[30] and, against the backdrop of this theoretical corpus, EA's insistence on an abstract approach to evaluation assumes the aspect of a refusal to listen to demands for justice.

In practice, the composite critique suggests that, within any domain in which they operate, charities guided by EA-ratings will in general direct funds towards simple interventions capturable with metrics such as income levels or health outcomes, and in a manner relatively insensitive to whether these interventions contribute to perpetuating the institutions that reliably produce the ills they address, while also disparaging as less 'effective' systematic attempts to change these institutions. This is what typically happens with EA-oriented organisations that rate animal charities. In addition to emphasising welfare improvements in the treatment of animals caught up in industrial 'farms', these organisations tend to depreciate pro-animal organisations that are dedicated to transforming social attitudes toward animals and whose achievements aren't demonstrable in EA's terms. This includes vegan organisations in Black and Brown neighbourhoods in the U.S. that seek to address people not through easily quantifiable methods like leafleting but through outreach to churches and regular participation in local markets and fairs; it includes many longstanding activist groups in the Global South working to contest the spread of factory farms; it includes many sanctuaries for domestic animals; and, more generally, it includes a vast array of grassroots pro-animal organisations and movements that, even when working in solidarity with larger networks, arrive at their methods in ways that are context-sensitive and bottom-up.

EA as moral corruption

EA is a movement based on a flawed conception of morality that encounters opposition not only from ethics, political theory and philosophy of the social sciences, but also from many critical theorists, organisers and activists who are committed to causes, such as animal protectionism, that effective altruists support. This raises the question of the source of its appeal. Effective altruists couch their moral assessments quantitatively in terms of doing the most good, trafficking in tropes of economic efficiency that align them with the institutions of neoliberal capitalism. It's no secret that EA urges its adherents to work within these institutions. Singer is openly dismissive of critiques of global capitalism in its current form,[31] and, along with MacAskill and many other proponents of EA, he encourages the practice of 'earning to give', that is, taking high paying jobs in business and finance in order to be able to give more.[32] Singer goes as far as to laud the billionaire philanthropists Bill Gates and Warren Buffett as 'the greatest effective altruists in human history'.[33] EA owes its success as a philosophical-philanthropic movement largely to its eagerness and ability to work within existing political-economic systems.

This source of EA's success is also its most grievous shortcoming. Effective altruists present their philanthropic program as the expression of an uncontextualised moral theory, in a manner that reflects no awareness of the significance of their situatedness within capitalist forms of life. How it happens that EA has at its disposal an audience of people with excess wealth is not a question that they take up. Within discussions of EA, it is difficult to find a hint of the plausible and well-grounded view – defended in the writings of many theorists of care, eco-feminists, ecological Marxists and other theorists of social reproduction – that the disproportionate material advantages of the wealthy in the global North depend on continuously treating as 'free resources' not only animals and other aspects of the non-human natural environment, but also the reproductive labour of women and the subsistence and care work of marginalised people the world over.[34] It is equally hard to find mention of the now extensive literature on how practices of 'internalising' these things into capitalist markets displace without halting or slowing the devastation of nature and the oppression of vulnerable humans.[35] Critical outlooks in which these ideas are at home have played no discernible role in discussions of EA, where there is rarely any suggestion of a tie between the forms of misery we are enjoined to alleviate and the structures of global capitalism. What is foregrounded instead is a paternalistic narrative about how the relatively wealthy should serve as benefactors of relatively poor and precarious humans and animals, and thus 'do good'.

Granted this tendency towards ahistorical theorising, it is unsurprising that enthusiasts of EA tend to regard reliance on ideals of economic efficiency as in itself unproblematic. Among other things, they betray no worry that the reach of these discourses into domains in which EA operates will displace political discourses shaped by values not capturable in terms of the logic of exchange. This insouciance about depoliticisation – another expression for EA's lack of any meaningful response to the institutional critique – is the counterpart of an inability to recognise how the instrumentalisation of public space can produce outcomes, rational only from the standpoint of capital, that reliably generate the forms of suffering EA aims to stamp out.[36]

This weakness is devastating when it comes to EA's capacity to make a positive contribution to animal protectionism. Effective altruists' pro-animal efforts are to a large extent devoted to attending to suffering visited upon animals in factory farms. But their characteristic theoretical stance prevents them from registering the significance of the fact that these 'farms' are capitalist phenomena. Alongside the unspeakable torments that factory farms visit on animals – bio-engineered for the growth-rates of their edible tissues, raised on unnatural diets, crammed mercilessly together with conspecifics, and slaughtered on assembly lines where they are all too often dismembered while still conscious – there are terrible costs to humans. The environmental impact of confined animal feeding operations is severe. They are sources of air and water pollution that disproportionately harms members of the already socially vulnerable human populations living in proximity to them; they produce approximately fifteen percent of global greenhouse gas emissions; and the need they generate for grazing land is a major factor in deforestation world-wide, which itself produces not only around a fifth of global greenhouse gas emissions but significant soil erosion and related polluting run-off. Industrial animal agriculture also poses serious threats to public health. It is a breeding ground for zoonoses, and, because it relies on the mass prophylactic use of antibiotics to mitigate its own disease-causing conditions, it adds to the prevalence of deadly infections of antibiotic-resistant bacteria such as salmonella. Industrial slaughterhouses are well-documented sites of systematic violations of the rights of 'kill floors' workers, a group that, in the U.S., has since the 1990s been in large part made up of Latin American immigrant and African-American men, and whose poor conditions, economic precariousness and vulnerability to abuse was exposed during the COVID-19 pandemic in which many industrial abattoirs continued to operate even while those working in them suffered disproportionate rates of illness and death. Industrial animal agriculture is a raging social pathology, intelligible only in terms of the protection and growth of meat companies' profits.

To note that effective altruists aren't guided, in their forays into animal protectionism, by insight into the capitalist origins of the 'third agricultural revolution' that gave us confined animal feeding operations and industrial abattoirs is not to say that their interventions on behalf of farmed animals are bound to misfire.[37] There is no reason to doubt that the welfare adjustments to the treatment of farmed animals that are favoured by EA-affiliated groups can lessen the pain of many such animals. It is even possible that in calling for these adjustments, effective altruists will hasten the demise of the industrial system that torments and kills billions of creatures annually. But it is also possible that the interventions of effective altruists will, because they affirm this system's underlying principles, contribute to its perpetuation, perhaps even precipitating the arrival of a further, more horrific 'agricultural revolution'. What is certain is that effective altruists' theoretical commitments lead them to approach animal protectionism without proper reference to political and economic forces that

sustain factory farms. Anyone seeking substantial steps toward shutting down these 'farms' would be well advised to exchange EA for efforts informed by an understanding of these forces. Only such interventions have a shot at being more than accidentally effective.

Drawing on a flawed understanding of the moral enterprise, EA directs its followers to respond to human and animal suffering in a manner that deflects attention away from how an image of humans as *homo economicus* contributes to the reliable reproduction of such suffering. At the same time, EA as a movement benefits from its embrace of those who 'earn to give', accumulating wealth in the economic arena that it leaves critically untouched. It is a textbook case of moral corruption.[38]

EA has not been wholly unresponsive to criticism. In addition to responding – unsatisfactorily – to the institutional critique, effective altruists have attempted to respond to the charge that EA has 'been a rather homogeneous movement of middle-class white men'[39] by placing new stress on inclusiveness. Two prominent effective altruists have urged effective animal altruists to 'consider how the history and demographics of the animal rights and effective altruist movements might be limiting their perspective',[40] and a number of EA-associated groups have made diversity a central institutional ideal. Animal Charity Evaluators, for instance, now includes diversity among the issues it considers both in its own staffing and in that of animal organisations it assesses, and Oxford EA has made a big push for diversity. These moves toward inclusiveness are typically presented as intended not just to bring in participants with different social identities, but to make room for their perspectives and ideas. Initially attractive as such gestures are, there is every reason to be sceptical about their significance. They come unaccompanied by any acknowledgment of how the framework of EA constrains available moral and political outlooks. That framing excludes views of social thought on which it is irretrievably perspectival – views associated with central strands of feminist theory, critical disability studies, critical race theory, and anti-colonial theory. Despite its signaling towards diversity of ideas, EA as it stands cannot make room for individuals who discover in these traditions the things they believe most need to be said. For EA to accommodate their voices, it would have to allow that their moral and political beliefs are in conflict with its guiding principles and that these principles themselves need to be given up. To allow for this would be to reject EA in its current form as fatally flawed, finally a step towards doing a bit of good.[41]

Alice Crary teaches philosophy at the New School for Social Research in New York, and is Visiting Fellow at All Souls College, Oxford, 2021-22. Her current projects include two books, Animal Crisis, *with Lori Gruen, and* Radical Animal.

Notes

1. Magnus Vinding, *Effective Altruism: How Can We Best Help Others* (Durham, NC: The Neuroethics Foundation, 2018).
2. Jeff McMahan, 'Philosophical Critique of Effective Altruism', *The Philosopher's Magazine* 73:2 (2016), 93.
3. Derek Parfit, *Reasons and Persons* (Oxford: Oxford University Press, 1984), 25.
4. See, for example, William MacAskill, *Doing Good Better: Effective Altruism and How You Can Make a Difference* (New York: Gotham Books, 2015), 34.
5. MacAskill, *Doing Good Better*, 34.
6. Peter Singer, *The Most Good You Can Do: How Effective Altruism is Changing Ideas about Living Ethically* (New Haven: Yale University Press, 2015), 84–85; Peter Singer and Katarzyna de Lazari-Radek, *The Point of View of the Universe: Sidgwick and Contemporary Ethics* (Oxford: Oxford University Press, 2014); the original source of the gesture is Sidgwick.
7. Peter Singer, 'Famine, Affluence, and Morality', *Philosophy & Public Affairs* 1:3 (1972), 231.
8. See Singer, *The Most Good You Can Do*, ch. 8 and MacAskill, *Doing Good Better*, 41 and ch. 9.
9. Avram Hiller, 'Consequentialism in Environmental Ethics', in *Oxford Handbook of Environmental Ethics*, eds. Stephen Gardiner and Allen Thomas (Oxford: Oxford University Press, 2017), 270.
10. Christine Korsgaard, *Fellow Creatures: Our Obligations to the Other Animals* (Oxford: Oxford University Press, 2018), 9 and 95.
11. For discussion of the work of these philosophers, see the website of the research group '(In Parentheses)', accessed 10 April 2021, https://www.womeninparenthesis.co.uk/about/. See also G.E.M. Anscombe, 'On Brute Facts', *Analysis* 18:3 (1958), 69–72; Philippa Foot, 'Moral Arguments', *Mind* 268 (1958), 502–13; Iris Murdoch, 'Vision and Choice in Morality', in *Existentialists and Mystics: Writings on Philosophy and Literature*, ed. Peter Conradi (New York: Penguin Books, 1997), 76–98. For the tradition's continuation, see Annette Baier, 'What Do Women Want in a Moral Theory', *Noûs* 19:1 (1985), 53–63; Cora Diamond, *The Realistic Spirit: Wittgenstein, Philosophy, and the Mind* (Cambridge, MA: MIT Press, 1991) and '"We are perpetually moralists": Iris Murdoch, Fact and Value', in *Iris Murdoch and the Search for Human Goodness*, eds. Maria Antonaccio and William Schweiker (Chicago: University of Chicago Press, 1996), 79–109; Philippa Foot, *Natural Goodness* (Oxford: Oxford University Press, 2001); John McDowell, *Mind, Value and Reality* (Cambridge, MA: Harvard University Press, 1998), ch. 3, 6, 7 and 10; David Wiggins, *Needs, Values, Truth*, 3rd ed. (Oxford: Oxford University Press, 2002), ch. 5.
12. See, for example, Brian Berkey, 'The Institutional Critique of Effective Altruism', *Utilitas* 30:2 (2018), 143–171.
13. See especially Emily Clough, 'Effective Altruism's Political Blindspot', *Boston Review*, 14 July 2015, http://bostonreview.net/world/emily-clough-effective-altruism-ngos; Angus Deaton, 'The Logic of Effective Altruism', *Boston Review*, 1 July 2015, http://bostonreview.net/forum/logic-effective-altruism/angus-deaton-response-effective-altruism. For critiques of humanitarian trends in development work that in some ways anticipate the institutional critique of EA, see e.g. Mark Duffield, *Global Governance and the New Wars: The Merging of Development and Security* (New York: Zed Books, 2001); Didier Fassin, *Humanitarian Reason: A Moral History of the Present* (Berkeley: University of California Press, 2010).
14. Berkey, 'The Institutional Critique of Effective Altruism', 160.
15. Jeff Sebo and Peter Singer, 'Activism', in *Critical Terms for Animal Studies*, ed. Lori Gruen (Chicago: University of Chicago Press, 2018), 34–35.
16. Sebo and Singer, 'Activism', 40–41.
17. For talk of an internal critique, see Sebo and Singer, 'Activism', 40; for similar responses on behalf of EA, see Berkey, 'The Institutional Critique of Effective Altruism'; Hauke Hillebrandt, 'Effective Altruism, Continued: On Measuring Impact', *Boston Review*, 31 July 2015, http://bostonreview.net/blog/hauke-hillebrandt-giving-what-we-can-effective-altruism-impact; McMahan, 'Philosophical Critique of Effective Altruism'.
18. Bernard Williams, 'A Critique of Utilitarianism', in J.J.C. Smart and Bernard Williams, *Utilitarianism: For and Against* (Cambridge: Cambridge University Press, 1973), 77–150; 'Utilitarianism and Moral Self-Indulgence', in *Moral Luck: Philosophical Papers 1973-1980* (Cambridge: Cambridge University Press, 1981), 40–53; *Ethics and the Limits of Philosophy* (London: Routledge, 1985), ch. 2 and 8. For references to Williams in philosophical critiques of EA, see, e.g., Nakul Krishna, 'Add Your Own Egg: Philosophy as a Humanistic Discipline', *The Point Magazine*, 13 January 2016, https://thepointmag.com/examined-life/add-your-own-egg; and Amia Srinivasan, 'Stop the Robot Apocalypse', *London Review of Books* 37:18, 24 September 2015.
19. See Berkey, 'The Institutional Critique of Effective Altruism', 169n67 and related text; McMahan, 'Philosophical Critique of Effective Altruism'; Singer, *The Most Good You Can Do*, 48–49, 85 and 102.
20. For evidence that these thinkers were an important source for Williams' attacks on point-of-viewlessness, see Williams, *Ethics and the Limits of Philosophy*, 141n7.
21. See Lisa Herzog, 'Can "effective altruism" really change the world?', *Open Democracy*, last modified 22 February 2016, https://www.opendemocracy.net/en/transformation/can-effective-altruism-really-change-world/; and Srinivasan, 'Stop the Robot Apocalypse' on how EA demands the wrong things.
22. Within the analytic tradition, Wittgenstein and Austin offer two of the most significant twentieth-century attacks on abstract conceptions of reason, and their efforts have been taken

up and elaborated by philosophers such as Stanley Cavell, Cora Diamond, John McDowell and Hilary Putnam. Wittgensteinian ideas have also resonated in debates about how to conceive of reason within history and philosophy of science. For one high-profile strike, from here, against conceiving reason abstractly, see Lorraine Daston and Peter Galison, *Objectivity* (New York: Zone Books, 2007).

23. Alice Crary, 'Objectivity', in *Wittgenstein on Philosophy, Objectivity, and Meaning*, eds. James Conant and Sebastian Sunday (Cambridge: Cambridge University Press, 2019), 47–61.

24. Philippa Foot, 'Utilitarianism and the Virtues', *Mind* 94:374 (1985), 205.

25. For a satirical version of this argument, see Annette Baier, 'A Modest Proposal', *Report from the Center for Philosophy and Public Policy* 6:1 (1986), 4.

26. Peter Winch, *The Idea of a Social Science and Its Relation to Philosophy* (London: Routledge, 2008), 99–99. For commentary, see e.g. Linda Zerilli, *A Democratic Theory of Judgment* (Chicago: University of Chicago Press, 2016), ch. 8.

27. See e.g. Theodor Adorno, et al., *The Positivist Dispute in German Sociology*, eds. Glyn Adey and David Frisby (London: Heinemann, 1977).

28. See e.g. Veena Das, *Life and Words: Violence and the Descent into the Ordinary* (Berkeley: University of California Press, 2007), and *Textures of the Ordinary: Doing Anthropology After Wittgenstein* (New York: Fordham University Press, 2020).

29. See e.g. Axel Honneth, *Freedom's Right: The Social Foundations of Democratic Theory* (New York: Columbia University Press, 2014).

30. For general discussions, see e.g. Charles Mills, 'Alternative Epistemologies', in *Blackness Visible: Essays on Philosophy and Race* (Ithaca: Cornell University Press, 1998), 21–39; and 'Ideology', in *The Routledge Handbook of Epistemic Injustice*, ed. Gaile Pohlhaus Jr., et al. (London: Routledge, 2020), 100–112. See also my article 'The Methodological is Political: What's the Matter with "Analytic Feminism"', *Radical Philosophy* 2.02 (2018).

31. See e.g. Singer, *The Most Good You Can Do*, 49–50.

32. Singer, *The Most Good You Can Do*, 39–40 and MacAskill, *Doing Good Better*, 76–77 and ch. 9.

33. Singer, *The Most Good You Can Do*, 50. Singer returns to these topics in a very recent interview, describing as merely 'realistic' the belief that we will continue to have billionaires and opining that 'it's much better to have billionaires like Bill and Melinda Gates or Warren Buffett who give away most of their fortune thoughtfully and in ways that are highly effective' ('Peter Singer is Committed to Controversial Ideas', an interview with Daniel A. Gross, *The New Yorker* (April 2021)). In this interview, Singer traces sources of many of his philosophical ideas, including his commitment to EA, to his sense of the lack of 'impact' of the ideas of an anti-capitalist Marxist group called Radical Philosophy that was at Oxford when he was a student there. Some of this group's members went on to found the current journal (see Chris Arthur et al., 'Reports', *Radical Philosophy* 1:1 (1972), 30–32). So, it is fitting to use this journal to observe that Singer owes his undeniable 'impact' substantially to his accommodating attitude toward neoliberal capitalism and that, far from vindicating his youthful impatience with radical philosophy, that

'impact' has been in large part a damaging one.

34. For some central treatments of these themes, see John Bellamy Foster, *Marx's Ecology: Materialism and Nature* (New York: Monthly Review Press, 2000); Joan Martinez-Alier, *The Environmentalism of the Poor: A Study of Ecological Conflicts and Valuation* (Cheltenham: Edward Elgar, 2002); Maria Mies and Veronika Bennholdt-Thomsen, *The Subsistence Perspective: Beyond the Globalized Economy* (London: Zed Books, 2000); and Ariel Salleh, *Ecofeminism as Politics: Nature, Marx and the Postmodern* (London: Zed Books, 1997).

35. For a helpful overview, see Johanna Oksala, 'Feminism, Capitalism, and Ecology', *Hypatia* 33:2 (2018), 216–234, esp. 223-229.

36. See Rupert Read, 'Must Do Better', *Radical Philosophy* 2.01 (2018).

37. For discussion of this 'third agricultural revolution', see John Bellamy Foster, 'Marx's Theory of Metabolic Rift: Classical Foundations for Environmental Sociology', *American Journal of Sociology* 105:2 (1999), 366–405.

38. For an account of the relevant – classic – idea of moral corruption, see the writings of Stephen M. Gardiner, especially *A Perfect Moral Storm: the Ethical Tragedy of Climate Change* (Oxford: Oxford University Press, 2011), ch. 9. Gardiner describes 'corruption that targets our ways of talking and thinking, and so prevents us from even seeing the problem in the right way' (301). To speak of such corruption is not to 'vilify any particular individuals' (6) but to highlight forms of moral evasion to which we are especially susceptible – and to which we can succumb in 'good faith' (307) – when we face circumstances of great urgency traceable to practices or institutions in which we participate, and when a clearsighted and responsible response would impose substantial demands. There is a particular danger in cases like these of sliding into reliance on distorting claims and methods that are themselves a 'manifestation of the underlying problem' (Stephen M. Gardiner, 'Geoengineering: Ethical Questions for Deliberate Climate Manipulators', in *Oxford Handbook of Environmental Ethics*, eds. Stephen M. Gardiner and Allen Thompson (Oxford: Oxford University Press, 2017), 501–514, 511). EA is a perfect fit for this familiar notion of moral corruption.

39. Srinivasan, 'Stop the Robot Apocalypse'.

40. Sebo and Singer, 'Activism.'

41. This article was prompted by conversations with directors of animal advocacy organisations and other animal advocates, at a February 2020 Miami meeting of the Brooks Institute for Animal Law and Policy, at which many described damaging effects of EA on their work. Accounts of EA-driven disparagement and funding loss convinced me of the need for a thoroughgoing philosophical and political critique of EA. I am grateful for helpful feedback I received at workshops at Oxford Public Philosophy, the Freie Universität, the University of East Anglia and Åbo Akademi. I have benefited from helpful discussions of these topics over the last several years with Jay Bernstein, Cora Diamond, Lori Gruen, Timothy Pachirat and Amia Srinivasan. I owe thanks to Carol Adams, Victoria Browne, Robin Celikates, Joel de Lara, Diamond, Aaron Gross, Gruen, Nathaniel Hupert and Pachirat for insightful comments on an earlier draft.

A liberal poetics of policy
The contemporary fortunes of Indian higher education
Debaditya Bhattacharya

In *The Evolution of Educational Thought* (1938), Emile Durkheim recounted the historical irony that undergirds the idea of institutionality – by pitting it against the birth of the university in medieval Europe. He noted how the coming into being of a corporative organisation – the *universitas* – was effectively an attempt at 'unionising' the body of teachers. It rose out of a conflict of jurisdictional authority between practicing teachers and the bishop, over the question of who had the *right* to teach. In that sense, the European university evolved from a discursive and executive dispute over the distribution of professional rights – insofar as the cathedral had until then empowered a Chancellor to arbitrarily decide on the conferment of the *licentia docendi* (the license to practice the teaching profession anywhere in Europe). Between 1210 and 1215, through a series of papal bulls, the teachers were recognised as an 'organisation of greater solidarity and of greater strength' capable of autonomously arbitrating on matters of academic practice.[1] The university was thus born into a structure of agonism, the ontological condition of a counter-institution. Interestingly, the weapon that the *universitas* used in this protracted litigious self-development was – as Durkheim succinctly maintains – 'systematic and widespread refusals to teach'.[2] In other words, the battle for recognition was historically won through the moral-political force of what is popularly understood as the strike.

There are three significant structural components about the university character that emerge from this originary parable, and all of them go against a common-sensical or current-day imagining of its role in society. First, the university cohered around a self-consciousness and not prior legislative sanction. To that extent, it was constituted by a political act of will and in direct opposition to the powers that be. Second, the corporative being of the *universitas* did not consist in a moral role or even a social calling; rather it was a definite coincidence of professional interests that brought it about. A practical bargain over teaching labour and its material corollary in an economy of minimum skills or vocational qualification (*sans* any transcendental aura of messianism, but with well-defined rights of access to the social surplus produced by such work) resulted in this transformation. Third and finally, the primary pedagogical legacy of this creature of medieval lore was informed by a rights-claim, and not a traditionally attributed ethic of duty. The modern Humboldtian instantiation of the university, in its co-optation of the incipient labour discourse within a fable of disinterested intellectuality as well as the relinquishment of all matters of appointment to the state,[3] had in fact substantially reneged on all these political promises immanent within its earliest conception.

Colonial pasts, nationalist futures

When, in colonial India, the demand for a national university was articulated along the lineaments of its modern European predecessor,[4] the fortunes of it were almost programmed into a self-fulfilling prophecy. To imagine an anti-colonial resistance taking root in a colonial import was flawed to begin with, in that the institution carried with it the burden of building a 'nation' in the image of one's oppressors. That the structural relationship between the university and the nation-state – both of which were historically conjoined by the imaginative project of colonial modernity[5] – will contort the possible futures of each was adequately warned against by none other than Rabindranath Tagore. In his efforts to experiment with a radically different idea of a 'world university',[6] he sought to escape the narrow distinctions of national spirit and utilitarian self-sufficiency at once. In his elaborate manifesto for 'The Centre of Indian Culture', Tagore presciently writes as early as 1919:

> Lately, most of our attempts to establish national schools and universities were made with the idea that it was external independence which was needed. We forget that the same weakness in our character, or in our circumstances, which inevitably draws us on to the slippery slope of imitation, will pursue us when our independence is merely of the outside. For then our freedom will become the freedom to imitate the foreign institutions, thus bringing our evil fortune under the influence of the conjunction of two malignant planets – those of imitation and the badness of imitation – producing a machine-made University, which is made with a bad machine ... [A]s soon as the idea of a University enters our mind, the idea of a Cambridge University, Oxford University, and a host of other European Universities, rushes in at the same time and fills the whole space. We then imagine that our salvation lies in a selection of the best points of each patched together in an eclectic perfection ...[7]

A hundred years on, the Tagorean caution seems to have achieved the force of a consummate truth – as public universities in India continue to be poised between an incomplete attempt at decolonisation and the compulsions of a global market. While a familiar lament about the absence of Indian higher education institutions in world ranking charts is regularly sounded,[8] the past six years of a Hindutva disciplining of public-funded universities have accused the latter of betraying a nationalist consensus. Faced with criticism on policy measures, the Indian Prime Minister has even actively abetted a climate of anti-intellectualism by pitting the *Harvard* pedigree of prominent scholar-critics (for example, the Nobel-winning economist Amartya Sen) against his own '*hard work*' of nation-building – and thus urging people to denounce such voices.[9] Consequently, study circles have

been proscribed, ruling-party bigots nominated to positions of institutional leadership, research fellowships blocked, Dalit students ghettoised, leading to suicide, a Muslim researcher assaulted and forced to disappear from campus, student leaders arrested on charges of sedition, teachers suspended for staging 'anti-national' plays or organising 'anti-government' talks, public intellectuals harassed and incarcerated for doubling up as 'urban Naxals', a campus library raided by riot action forces and student hostels bombed with stun grenades.[10] Alongside all this, student fees have been periodically hiked,[11] departments defunded and threatened with closure,[12] universities empowered to open self-financed courses[13] and foreign institutions encouraged to set up shop in the name of internationalising higher education.[14] Not surprisingly, the very same universities and colleges that were subjected to regular governmental crackdowns came to be subsequently anointed as the 'best performing' institutions through annual surveys and audit-routines – only to then allow them to generate their own resources and work towards a cherished ideal of financial autonomy.[15]

Walking a neoliberal tightrope

Soon after the electoral ascendancy of the Hindu right in 2014, the Narendra Modi government promised a structural refashioning of the education sector through a new national policy. The first committee set up for the purpose, under the chairmanship of a now-deceased bureaucrat TSR Subramanian, spent more than a year drafting a neoliberal manual for successive privatisation. It was in following its recommendations that colleges began being ranked by a state agency, and those occupying either end of the grading spectrum were eventually delinked from state resources. Top-ranked colleges could find investors in the private equity market through appropriate branding measures, while the lowest in the range were to be considered a waste of public money and therefore earmarked for imminent closure.[16] The same policy document, popularly referred to as the *Draft National Policy on Education 2016*, ominously noted in Section 5.4:

> [O]ne finds unions or associations of subsets of students, or teachers, or other employees, who aggressively pursue their special political or other interests, within the arena of the campus, and the college/university ambit. It is

not infrequent that two or more of such groups of students or faculty members come into serious opposition with each other on this or [an]other issue, and have no hesitation in blocking the main-line work of the university; they may have real or imagined grievances, but the collateral damage to the serious students can be heavy indeed ... Universities and colleges are temples of learning. Some self-imposed restrictions surely should be in place to ensure that the primary work of the universities should be conducted without hindrance. Ideally the universities ought not to lend themselves as play grounds for the larger national rivalries, inequalities, inequities, and social/cultural fault-lines; these need to be tackled by society as a whole in other fora such as parliament, courts, elections, etc. The point in short is that it is now essential to review the current situation, and find the balance between free speech and freedom of association guaranteed by the Constitution, the needs of various sections of society, and balance them with the primary purpose for which the universities and institutions of higher learning have been established.[17]

Nothing about this recommendation sounds surprising though. In its debunking of the university's relationship with social/cultural fault-lines and an imaginary self-referentiality of assumptions about so-called primary work or primary purpose lies a vehement denial of histories of caste-apartheid underwritten into structures of cognitive labour. This call for a de-politicisation of the university not only responds to the neoliberal pathology of self-aggrandising individualism, but also distorts the story of its medieval origins. By repeatedly emphasising that the 'main-line work of the university' is counterposed to the task of social or political transformation, the Draft of 2016 lent credence to nearly three decades of policy orientation towards human resource development. One would have assumed that the government would lap up such a manifesto, given the latter's careful conjuring of an exit-route for state participation in higher education.

The sequence of events that followed however turned out to be quite contrary. The ruling-party dumped this proposal for following the financialisation plot too manifestly, and appointed a second committee to draw up a renewed roadmap for the nation's educational futures.

Falling into a liberal phantasm

Chaired by renowned space scientist K. Kasturirangan, the new policy-making body spent another one-and-a-half years to reconfigure a national vision in the field – and employed the services of a four-member Drafting Committee, three of whom represented interests of Amer-

ican and Indian private universities as well as corporate-funded think-tanks.[18] The animating spirit of the exercise had evidently not changed, though the terms of public reference – one could guess – would have to be distinctly different this time around.

What emerged from these deliberations – which did not involve representations by any teachers' association or even student bodies (barring the ruling-party's off-shoot)[19] – advocated a wholesale reinvention of universities and colleges as sites of liberal education.[20] The government was initially unsure of the public traction of such a recommendation, and shelved the report until the political harvest of the next general elections was settled in May 2019. Within a week of the Modi government's re-installation at the Centre, the *Draft National Education Policy* was unveiled and placed in the public domain. A year of intense debates followed and several excisions were made in the original *Draft*, until the peak of the pandemic helped the government bypass the parliamentary route and approve the final *National Education Policy (NEP) 2020* through Cabinet fiat. Notably, while the original framework submitted by the Committee had been slashed to one-eighth its size and all documentary attempts at a stock-taking of the existing systems had been edited out, the overwhelming 'liberal' thrust in the retooling of tertiary education was left untouched.

In the name of an intellectual holism, the *NEP 2020* stressed that the 'notion of a "knowledge of many arts" or what in modern times is often called the "liberal arts" (i.e., a liberal notion of the arts) must be brought back to Indian education, as it is exactly the kind of education that will be required for the 21st century'.[21] To this effect, it suggested that compulsory training in the liberal arts, humanities and social sciences be introduced within routines of technical, professional and vocational education – such that all single-stream institutions of the latter kind may be integrated with multidisciplinary pedagogical practice.[22] The ideal of democratic citizenship was harnessed to the policy *telos* of university education, and it was maintained – almost in stark contrast to the now-junked *Draft* of 2016 – that the purpose of higher studies is 'more than the creation of greater opportunities for individual employment'.[23] The litmus-test of employability that had – since the previous *National Policy on Education 1986* and its subsequent revisions in 1992 – steered the fortunes of higher learning

in intimate partnership with the global marketplace of auctionable labour suddenly became the 'by-product' of institutionalised college curricula.[24] Instead, it was mandated that 'Departments in Languages, Literature, Music, Philosophy, Indology, Art, Dance, Theatre, Education, Mathematics, Statistics, Pure and Applied Sciences, Sociology, Economics, Sports, Translation and Interpretation, and other such subjects needed for a multidisciplinary, stimulating Indian education and environment will be established and strengthened at all HEIs'.[25]

Such a happy marriage of disciplinary *silos* was not only visibly ranged against recent archives of policy-planning in terms of university pedagogy, but it also went against the prerogatives sounded since the first *National Policy on Education (NPE)* of 1968. Hailing higher education as an instrument of economic growth and source of 'manpower' within a developmentalist imagination, the second *NPE* of 1986 was preceded by a re-christening of the education department as the Ministry of Human Resource Development (MHRD).[26] This was to clearly enunciate the priorities of a developing economy in reaping the potential surplus of its labour-power – refashioned as human capital – and, in close alliance with such goals, there were special packages announced for the productivity-enhancing STEM disciplines.[27] In a classic tokenistic inversion of such a scheme of policy wisdom, the final version of *NEP 2020* declaimed:

> To bring the focus back on education and learning, it is desirable that the Ministry of Human Resource Development (MHRD) be re-designated as the Ministry of Education (MoE).[28]

The question that begs to be asked at this point is: what are those structures of desire that necessitate a semiotic shift from the *neoliberal* to the *liberal* within Indian policy-imagination, and especially in the face of continued fascist onslaughts on the university sector? Why must a government, which has faced the stiffest opposition from a secular liberal intelligentsia for its persistent illiberalism and has commandeered all repressive arms of the state to criminalise such opposition for more than six years now, suddenly sing reformist paeans to 'critical thinking and higher-order thinking capacities'?[29] To put it rather aphoristically, how does a training in liberal citizenship become the normative logic of authoritarian rule?

The great Indian educational marketplace

One might fathom a two-part answer to this – the parts interconnected by their simultaneity in historical and ideological terms. The first part calls for a detour into the trajectories of international finance, and a gradual unfolding of the concurrent but differentiated histories of globalisation in the North and South. Though the Indian economy officially opened itself up to transnational investments within key industrial sectors in 1991, it inspired relatively little confidence until about the turn of the century. The structural adjustment programmes demanded by the Washington consensus of 1989 saw a desperate reconfiguration of regulatory regimes through legislative incursions, but the Western markets were yet to shed their apprehensions about the adventure it promised. As a result, the influx of foreign capital was slow and largely conditioned by financial perceptions of risk. It was only with the stock-market upheavals portended by the 'dotcom' and Enron scandals between 2001 and 2004 that the recessionary wave hit the high havens of development. The aleatory *outsides* to the downturn were identified in the emerging market economies (EMEs) and the 'third world' nations – now fancifully picking up in crisis-management discourse as the 'global South'. Insofar as these new investment-destinations had hardly resisted the dominant model of globalisation and had instead become its bailout zone, the neoliberal experiment finally found an opportune reincarnation in countries like India. Given its population statistics and a ready market of cheap but over-available labour-power, all that India needed in order to translate its super-power fantasies was a reaping of the demographic dividend through mass-skilling exercises.

While the leash of austerity cuts plagued resource allocations for education in the West, Indian policy-makers spelt out a rare variety of enthusiasm for democratising educational outreach and delivery through the first decade of the millennium. Universities and colleges were marked out as factories for producing flexible but specialised labour for the low-wage service-industries, which had – since the aftermath of the oil/energy crisis in late-1970s USA – been outsourced by international markets in order to reduce cost liabilities. India's offer of higher education under the World Trade Organisation's General Agreement on Trade in Services (WTO-GATS), in the 2001 Doha Round of negotiations invited multilateral trade in the sector and pledged a curtailment of national subsidies in order to ease the move.[30] This was followed by a *Model Universities Act 2004* that urged institutions towards competitive regimes of resource-generation through diversification of curricula.[31] The push for vocational and basic skilling courses – within the precincts of the traditional university – saw a strategic neglect for the liberal disciplines.[32] And yet, more and more universities were established in relatively remote locations in the name of democratising higher education. The Eleventh Five Year Plan (2007-2012), the National Knowledge Commission Reports (2006-2009) and the Yash Pal Committee Report (2009) culminated in the setting up of 15 new central universities across the country through a single piece of legislation in 2009.[33] Ironically, the Euro-American academy was in the vortex of a large-scale delegitimisation at exactly the same moment in history. In terms of pedagogical reform however, the forceful and mindless mimesis of American paradigms – like the semester system, the four-year undergraduate programme and a cafeteria model of choice-based credit transfer – continued without respite.[34] By peddling employability and global relevance as the only governing shibboleths of educational planning, there were even attempts at passing a Foreign Education Providers Bill in parliament on two successive occasions in 2010 and 2013.[35]

Post-productionist paranoias

The forced expansion of the higher education market, coupled with ill-suited structural changes within pedagogy – such as a wholesale import of the semester system and reduced teaching time for masses of systemically deprived students, or adding an extra year of college in order to impart low-level cognitive skills across motley subjects – soon started showing its effects. An economy of mass-producing specialised labour from within the college sector had its direct impact on the conditions of employment and dignity of work: rates of wage-compensation were depressed, whole-scale informalisation of job contracts followed, social security measures were withdrawn and there was a growing loss of jobs proportionate to one's skills/qualifications. Understandably,

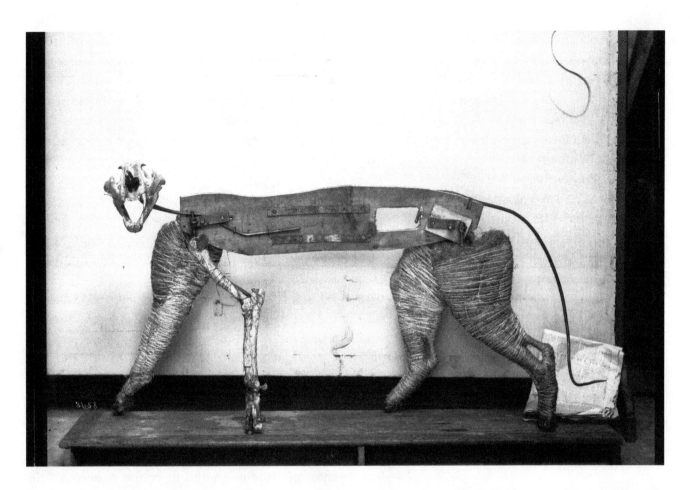

domestic consumption contracted and global investors started seeking an exit in the fear of potential losses. The plummeting indices of economic growth, coupled with the optics of major financial scams involving an erstwhile ruling-party leadership between 2010 and 2013, became the cause for a cultural triumphalism on the part of the Hindu right. A widespread climate of economic disaffection within the country was not only converted into a spectacular failure of the developmentalist state, but was more accurately channeled into cultural anxieties about how jobs and lands of the 'sons of the soil' were under threat from foreign 'infiltrators' from the neighbouring Muslim nations. The general elections of 2014, which saw rioteering communal forces thump their way into power, became in effect the demand for a grand plebiscite on the Hindu nation. Predictably, as the economic emergency deepened, the political narrative was engineered to seek an identification of the 'illegal migrant' and a securitisation of national interest by re-codifying the imaginative limits of being-citizen. State-supported instances of local vigilantism, aided by a series of mob lynchings and extra-judicial action, turned the most vulnerable (and hence, incessantly mobile) forms of labour into spectres of civilisational terror and scavengers on national wealth.

On the other hand, a continued spate of ill-thought economic reforms – like demonetisation of high-value legal tender in 2016 and the 2017 imposition of a centralised tax regime in violation of the distributive federal powers of local state governments – ushered the economy into an irrecoverable crisis and forced millions of jobless workers into chronic precarity.[36] That the Subramanian Committee's 2016 recommendations for market-oriented reforms in education found no takers in the government at the time assumes its true import in the context of this history – insofar as the economic mobility rationale of higher learning was already busted. A narrative nauseatingly recycled since the Ambani-Birla Report of April 2000 – that a college degree leads to higher private lifetime incomes or greater creditworthiness in the debt market[37] – was apodictically exposed as a hoax. Education now had to be an end in itself and not a means to employment. In other words, the distribution of its surplus had to be limited to the use value of the commodity purchased, while imploding the potential for any productive exchange in the future.

With Indian universities belching out a surplus population of exploitable labour, rates of unemployment in 2017-18 touched a 45-year peak according to initially-censured government data.[38] Labour Bureau Surveys from consecutive years (2014 to 2016) proved that there were three times the quantum of formally-trained skills available in the market than there were jobs.[39] The All India Survey on Higher Education (AISHE) Report 2017-18, when read in conjunction with the Periodic Labour Force Surveys (PLFS) from the same period, betrayed similar statistical shockers – for example, 18 out of 26 college-educated men in India were not even informally employed while for women the corresponding rate was 20 out of every 25.[40] Under such circumstances, what could a promised National Education Policy pronounce as immediate panacea? The *NEP 2020* is meticulously calculated to re-enchant the loss of a 'normative justification' for higher education. How it performs this function comprises the second part of my promised explanation here.

Reimagining citizenship

The policy document's inspired prose around a newfound liberal agenda is shaped into this much-needed epistemological therapy for the ailing public university in India. It involves a training in civic behaviours that can seek legislative articulation in the parliament and courts, but must garner the ideological force of hegemony through institutionalised higher education. The new citizenship laws of the country set the limits of the epistemic forecast for the public university through its definition of the 'national public'. That an amendment to India's citizenship routines preceded the publication of a liberal education policy is, therefore, far from fortuitous.

In early December 2019, the Citizenship Amendment Act (CAA) was passed by brute numerical force in the Indian parliament and mandated the conferral of citizenship to 'illegal migrants' of all religious faiths barring Muslims.[41] Repeatedly publicised as part of an accompanying chronology of bureaucratic tests of citizenship – through integration with population census and compulsory registration of lineage – the said Act specifically threatened the Muslim poor with judicial and administrative harassment, detention and deportation.[42] Students of public universities from across the country

joined in with mass uprisings against this slew of discriminatory civic rights-reforms, to which the state responded with terror and a communal massacre in the month of February 2020.[43] While the pandemic foreclosed the possibility for physical demonstrations for months thereafter, it also provided the government an opportunity to re-instrumentalise its biggest detractors within intellectual professions with the civic malcontents of its political ideology. Since the process of accruing legitimacy for laws – through the production of citizen-subjects – is the stated vocation of the liberal university, the *NEP* proposes a nationalist fantasy as the democratic consensus.[44]

In this, it is neither paradoxical nor accidental that the interpellative terms of Indian higher education discourse that have gone completely missing between *NPE 1986/92* and *NEP 2020* include both 'human resource' as well as 'secularism' or 'reservation policy'.[45] Placed against the present context, the university is not obligated to provide social mobility or social justice – and yet garbs itself in the literal mystification of liberalism.

This exhibitionism of liberalism – as either a guarantor of citizenly sentiment or the preserve of the class/caste-elite in expensive private universities – does not require us to go very far to understand its eventual destiny. In mid-March 2021, there was much media uproar over the purportedly forced resignations of key intellectual voices from a certain private university that has not only been touted as the leading liberal arts institution in the country, but had also generated effusive enthusiasm for the *NEP*'s advocacy of liberal training.[46] In fact, one of these intellectuals – a leading political commentator and an erstwhile Vice Chancellor of the same university – had even been part of the consultative process that gave shape to the Draft *NEP 2019*. On his exit from the university, much was written in the popular press about the survival struggles of a dissensual consciousness in these lone private universities and how that too is under siege from the current ruling dispensation. The founders of the university perceived a political liability in associating with overly outspoken professors, and have been severally and deservedly charged with violation of due process as well as the institution's haloed founding-principle. But there is an evil irony here. The working committee of the Draft *NEP 2019* – as I have already shown – included an overwhelming majority representation from national/global private institutions and entities. If a privatised order of institutional liberalism can be the legitimate ground for manufacturing nationalist consent (in the exact terms of a Vedic 'golden age' theory, found in the *NEP)*, why must it be expected to curate dissent beyond digitally-administered doses of vision-and-mission statements?

Reproducing surplus labour

By way of concluding, it is perhaps important to query whether the *NEP*'s acknowledgment of the redundancy of employment-concerns within higher education is really antithetical to the neoliberal character of development. Put differently, does the reinstatement of a liberal penchant at the heart of the university's self-imagining mark a definite departure from neoliberal fortunes? It would seem to confirm quite the opposite, in fact. And the key to this rhetorical paradox lies in the policy-muddle of what has been called multidisciplinarity. A liberal education, the *NEP* framework contends, may only be possible through a default 'multidisciplinary' focus that 'would aim to develop all capacities of human beings – intellectual, aesthetic, social, physical, emotional, and moral in an integrated manner'.[47] To achieve this goal, not only must smaller institutions be merged and swallowed within college complexes, but

> [ev]en engineering institutions, such as Indian Institutes of Technology (IITs), will move towards more holistic and multidisciplinary education with more arts and humanities. Students of arts and humanities will aim to learn more science and all will make an effort to incorporate more vocational subjects and soft skills.[48]

Borrowing explanatory registers from the policy document, a multidisciplinary undergraduate programme requires a student to study different subjects at distinct points of time – for example, a physics major opting for a paper in Sanskrit poetry or an enrolment in sociology being offered a semester's worth of management studies. On the face of it, this might sound invigoratingly close to what we identify as interdisciplinary intellectual practice.

But I would insist that the politics of radical interdisciplinarity is as far removed from a liberal multidisciplinary curriculum as possible – inasmuch as the former probes the limits of a discipline through counterfactual intersections, while the latter dabbles in a cognitive skilling across multiple disciplines without necessarily questioning the self-composition of either. In the process, what it prepares for is a multi-tasking workforce with minimal cognitive competence in varied disciplines of dubious (and understandably diluted) quality.[49] Universities and colleges are effectively (re)turned to their fate as factory-units for mass-producing semi-skilled, cheap, informal labour – lacking substantive depth in any subject while potentially manoeuvring the know-how demanded by low-paying jobs in multiple sectors. This was explicitly spelt out in the original report of the Kasturirangan Committee thus:

> Simply tailoring people into jobs that exist today, but that are likely to change or disappear after some years, is suboptimal and even counterproductive.... Single-skill and single-discipline jobs are likely to become automated over time. Therefore, there will be a great need to focus on multidisciplinary and 21st century competencies for future work roles.... By focusing on such broad based, flexible, individualised, innovative, and multidisciplinary learning, higher education must aim to prepare its students not just for their first jobs – but also for their second, third, and all future jobs over their lifetimes.[50]

By admitting to a permanent informalisation of employment opportunities, the expansive vision behind *NEP 2020* stitches up the logic of multidisciplinarity as an emergency-antidote to economic precarity. It confirms the recessionary demands of the present, and proposes a model of cognitive citizenship as perfect condition for maximal human resource exploitability.

Why else, one must posit, would a policy-template that waxes eloquent about the need for breaching disciplinary *silos* not name for once those sites of interdisciplinary intellectual practice that currently exist across Indian universities – such as women's studies, studies in social exclusion, human rights studies, economic and social planning, comparative literature, etc.? More urgently, why does the *NEP* not say a word about the systematic threats of closure to more than 167 Centres for Women's Studies and 35 Centres for Studies in Social Exclusion and Inclusive Policy since 2017?[51] These interdisciplinary programmes of social scientific study, instituted for the most part as schemes incorporated between the Eighth (1992-1997) and Tenth Five Year Plans (2002-2007), have functioned effectively for decades before being hounded by annual reviews and pleas for extension since the abolition of the Planning Commission.[52] The latest in the chronicle of such attacks saw the Saroijini Naidu Centre for Women's Studies in Jamia Millia Islamia University – a public institution now identified as having spearheaded the movement against *CAA 2019* – issued cursory notices for dissolution in the middle of the pandemic, which were then later withdrawn in the face of a public outcry.[53]

The reason for a policy bulletin's studied silence on the place of these long-repressed undersides to secular-liberal social sciences within the university is due to a fundamental distinction between the scourge of the multidisciplinary vis-à-vis the scope of the interdisciplinary. True interdisciplinarity is about honing a condition of epistemic immigrancy. It interrogates the methodological violence(s) of *borders* on/against disciplines, instead of reveling in a touristic uncriticality of wonder and museumised charades of difference. Studying literature and sociology and politics as separate curricular components does not on its own produce the alchemical charge of gender studies, and can therefore be easily made to replace existing departments of women's studies. The corollary benefits of such a substitution would include a complete exorcism of the understanding of sexual harassment from within the feudality of academic practice, and in the process forestall the possible futures of #MeToo movements across our universities. It appears that India's official vision for national education – in completing Tagore's century-old angst – echoes the *double dangers* of a nation of 'mimic *men*' and of the machines with which they are mimed.

Debaditya Bhattacharya teaches literature at Kazi Nazrul University, India. His current interests revolve around a 'historical sociology' of the Indian university. He is editor of The Idea of the University: Histories and Contexts *(2019) and* The University Unthought: Notes for a Future *(2019), and co-editor of* Sentiment, Politics, Censorship: The State of Hurt *(2016).*

Notes

1. Emile Durkheim, 'The Birth of the University: The *inceptio* and the *licentia docendi*', in *The Evolution of Educational Thought: Lectures on the formation and development of secondary education in France*, trans. Peter Collins (London: Routledge and Kegan Paul, 1977 [1938]), 75–87.
2. Durkheim, 'The Birth of the University', 83.

3. Wilhelm von Humboldt, 'On the Internal and External Organisation of the Higher Scientific Institutions in Berlin', in *Works in German, Volume 4: Writings on Politics and Education*, eds. Andreas Flitner and Klaus Giel, trans. Thomas Dunlap (Darmstadt: Wissenschaftliche Buchgesellschaft, 1982 [1810]). Humboldt maintains: 'Since these institutions can thus achieve their purpose only if each one, as much as possible, faces the pure idea of science, solitariness and freedom are the predominant principles in their circle ... [A]s far as the externality of the relationship to the state and its activity in all of this is concerned, it must only ensure the wealth (strength and variety) of mental power through the choice of the men that should be assembled ... The appointment of university teachers must be reserved exclusively to the state, and it is surely not a good practice to allow the faculties more influence on it than a perspicacious and reasonable committee would exercise on its own ... Moreover, the make-up of the universities is too closely tied to the immediate interests of the state' (3–5).
4. For an understanding of the context, see Aurobindo Ghose, 'A National University', in *Sri Aurobindo Birth Centenary Library, Volume 1: Early Political Writings 1890 – May 1908* (Pondicherry: Sri Aurobindo Ashram, 1973 [1908]). Ghose articulates his demand in contradistinction to Annie Besant's, and sees the early lineaments of a 'national institution' in the National Council of Education in Bengal: 'National education cannot be defined briefly in one or two sentences, but we may describe it tentatively as the education which starting with the past and making full use of the present builds up a great nation ... So shall the Indian people cease to sleep and become once more a people of heroes, patriots, originators, so shall it become a nation and no longer a disorganised mass of men' (895).
5. Bjorn Wittrock, 'The Modern University: The Three Transformations', in *The European and American University since 1800: Historical and Sociological Essays*, eds. Sheldon Rothblatt and Wittrock (Cambridge: Cambridge University Press, 1993), 303–362.
6. For more on Tagore's pedagogical experiments at Visvabharati in a provincial *ashram*-location of Shantiniketan, see Himangshu B. Mukherjee, *Education for Fullness: A Study of the Educational Thought and Experiment of Rabindranath Tagore* (New Delhi: Routledge, 2013 [1962]); see also Kumkum Bhattacharya, *Rabindranath Tagore: Adventure of Ideas and Innovative Practices in Education* (Heidelberg and New York: Springer, 2014).
7. Rabindranath Tagore, 'The Centre of Indian Culture', in *The English Writings of Rabindranath Tagore, Volume Two: Plays, Stories, Essays*, ed. Sisir Kumar Das (New Delhi: Sahitya Akademi, 1996 [1919]), 470–71.
8. Jayanta Gupta, 'President Pranab Mukherjee Rues No Indian University in World's Top 200', *The Times of India*, 16 September 2012.
9. Lalmani Verma, 'Harvard vs Hard Work: With GDP Data, PM Narendra Modi Snubs Note Ban Critics', *The Indian Express*, 2 March 2017.
10. For a ready reckoner on how Indian universities have become the battleground for a muscular right-wing fanaticism over the past six years, see Sruthisagar Yamunan, 'IIT-Madras derecognises student group', *The Hindu*, 28 May 2015; 'Rohith

Vemula didn't get fellowship for past 7 months, says letter', *The Economic Times*, 19 January 2016; 'My Birth is My Fatal Accident: Rohith Vemula's Searing Letter is an Indictment of Social Prejudices', *The Wire*, 17 January 2019; 'Police crack down at JNU, arrest student leader for sedition', *The Hindu Business Line*, 12 February 2016; Munish Chandra Pandey, 'JNU student Najeeb Ahmed's disappearance to remain mystery, CBI ends search', *India Today*, 16 October 2018; Aman Sethi, 'Reading Foucault in Mahendragarh, or Why We Need a Public University System', *The Wire*, 10 May 2016; Prajakta Hebbar, 'Haryana Professors Reprimanded For Staging Play Based On Mahasweta Devi Story', *Huffpost*, 9 November 2016; 'After national flag, Smriti Irani ropes in Army to teach nationalism on campus', *India Today*, 15 March 2016; 'Who is an urban naxal, asks Romila Thapar', *The Hindu*, 30 September 2018; 'Purported CCTV Footage Shows Police Attacking Students in Jamia Library on Dec 15', *The Wire*, 17 February 2020.

11. 'Education for all? Universities across India fight fee hikes', *India Today*, 19 December 2019; Aranya Shankar, Dipti Nagpaul and Ankita Dwivedi Johri, 'Not just JNU: How India's public universities becoming costlier hurts the most vulnerable', *The Indian Express*, 1 December 2019.

12. Mridula Chari, '35 staff at Mumbai's TISS are fired because of UGC funding ambiguity', *Scroll*, 26 March 2017; Sushmitha Ramakrishnan, 'All for a name? JNU centre on UGC fund exclusion list', *The New Indian Express*, 17 March 2017; Priyanka Dasgupta, 'JU School of Women's Studies Staffers Brace for Uncertain Future', *The Times of India*, 31 March 2017.

13. 'UGC grants full autonomy to 62 higher educational institutes', *The Times of India*, 20 March 2018; Debaditya Bhattacharya and Rina Ramdev, 'Autonomy in Higher Education, a Trojan Horse for Privatisation', *The Wire*, 23 March 2018.

14. Government of India, *The Foreign Educational Institutions (Regulation of Entry and Operations) Bill* (New Delhi: Ministry of Human Resource Development, 2010); S. Vaidhyasubramaniam, 'Foreign Universities Bill, an Unprescribed Pill', *The Hindu*, 1 August 2010; Ministry of Human Resource Development (MHRD) and Confederation of Indian Industry (CII), 'FDI in Indian Higher Education', in *Annual Status of Higher Education in States and Union Territories in India* (New Delhi: CII, 2014), 15–20.

15. Debaditya Bhattacharya, 'What Makes the Public University Anti-National?', *The Wire*, 18 December 2018.

16. *Draft National Policy on Education 2016: Report of the Committee for Evolution of the New Education Policy* (New Delhi: Ministry of Human Resource Development, 2016), Section 7.5.19, 143.

17. Draft *NPE 2016*, 51–52.

18. See 'Appendix I' of the *Draft National Education Policy 2019* (New Delhi: Ministry of Human Resource Development, 2019), 439, which states the composition of the Drafting Committee as including a professor of mathematics at Princeton University, an employee of Wipro Industries Limited and a functionary of a think-tank funded by Reliance Industries. The Indian government was represented by a lone Advisor to the National Institute Educational Planning and Administration (NIEPA) on that body. See also 'The curious case of Azim Premji Foundation and the new NEP 2020: How and why big business takes over education policy during post-Fordism', On Human Condition

Blog, accessed 31 July 2020.

19. 'Appendix VII' of the Draft *NEP 2019*, 453 – which furnishes 'Details of Consultations by the Committee for Draft National Education Policy (July 2017 onwards)' – does not name any teachers' or students' union barring the Akhil Bharatiya Vidyarthi Parishad (ABVP). The ABVP is a Hindu nationalist organisation affiliated to the Rashtriya Swayamsevak Sangh (RSS) and responsible for much of the recent lumpen violence on public university campuses referenced elsewhere in the essay.

20. Part II, Chapter 11 ('Towards a More Liberal Education') of the Draft *NEP 2019* notes: 'The purpose and importance of a liberal arts education today – i.e. an education across the *kalas* – is to enable students to explore the numerous remarkable relationships that exist among the sciences and the humanities, mathematics and art, medicine and physics, etc. – and more generally, to explore the surprising unity of all fields of human endeavour. A comprehensive liberal arts education develops all capacities of human beings – intellectual, aesthetic, social, physical, emotional and moral – in an integrated manner. Such education, which develops the fundamental capacities of individuals on all aspects of being human, is by its very nature liberal education, and is aimed at developing good and complete human beings' (224).

21. *NEP 2020*, 36.

22. *NEP 2020*, Section 10.11, 35.

23. *NEP 2020*, 33.

24. *NEP 2020*, Section 11.8, 37.

25. *NEP 2020*, 37.

26. Shyamlal Yadav, 'Explained: How India's Education Ministry became "HRD Ministry", and then returned to embrace Education', *The Indian Express*, 1 August 2020.

27. Section 7 of the first *National Policy on Education 1968* (Government of India: Ministry of Education, 1968) holds that '[w]ith a view to accelerating the growth of the national economy, science education and research should receive high priority.' Section 6.13 of the second *National Policy on Education 1986* (GoI: Ministry of Human Resource Development, 1986) continues this strain of policy wisdom by enlisting research as a prerogative of 'higher technical institutions' alone, in the cause of 'producing quality manpower' (22).

28. *NEP 2020*, 60.

29. *NEP 2020*, 36.

30. All India Forum for Right to Education (AIFRTE), 'Fight against inclusion of higher education in WTO', *The Companion*, 5 April 2015.

31. 'Commercialisation of Education – Teachers Protest Against UGC Model Act', *Labour File* 2:1 (January-February 2004); 'Protest against UGC Act continues', *The Times of India*, 22 January 2004.

32. *National Knowledge Commission: Report to the Nation 2006-2009* (New Delhi: Government of India, 2009) dedicated elaborate chapters to discussing 'Vocational Education and Training', 'Management Education', 'Engineering Education' – and even two separate sections on attracting 'More Talented Students in Maths and Science' (96-110) – but spared not a word on the fate of liberal arts disciplines.

33. See Central Universities Act 2009, *The Gazette of India Part II, Section I* (New Delhi: Ministry of Law and Justice, 2009).

34. For a chronology of how half-baked curricular imports have been imposed in the most unilateral fashion across Indian higher education – often using the 82 colleges of Delhi University as the testing ground for infamous 'reform-agendas' – see Mukul Mangalik, '"Up Against the Wall'5" but Not "Down and Out" at Delhi University', *The Wire*, 26 June 2018; Pratik Kumar, 'FYUP to CBCS, game of choices', *Deccan Herald*, 9 August 2015.

35. GoI, *Foreign Educational Institutions Bill*. See Nandini Chandra, 'Private Nation, Public Funds: The Case of the Foreign Education Providers (Regulation of Entry and Operation) 2010 Bill', *Sanhati* (2011) – for a deeper analysis of the Bill, reintroduced in the Indian parliament in 2013.

36. For analyses of the economic impact of these hastily-implemented authoritarian moves, see Arun Kumar, 'Economic Consequences of Demonetisation', *Economic and Political Weekly* 52:1 (January 2017) and 'The Structurally Flawed GST', *Economic and Political Weekly* 54:9 (March 2019).

37. Mukesh Ambani and Kumarmangalam Birla, 'Report on a Policy Framework for Reforms in Education', *Journal of Indian School of Political Economy* 15:4 (2003), 840–45.

38. 'Unemployment rate at 45-year high, confirms Labour Ministry data', *The Hindu*, 31 May 2019; for factors leading to such 'jobless growth', see also Jayan Jose Thomas, 'Missing the Demographic Window of Opportunity? Labour Market Changes in India, 2005-2018', *Economic and Political Weekly* 55:34 (22 August 2020); Indrajit Bairagya, 'Why is Unemployment Higher among the Educated?', *Economic and Political Weekly* 53:7 (17 February 2018); Rahul Menon, 'Never Done, Poorly Paid, and Vanishing: Female Employment and Labour Force Participation in India', *Economic and Political Weekly* 54:19 (11 May 2019); 'Editorial – The Unemployment Paradox: Looking at Growth Without Jobs', *EPW Engage*, accessed 30 October 2020.

39. For details, see *Report on Education, Skill Development and Labour Force, Volume III, 2013-14* (Chandigarh: Labour Bureau, Government of India, 2014); *Economic Survey 2014-15* (New Delhi: Ministry of Finance, Government of India, 2015); *Report on Education, Skill Development and Labour Force, Volume III, 2015-16* (Chandigarh: Labour Bureau, Government of India, 2016); see also Subodh Varma, 'Survey: Even Among Skilled Workers Joblessness Is High', *The Times of India*, 20 July 2015.

40. Compare Section 2.3, *All India Survey on Higher Education 2017-18* (Government of India: Department of Higher Education, Ministry of Human Resource Development, 2018) with Section E, *Periodic Labour Force Survey 2017-18* (Government of India: National Statistical Office, Ministry of Statistics and Programme Implementation, 2019).

41. For an understanding of the fuller implications of the Amendment, see Soumya Shankar, 'India's Citizenship Law, in Tandem with National Registry, Could Make BJP's Discriminatory Targeting of Muslims Easier', *The Intercept*, 30 January 2020; Saba Naqvi, 'Citizenship Amendment Bill: A Noose Around Necks of Muslims', *Outlook*, 11 December 2019; Rohit De and Surabhi Ranganathan, 'We Are Witnessing a Rediscovery of India's Republic', *The New York Times*, 27 December 2019.

42. '"Aap chronology samajh lijiye": Amit Shah's phrase on NRC-CAA is the internet's favourite meme', *The Free Press Journal*, 30 December 2019; Venkitesh Ramakrishnan, 'What is the BJP up to?', *Frontline*, 17 January 2020.

43. Ankita Dwivedi Johri, 'From anti-CAA protests, to JNU and Jamia, why women are leading the fight', *The Indian Express*, 19 January 2020; 'Resistance, revolution and resolve: How Indian students led the anti-CAA protests', *Sabrang*, 23 December 2019. For a detailed report on the role of the state machinery and police authorities in the planning and abetting of the 'pogrom', see *Report of the DMC Fact-Finding Committee on North-East Delhi Riots of February 2020* (New Delhi: Delhi Minorities Commission, Government of NCT of Delhi, 2020). A complete catalogue of events and the deliberate provocations that engineered the murderous communal violence may be found in 'Investigative Briefing: Six Months since Delhi Riots, Delhi Police Continue to Enjoy Impunity despite Evidence of Human Rights Violations', Amnesty International India (28 August 2020), accessed 4 April 2021.

44. The *NEP 2020* articulates its 'Vision' in the introductory section of the final document thus: 'This National Education Policy envisions an education system rooted in Indian ethos that contributes directly to transforming India, that is Bharat, sustainably into an equitable and vibrant knowledge society, by providing high-quality education to all, and thereby making India a global knowledge superpower.' Continuing in the same breath, it then enjoins this 'superpower'-fantasy and desire for 'globality' to the task of 'instill[ing] among the learners a deep-rooted pride in being Indian, not only in thought, but also in spirit, intellect, and deeds, as well as to develop knowledge, skills, values, and dispositions that support responsible commitment to human rights, sustainable development and living, and global well-being, thereby reflecting a truly global citizen.' (6)

45. See Basant Kumar Mohanty, 'Out: Secularism In: Gita ideal', *The Telegraph*, 2 August 2020; Kumkum Roy, 'National Education Policy needs close scrutiny for what it says, what it doesn't', *The Indian Express*, 31 July 2020; Prem Singh, 'National Education Policy for the elites', *The Indian Express*, 22 October 2020.

46. See 'Pratap Bhanu Mehta, Critic of Government Policies, Resigns as Professor at Ashoka University', *The Wire*, 17 March 2021; Shradha Chettri, 'After Pratap Bhanu Mehta, ex-CEA also resigns from Ashoka University', *The Times of India*, 19 March 2021.

47. *NEP 2020*, 36.

48. *NEP 2020*, 37.

49. See Akshita Jain, 'How NEP Will Increase Cost Of Good Education And Produce A Semi-Skilled Workforce', *Huffpost*, 7 August 2020.

50. *Draft NEP 2019*, 202-203.

51. See Pranita Kulkarni, 'Centres for social exclusion and women's studies face uncertain future', *Governance Now*, 29 September 2017.

52. For the history behind this onslaught and the immediate policy-precedents that underpin it, see Debaditya Bhattacharya, 'Between disciplines and interdisciplines: the university of in-discipline', in *The University Unthought: Notes for a Future*, ed. Debaditya Bhattacharya (London: Routledge, 2019), 183–208.

53. See Ismat Ara, 'As Students and Teachers Panic, Jamia Withdraws Notice Disbanding Two Departments', *The Wire*, 7 April 2020.

Authoritarian and neoliberal attacks on higher education in Hungary

Céline Cantat and Pınar E. Dönmez

In April 2017, a law adopted by the Hungarian authorities, and promptly nicknamed 'Lex CEU', made the operation of the Central European University (CEU) impossible. The CEU is an English language graduate university with accreditation both in Hungary and in the USA, which was based in Budapest from 1991. Following a long process of attempted negotiations on the part of the university's management, the decision was eventually taken in January 2018 to move the institution across the Austrian border, to Vienna, where it started some educational activities in Autumn 2019. By the start of the present academic year, virtually all of CEU's teaching activities and most of its research had been moved, leaving behind only a few units whose workers operate at a distance, and a newly created 'Democracy Institute', hosting some of the researchers the university had not taken with it to Vienna and presented as a moral and political legacy of CEU in Hungary.

CEU's displacement received much attention as the only university to have been expelled from a European country. The story of the confrontation between the institution and the Hungarian authorities was essentially told as one of violation of academic freedom and freedom of expression. Indeed, the attacks against the university took place in the broader context of an authoritarian shift in the country, targeting both a range of social groups seen as deviant and undesirable (migrants, of course, but also the Roma, LGBTQI+, homeless and unemployed people, among others) and the production of critical knowledge, with the abolition of gender studies as a certified discipline and the harassment of various critical scholars working on issues related to migration, race, sex and sexuality. In this sense, the evacuation of CEU was seen as the apex of the repressive politics of the ultraconservative party in power, Fidesz, and its strongman and Hungary's Prime Minister, Viktor Orbán.

While there certainly is a lot of truth to this account, it tends to isolate CEU's move to Austria from the politics of education that have emerged in Hungary over the last few decades, which are underpinned by a broader transformation of social relations in the country. It does so in at least two ways. First, the emphasis that was placed on CEU had a tendency to invisibilise struggles happening in other institutions, particularly in Hungarian public higher education. Most notably perhaps, while publicity was given to CEU's President and Rector, former Canadian politician Michael Ignatieff, in order to expose the plight of his institution and call on international solidarity, much less was said about the dismantling of the Hungarian Academy of Sciences and the pressure exercised over its members engaged in critical research and teaching. Second, the discourse on academic freedom has largely ignored structural transformation of higher education regimes, and in particular the changing conditions of academic labouring and knowledge production within CEU itself. This article argues that the story of CEU and the politics of education that it entails cannot be understood outside a critical analysis of the neoliberal restructuring of education.[1]

After presenting a short timeline of the adoption of 'Lex CEU' and the series of events that eventually led to the departure of the university from Hungary, we suggest that relocating the attacks against CEU within a broader assessment of the politics of higher education in Hungary is a useful entry point to complexify and destabilise the dominant discourses of academic freedom that were deployed to support the university. In turn, we examine the way in which such discourses concealed both structural hierarchies in Hungarian higher education and important evolutions within CEU, notably an ongoing process of marketisation and neoliberalisation.

Illiberal democracy, technocratic politics and the control of higher education

On 10 April 2017, the President of the Republic of Hungary signed a set of amendments to Hungary's national higher education law that effectively rendered impossible the operation of CEU in the country. The adoption of the law was accompanied by attacks on the university in pro-government media outlets, which routinely referred to it as 'Soros University' in reference to its founder and main benefactor George Soros. CEU's Gender Studies department and its newly running Open Learning Initiative unit (OLIve), which provided study programmes to refugee students – and in which both authors of this article were involved at the time and in subsequent years – were recurrent targets of these attacks.[2]

The authorities' rhetoric around CEU and Soros was underpinned by a range of mutually reinforcing narratives. Most notably, it brought Islamophobic and anti-migrant discourses, which had gained currency in the country since 2015 and were premised on the identification of new figures of 'external enemies', together with long-standing tropes of the 'enemies within', drawing on historic antisemitic and anti-Roma politics.[3] Fidesz's positioning in regard to antisemitism is worth highlighting; the party in power simultaneously invoked an antisemitic imaginary, most notably perhaps in its 2017 anti-immigration campaign,[4] while pretending to distance itself from antisemitism in order to sideline and discredit the main opposition party, the overtly antisemitic Jobbik.[5] The coupling of a nationalist, racist and xenophobic political agenda and of revanchist, capitalist social and economic policies has led scholars to draw parallels between Orbán and Hungary's interwar leader and close ally of Hitler, Miklós Horthy.[6]

Against this backdrop, the attacks against CEU were immediately relayed to the international media. Its President and Rector, Michael Ignatieff, became the visible face of a larger campaign condemning Hungary for its breach of academic freedom and its weakening of free speech. Presented in the *New York Times* and the *Washington Post* as attempting to save a last bastion of 'Europe's multicultural, tolerant liberalism', the fight of CEU against the Hungarian authorities attracted widespread support under the rubric #aCEUvalvagyok

(#IstandwithCEU) and was turned into a symbol of enlightened resistance to authoritarianism. Mayors from a range of cities across Eastern Europe broadcast open invitations for the institution to relocate to their municipality,[7] while within Hungary, a wave of support emerged, bringing together tens of thousands for solidarity protests in Budapest.

Throughout the controversy that followed, the official position of the Hungarian government, as repeatedly conveyed by Orbán, was that the reasons for targeting CEU were purely legal. The institution, he claimed, was involved in regulatory infringements which it needed to redress if it wanted to remain operative. Yet even as the university adjusted its institutional structures in order to comply with new requirements over the following years (opening a campus in the US state of New York, among other things), the government refused to sign an agreement allowing it to continue teaching its US-accredited programmes in Hungary. The ways in which Hungarian authorities have pushed an openly racist, capitalist and heteropatriarchal agenda under the depoliticising guise of administrative and technocratic reforms in certain areas,[8] coupled with the imposition of direct executive control in several other policy areas are well-documented.[9] Indeed, the declaration in January 2017 by governing party Fidesz' vice chairman, Szilárd Németh, that Soros-funded organisations had to be 'swept out of Hungary' serves as a clear indicator of the highly political nature of the move against CEU.[10]

The fact that the media attacks that accompanied the adoption of 'Lex CEU' focused on initiatives within the institution that denounced gender inequality and advocated for LGBTQI+ and refugees' rights was not coincidental. It rather reflects the broader project of an illiberal democracy dear to Orbán and which he has described as a way to make the state more competitive and efficient, notably by erasing the obstructive activities of NGOs, civil society groups and critical scholars.[11] With a two-thirds majority in Parliament since its victory in the 2010 general election, Fidesz has been working to operationalise this vision through sweeping reforms in several sectors.[12] The Hungarian Constitution now begins with a statement that highlights the 'role of Christianity in preserving nationhood',[13] and has adopted Cardinal laws (which can only be changed by a two-thirds majority) that define marriage as the union 'of a man and a woman'.[14] In October 2018, a government decree signed by Orbán removed gender studies from the list of approved master's degrees in the country, effectively ending all related programmes.[15]

In this sense, governmental attacks against CEU must be understood within the broader context of an increasingly authoritarian practice of state power, in which organisations involved in rights-based advocacy or critical education have been portrayed and interpellated as traitorous to the national project. Indeed, while much attention was paid to the situation of CEU, in ways that reproduced a distinction between a backward and illiberal East and a progressive and modern West, attacks waged against other higher education institutions and critical researchers in the country attracted much less support. These politics of differentiated (in)visibility are all the more disturbing when we consider that the possibility enacted by CEU to move to and continue its operation in another country – while of course a testimony to the violence of the state and its attacks against higher edu-

cation – remains a privilege inaccessible to Hungarian public institutions.

A year after the adoption of 'Lex CEU', in June 2018, the Hungarian government adopted changes to its research funding system that put a newly formed Ministry for Innovation and Technology (headed by a close ally of Orbán) in charge of decisions over public research funding. In particular, the new law has meant that funding going to the Hungarian Academy of Sciences, the oldest public research institution in the country, would effectively be overseen by the new Ministry. Here as well, the official line was that the logic behind the law was efficiency regarding research funding allocation and management. Yet, a few days following the law proposal, an article published in pro-government outlet Figyelő and titled 'Immigration, homosexual rights and gender theory: these are the topics which occupy the researchers of the Academy', targeted a range of researchers in the Academy's Centre for Social Sciences as politically suspicious and suggested that the government would now

perform greater oversight of their work. In August 2018, a plan to restructure the Academy, introduced by the new Ministry, introduced increased centralisation and further government control over the institution, primarily by abolishing core funding and replacing it exclusively with tender-based financing through thematic focus areas selected by the government.[16]

State attacks on public higher education and research via the control of funding has continued since. After testing the model on the Corvinus University of Budapest, virtually all major public universities have by now been restructured through the setting up of private foundations whose boards of trustees, typically headed by Fidesz loyalists, oversee the funds and budgets of the institutions. Attempts at imposing the new model on the Theatre and Film University (SzFE) led to a series of violent confrontations between the university community and the authorities at the start of the 2020-21 academic year. The restructuring of SzFE must also be understood as an attempt by Fidesz to gain control over a key strategic area for its ultraconservative national project – that of cultural production. In the same vein, the government has made plans to move one of Hungary's main teacher training institutions, the Eszterházy Károly University of Applied Sciences in Eger, under the supervision of the church.[17]

These attacks are in fact part of a long-standing assault by Fidesz against public higher education: as early as 2011, a law introducing draconian reforms and threatening academic freedom and institutional autonomy had set off a strong wave of protests and bottom-up organising of university communities across the country.[18] Yet, attacks on research and higher education, including via the restructuring of public funding, have been all together absent from the international discourse on academic freedom that developed around Hungary and that centred almost exclusively on the evacuation of CEU from the country.

The limits of (neo-)liberal academic freedom

In order to unravel the complex layering of inequalities, hierarchies and struggles that were rendered invisible through the dominant discourse, it is necessary to think beyond (neo)liberal notions of academic freedom

that disconnect its politics from the material conditions that are needed for genuinely free teaching, learning and knowledge production.[19]

Adopting an expansive reading of academic freedom allows us to challenge the contours of capitalist enclosures and recolonisation of the university.[20] In the case of Hungary, it pushes us to examine at least three scales of inequality that become muted in mainstream and hegemonic narratives on higher education: first, the positioning of Hungary in global hierarchies and corresponding hegemonic East/West narratives, which we have touched upon above by contrasting the international response to attacks against CEU, perceived as a primarily US university, *versus* those on local public institutions; second, the social and economic inequalities prevalent within Hungarian society and in public (higher) education; and third, internal hierarchies and resulting invisibility within CEU itself.[21]

With respect to the second and third dimensions, the myopic perspective of a (neo)liberal conception of academic freedom tends to sideline the unequal characteristics of knowledge production and of teaching and learning activities, both in relation to the Hungarian public (higher) education system as well as within CEU. As a private, US-accredited institution, CEU has increasingly been shaped by its embeddedness within a global trend towards commodification and privatisation of higher education, on the one hand, and precaritisation and casualisation of academic labour, on the other.[22] Indeed, the very establishment of CEU and other private universities in Hungary (and more broadly in Central and Eastern Europe) was decisively made possible by structural transformations in the Hungarian HE context from the early 1990s onwards.[23]

Moreover, the institutional nature of CEU and its positioning at the heart of the East/West hierarchies outlined above, have perpetuated the conventional view that *all* its faculty, staff and students benefited from its prestige and privilege in material and symbolic ways. This perception of a homogeneous community, characterised by widespread advantages, contributed to invisibilising a range of hierarchies and inequalities within the institution and diminished the possibilities for greater solidarity with higher education workers outside CEU in the public sector.[24] In particular, the processes of casualisation and fragmentation of academic labour introduced and entrenched new hierarchies and divergent positions within the academic, administrative and subcontracted workforce, which could also be contrasted with those existing within senior university management. The articulation of these positionalities across class, race and gender axes have not been fully acknowledged. The lack of consideration, for instance, of the dramatic rise in problems faced by non-EU university workers and students in securing visa and residence permits after CEU's departure from Hungary to Austria, reflects the intensification of global, national and institutional asymmetries and inequalities.[25] At the same time, the limited acknowledgment of this problem indirectly strengthened the hegemonic governmental narrative by distancing CEU (imagined as a homogeneous block) from the broader society and university communities within public institutions and by overshadowing their shared interests in access to free education, decent and stable work and pay, and intellectual freedom. Another contributing factor to this distancing process has been the relative absence of active solidarity from CEU towards Hungarian public HE institutions in the context of the repeated governmental attacks mentioned above. While solidarity-building improved considerably in the post-2017 period, when the governmental attacks intensified and spread further into several public universities and degree programmes as well as the Hungarian Academy of Sciences, long-entrenched structural hierarchies impacted negatively on the formation of strong bridges between these university communities.

Crisis and the neoliberal restructuring of CEU

Meanwhile, within CEU, senior management's insistence that it was the sole appropriate authority to represent the institution and to respond to governmental attacks yielded a defensive posture, which contributed to the relegation of several crucial matters to a hypothetical future, when the existential crisis triggered by Lex CEU would be overcome.[26] The cultivation of highly individualised, atomised, yet hierarchised neoliberal subjectivities in the global university,[27] coupled with persistent governmental attacks, thus triggered a set of specific and noteworthy trends.

First, it produced significant challenges for attempts to address a range of concerns in a collective fashion. Academic workers in neoliberal universities often find themselves in a double bind. On the one hand, their labour is increasingly subject to casualisation and devaluation – notably characterised by the deterioration of *actual* working conditions – while being pitted against one another in the highly competitive higher education environments fuelled and maintained by alienated academic labour.[28] On the other hand, the alleged prestige and privilege attributed to HEIs and to the products of academic work, as well as the commonly held view that job security is attainable following a period of stoic endurance and perseverance through precarity, often keep many early career scholars, PhD students, and others on insecure contracts and feeling perpetually disempowered.[29]

The hierarchies and marginalisations are further entrenched (and at times weaponised) through uneven, gendered and racialised regimes of care.[30] As teachers and academic supervisors in OLIve – a set of education initiatives for students who had experienced displacement initially formed in a grassroots fashion but which became a CEU unit in 2016 – our experience was shaped in specific ways by such regimes, both because our own institutional positions were made unstable due to the precarity of our unit (which relied in large part on external funds), and because our students tended to be relegated to the margins through disqualifying and exclusionary administrative and/or pedagogical processes.[31]

Moreover, in such an environment, which elevates and prioritises the interests of the abstract individual as its *modus operandi*, attempts at collective claim-making are forced to wage a double-struggle: against the liberal individualistic paradigm that continuously (mis)represents shared grievances and concerns as intending to advance particular interests of individuals/groups *vis-à-vis* the general interest of the university community; and against the existing conditions of precarity and alienation that perpetuate a chronic sense of anxiety and worry about everyday subsistence and the possibilities of meaningful, sustainable work.[32] The subsuming of the collective university voice within that of its President/Rector, as noted earlier, reinforced these internal dynamics, perhaps partly unintentionally, thus sustaining the politics of invisibility that played out at the global and national scales.

A striking manifestation of the intersection between neoliberal politics and authoritarian attacks can be found in the 2018 suspension of the OLIve programmes and of the European Commission-funded research project on migration solidarity.[33] The authoritarian legal backdrop was a series of laws, evocatively labelled the 'Stop Soros' package, rushed through the parliament by the Hungarian government over the course of 2018 and which targeted civil society organisations in the field of migration and actions putatively pertaining to the nebulous notion of 'migration propaganda'. The instrument of repression that led to the suspensions, on the other hand, was economic as it manifested in the form of a tax on the budgets of the organisations whose primary funding source originated from outside Hungary.[34] Even though the legality and constitutionality of the legislation were the subject of much controversy, and were eventually declared in violation of European legislation by the European Court of Justice in 2021, the risk of enforcement proved sufficient to close down projects on migration at CEU.[35] Indeed, the question of who can exercise their right to practice academic freedom gains a whole new meaning from the vantage point of those whose education programmes and research were interrupted and suspended in this period.

In turn, CEU's move to Vienna, against the backdrop of governmental attacks on the institution, accelerated and justified an ongoing internal restructuring process and provided new openings for it. While the seeds of these structural transformations were planted prior to the crisis inaugurated in 2017, it acted as a catalyst to bring them to completion. It also worked as a means to stifle the articulation of a collective, internal critique by the university faculty, staff and students. A concrete manifestation of how these dynamics have impacted the livelihoods of university community members is the limited financial support and scholarships extended to students who cannot otherwise self-fund their studies, accommodation and living expenses in Vienna following the institutional move. This testifies to the evolution of what has been called the student funding model of CEU, which has evolved from a system where virtually every student received a full scholarship when the university opened in the early 1990s to one where most now have to pay tuition fees. Referring to this process as pertaining to CEU's 'changing funding model' is in itself a discursive strategy that localises a broader structural pattern and erases its connection to the global project of neo-

liberalising the university. While it may be thought that any support is still better than no support at all, this reorganisation privileges the enrolment of fee-paying students who have the necessary financial means to fund their studies. This indeed constitutes a sharp move away from CEU's historic student population, which has included many from disadvantaged backgrounds within and beyond Central East Europe. It is evident, therefore, that the impact of this process will be (and is already) felt drastically by those students whose access to funded graduate study has become limited and that this is ultimately transforming the overall spirit and ethos of the university.[36]

Critical contextualisation

We have attempted above to critically reflect on a widely publicised case of direct governmental attacks against a higher education institution in Europe. While fully acknowledging the catastrophic impact of the authoritarian turn in Hungarian politics, we have argued that dominant discourses around the eviction of CEU need more critical contextualisation. In particular, such discourses tend to isolate the plight of CEU from broader processes unfolding within higher education, locally and globally. Exceptionalising CEU makes it difficult to carry out an analysis in relation to what has happened and keeps happening to other academic institutions in Hungary and to universities elsewhere. In contrast, we believe that placing more emphasis on the broader social and political dynamics within which attacks against CEU were embedded allows us to understand better not just the events in themselves, but also the contemporary politics of higher education in the country and beyond.

For this purpose, we have attempted to shed light on a set of social and political layers that tend to go unmentioned in mainstream accounts – namely, the inscription of the CEU events within East/West hierarchies, their relationship with longstanding attacks on Hungarian public higher education, and the way they impacted on the rights and conditions of university workers and students within CEU. This rethinking of the politics of higher education in Hungary from the margins of a neoliberalising university is a call for recentring structurally muted voices and accounting for the diverse constituencies that make up university communities. It is thus part of broader efforts at rethinking the role of universities and academics 'as critic and conscience of society'.[37] We believe that this reflexive exercise is a necessary first step towards building further resistance to the acute sense of alienation and anxiety prevalent across academia in neoliberal and authoritarian times.[38]

Céline Cantat works at the Paris School of International Affairs, where her research focuses on migration, humanitarianism and solidarity. Pınar E. Dönmez works at De Montfort University, where her research focuses on the (de)politicisation of governance and social processes from a critical political economy perspective.

Notes

1. Eszter Neumann and György Mészáros, 'From public education to national public upbringing: the neoconservative turn of Hungarian education after 2010', in *Austerity and the Remaking of European Education*, eds. A. Traianou and K. Jones (London: Bloomsbury Academic, 2019), 117–14. For a recent exploration of the cases of Hungary and Turkey through such a lens, see Pinar E. Dönmez and Anil Duman, 'Marketisation of Academia and Authoritarian Governments: The Cases of Hungary and Turkey in Critical Perspective', *Critical Sociology* (2020), doi: https://doi.org/10.1177%2F0896920520976780.

2. Elissa Helms and Andrea Krizsan, 'Hungarian Government's Attack on Central European University and its Implications for Gender Studies in Central and Eastern Europe', *Femina Politica* 2 (2017), 169–173.

3. Prem Kumar Rajaram, 'Europe's "Hungarian Solution"', *Radical Philosophy* 197 (2016), 2–7. Zsuzsanna Vidra, 'Dominant Counter-Narratives to Islamophobia – Hungary', *Working Paper 12, Centre for Ethnicity and Racism Studies*, 2018, https://cik.leeds.ac.uk/wp-content/uploads/sites/36/2018/04/2018.04.09-WS2-Hungary-ZV-Final.pdf. Ivan Kalmar, 'Islamophobia and anti-antisemitism: the case of Hungary and the "Soros plot"', *Patterns of Prejudice*, 54:1–2 (2020), 182–198.

4. Krisztina Than, 'Hungary's anti-Soros posters recall "Europe's darkest hours": Soros' spokesman' *Reuters*, 11 July 2017, https://www.reuters.com/article/us-hungary-soros-idUSKBN19W0XU.

5. Vidra, 'Dominant Counter-Narratives', 6. Kalmar, 'Islamophobia and Anti-antisemitism'.

6. Tamás Krausz, 'A neo-Horthyist restoration', *Radical Philosophy* 197 (2016), 8–12.

7. Romania Insider, 'Two Romanian cities volunteer to host the Central European University', 7 April 2017, https://www.romania-insider.com/two-romanian-cities-volunteer-host-central-european-university.

8. On the 'quiet' abuse of asylum-seekers, see Céline Cantat, 'Governing Migrants and Refugees in Hungary: Politics of Spectacle, Negligence and Solidarity in a Securitising State', in *Politics of (Dis)Integration*, eds. S. Hinger and R. Schweitzer (Cham: Springer, 2020).

9. On the transformation of monetary policy along these lines, see Pinar E. Dönmez and Eva J. Zemandl, 'Crisis of Capitalism and (De-)Politicisation of Monetary Policymaking: Reflections from Hungary and Turkey', *New Political Economy*, 24:1 (2019), 125–143.

10. Reuters, 'Ruling Fidesz party wants Soros-funded NGOs "swept out" of Hungary', 11 January 2017, https://www.reuters.com/article/us-hungary-fidesz-soros-idUSKBN14V0P2.

11. EUobserver, 'Orbán Wants To Build "Illiberal State"', 28 July 2014, https://euobserver.com/political/125128.

12. On social policy, see Dorottya Szikra, 'Democracy and Welfare in Hard Times: The Social Policy of the Orbán Government in Hungary Between 2010 and 2014', *Journal of European Social Policy*, 24:5 (2014), 486–500. On the criminalisation of homelessness, see Katalin Ámon, 'Revanchism and Anti-revanchism in Hungary: The Dynamics of (De)Politicisation and the Criminalisation of Homelessness', in *Comparing Strategies of (De)Politicisation in Europe*, eds. J. Buller, P. E. Dönmez, A. Standring and M. Wood (Cham: Palgrave Macmillan, 2019), 209–236.

13. Krausz, 'A neo-Horthyist restoration'.

14. For a legal analysis from a constitutional perspective, see Mauro Mazza, 'The Hungarian Fundamental Law, the new cardinal laws and European concerns', *Acta Juridica Hungarica* 54:2 (2013), 140–155. For the most recent developments on this front, see Reuters, 'Hungary government proposes constitutional amendment mandating Christian gender roles', 10 November 2020, https://www.reuters.com/article/us-hungary-lgbt-constitution-idUSKBN27Q34Z.

15. Clare Hemmings, 'Unnatural feelings: The affective life of "anti-gender" mobilisations', *Radical Philosophy* 2.09 (Winter 2020).

16. Zoltán Gábor Szűcs, 'The Battle of the Academy: The war on academic freedom in Hungary enters its next phase', 12 March 2019, https://www.boell.de/en/2019/03/12/battle-academy-war-academic-freedom-hungary-enters-its-next-phase.

17. Ábrahám Vass, 'Outsourcing of Higher Education Continues Despite Uncertainties', 9 April 2021, https://hungarytoday.hu/hungary-universities-higher-education-outsourcing/.

18. Gergely Kováts, 'Trust and the governance of higher education: the introduction of chancellor system in Hungarian higher education', in *European Higher Education Area: The Impact of Past and Future Policies*, eds. A. Curaj, L. Deca and R. Pricopie (Cham: Springer, 2018), 651–669. Alexandra Zontea, 'The Hungarian student network: a counterculture in the making', in *The Hungarian Patient: Social Opposition to an Illiberal Democracy*, eds. P. Krasztev and J. Van Til (Budapest and New York: Central European University Press, 2015), 263–289.

19. Henry A. Giroux, 'Public Pedagogy and the Politics of Resistance: Notes on a critical theory of educational struggle', *Educational Philosophy and Theory*, 35:1 (2003), 5–16. George Caffentzis, 'Academic freedom and the crisis of neoliberalism: some cautions', *Review of African Political Economy* 32:106 (2005), 599–608. Kathleen Lynch and Mariya Ivancheva, 'Academic freedom and the commercialisation of universities: a critical ethical analysis', *Ethics in Science and Environmental Politics* 15:1 (2015),

71–85. Leyla Safta-Zecheria, 'The Authoritarian Turn Against Academics in Turkey: Can scholars still show solidarity to vulnerabilized groups?', in *Opening Up the University: Teaching and Learning with Refugees*, eds. C. Cantat, I.M. Cook and P. K. Rajaram (Oxford: Berghahn Books, 2021).

20. Silvia Federici, 'Education and the enclosure of knowledge in the global university', *ACME: An International Journal for Critical Geographies* 8:3 (2009), 454–461.

21. Dönmez and Duman, 'Marketisation'. Attila Melegh, *On the East-West Slope: Globalization, Nationalism, Racism and Discourses on Eastern Europe* (Budapest and New York: Central European University Press, 2016). Agnes Gagyi 'Hungary's "Lex CEU" and the state of the open society: looking beyond the story of democratic revolutions', *Cultures of History Forum*, 2017, http://www.cultures-of-history.uni-jena.de/focus/lex-ceu/hungarys-lex-ceu-and-the-state-of-the-open-society-looking-beyond-the-story-of-democratic-revolutions/.

22. Sarah S. Amsler and Chris Bolsmann, 'University ranking as social exclusion', *British Journal of Sociology of Education* 33:2 (2012), 283–301. Hugo Radice, 'How We Got Here: UK Higher Education under Neoliberalism', *ACME: An International Journal for Critical Geographies* 12:3 (2013), 407–418.

23. Relatedly, the 'Lex CEU' was ultimately struck down in October 2020 by the European Court of Justice (Grand Chamber) on the basis that it violated Hungary's commitments under the WTO as well as infringing certain provisions of the Charter of Fundamental Rights of the European Union relating to academic freedom. See *Commission v Hungary* (C-66/18).

24. Dönmez and Duman, 'Marketisation'.

25. Sukaina Ehdeed, 'The Impact of Visa Denial in Academia', 27 August 2019, https://blogs.lse.ac.uk/mec/2019/08/27/the-impact-of-visa-denial-in-academia/; Bathsheba Okwenje, 'Visa applications: emotional tax and privileged passports', 10 July 2019, https://blogs.lse.ac.uk/africaatlse/2019/07/10/visa-applications-emotional-tax-privileged-passports/.

26. This meant that, at first, official institutional guidelines instructed the university community not to respond, either through protests, organising or communication around 'Lex CEU'. These were soon dropped due to the continuous mobilisation in support of CEU, notably with several large protests in spring 2017, yet the claim by senior management to have a monopoly over the legitimate representation of CEU and its policing of autonomous actions remained a strong characteristic throughout our time in the university.

27. Jana Bacevic, 'Universities, neoliberalisation, and the (im)possibility of critique', *The Practice of Social Theory*, 1 September 2017, https://medium.com/@TheorySchool.

28. Aline Courtois and Theresa O'Keefe, 'Precarity in the ivory cage: Neoliberalism and casualisation of work in the Irish higher education sector', *Journal for Critical Education Policy Studies* 13:1 (2015), 43–66. Richard Hall, *The Alienated Academic: The Struggle for Autonomy inside the University* (Cham: Palgrave Macmillan, 2018).

29. Ross Clare, 'How Working-Class Academics Are Set Up to Fail', 13 October 2020, https://tribunemag.co.uk/2020/10/how-working-class-academics-are-set-up-to-fail. Ian M. Cook, 'Fuck prestige', in *Opening Up the University: Teaching and Learning with Refugees*, eds. C. Cantat, I. M. Cook and P. K. Rajaram (Oxford: Berghahn Books, 2021).

30. Akanksha Mehta, 'Teaching Gender, Race, Sexuality: Reflections on Feminist Pedagogy', *Kohl: a Journal for Body and Gender Research* 5:1 (2019), 28–9.

31. Celine Cantat, Ian M. Cook and Prem K. Rajaram, *Opening Up the University: Teaching and Learning with Refugees* (Oxford: Berghahn Books, 2021).

32. Richard Hall and Kate Bowles, 'Re-engineering Higher Education: The Subsumption of Academic Labour and the Exploitation of Anxiety', *Workplace* 28 (2016), 30–47.

33. Florin Zubaşcu, 'Horizon 2020 grant suspended as Hungarian government levy on "migration propaganda" comes into effect', *Science Business*, 30 August 2018, https://science-business.net/news/horizon-2020-grant-suspended-hungarian-government-levy-migration-propaganda-comes-effect.

34. To our knowledge, there has been no known case of the imposition of the tax on any civil society organisation, initiative, research project or educational programme under this legislation on grounds of their engagement with 'migration propaganda'.

35. Balázs Majtényi, Ákos Kopper and Pál Susánszky, 'Constitutional othering, ambiguity and subjective risks of mobilization in Hungary: examples from the migration crisis', *Democratization* 26:2 (2019), 173–189. For an account of a similar enforcement of bordering practices through universities in the UK context, see Matt Jenkins, 'On the effects and implications of UK Border Agency involvement in higher education', *The Geographical Journal* 180:3 (2014), 265–270.

36. Radical Student Collective, 'Manifesto of the CEU Radical Student Collective', 14 March 2019, https://lefteast.org/manifesto-of-the-ceu-radical-student-collective/.

37. Tony Harland, Toni Tidswell, David Everett, Leigh Hale and Neil Pickering, 'Neoliberalism and the academic as critic and conscience of society', *Teaching in Higher Education* 15:1 (2010), 85–96.

38. Richard Hall, 'On Authoritarian Neoliberalism and Poetic Epistemology', *Social Epistemology* 33:4 (2019), 298–308. Mariya Ivancheva and Kathryn Keating, 'Revisiting precarity, with care: Productive and reproductive labour in the era of flexible capitalism', *Ephemera* 20:4 (2020), 251–282.

Who will survive the university?

Aimée Lê and Jordan Osserman

We write as organisers of #CoronaContract, a campaign we co-founded shortly after the UK's first COVID-19 lockdown in March 2020, demanding a two-year contract extension for all casualised university staff (academic and non-academic). In the early days of COVID-19, when previously unthinkable forms of economic rescue took place, this demand functioned as a 'transitional demand' in the sense both Leon Trotsky and Slavoj Žižek have elaborated: a 'reasonable' goal that workers can agree on, yet which is unlikely to be accommodated by the existing constraints of the situation, pointing towards structural flaws around which a transformative movement can be built.

#CoronaContract emerged under particular circumstances. As COVID-19 hit the UK, we were on the picket lines for the University and College Union (UCU)'s second period of national strike action in higher education over casualisation, inequality, cuts to pensions, and workloads during the 2019-20 academic year. In response to the pandemic, the leadership of our union looked to make gestures of goodwill towards management: calling us off the picket line without proposing a viable alternative and essentially abandoning action short of a strike ('ASOS', or working to contract). While the argument of UCU leaders was that we needed to shore up universities in an 'unprecedented crisis', our own sense was that staff as a whole needed to seize this opportunity to show management that they depend on us to function and to refuse the additional labour involved in transitioning to online working as a bargaining tool. That we didn't do this has emboldened universities to impose more punitive conditions on staff, and to press for redundancies at unprecedented rates.

While the general mood shifted towards collective sacrifice, which many staff presumed would be recognised by their university management, we and other casualised staff, acutely aware of our employment's 'ticking clock', turned in the opposite direction, launching campaigns and mass online meetings to take action, strategise and share tactics immediately while the national union and many local branches were unwilling to meet. This led to a successful vote to carry on our official dispute with our employers (despite resistance from conservative forces in our union), giving us the basis to reballot for further industrial action. UCU also eventually launched a jobs campaign which, although belated and focused on parliamentary lobbying, was spurred by casualised staff's momentum from below. Perhaps most significantly, two-year minimum contracts were incorporated into our national negotiators' pay claim, meaning that #CoronaContract's 'transitional demand' on casualisation has now become official union policy.

This demand was not without its critics. For example, during our union's last leadership election, anti-casualisation candidate Ben Pope and others opposed the demand for minimum contract lengths, proposing instead that employers offer casualised staff 'internships' and 'fellowships' that will assist in our 'professional development', in keeping with a portrayal of union members as 'educational professionals'.[1] Yet, for reasons that we set out below, we do not believe we can afford to put our hopes in technocratic visions of 'progress' that ultimately hinge on maintaining or securing professional status.

UCU estimates that between 25-30% of teaching in universities is done by casualised staff, while around 70% of researchers in the sector are casualised.[2] However, the economic structure which has introduced this 'flexible' labour force represents a dynamic that affects all university workers, precarious and 'permanent' alike (the latter of whose work conditions have become notably less secure in the UK due to the removal of protections against redundancy). In what follows, we want to consider how, in this context, university professionals experience tensions around demands stemming from contradictory class interests, and to raise a question – already posed more

generally during the Corbyn project – about the role of 'professionals' in bringing about political and economic change for the working class as a whole.

Are we professionals?

While universities also employ workers in 'traditional' working class occupations (such as cleaners and catering staff), by far the largest layer of university staff is 'professional' academic and academic-related staff.[3] Although these have historically been drawn from the privileged elite, recent years have seen some degree of demographic change and diversification, concomitant with deteriorating working conditions. Unsurprisingly, the most insecure staff are more likely to be female and non-white.[4]

When Barbara and John Ehrenreich first coined the term 'professional-managerial class' in the journal *Radical America* in 1977, it was meant to encompass precisely these workers in the professions.[5] The 'PMC', the Ehrenreichs wrote, consisted of:

salaried mental workers who do not own the means of production, and whose major function in the social division of labour may be described broadly as the reproduction of capitalist culture and capitalist class relations ... scientists, engineers, teachers, social workers, writers, accountants, lower- and middle-level managers and administrators, etc.[6]

The Ehrenreichs' analysis was particularly concentrated on the university setting, to account for the cultural differences between student radicals and the traditional working class. These radicals were 'professionals in training', who, while exposed to capitalist greed and irrationality, in their potential future roles as rationalisers and managers of capitalist systems simultaneously had an interest in suppressing the working class. The Ehrenreichs mapped out two paths for those who wanted to escape this destiny: either actively working against their own class background through joining the new Communist parties and disavowing their PMC origins, or becoming 'radicals in the professions' whose attempts to popularise and politicise (to say nothing of 'proletarianise') their white-collar work largely failed despite their best efforts.

The idea of the PMC as a separate class was, and remains, controversial. Debates around the term have re-emerged on the left today in relation to growing militancy among members of the professions, such as nurses, journalists, tech workers and teachers, alongside a renewed scepticism about how professional status conditions workers ideologically and differentiates them from those who are most exploited.[7] These debates re-pose the question of whether these workers compose a separate class or are in essence still part of the expropriated working class in the traditional Marxist two-tier system. The most compelling analysis in our view is that the PMC is not a full class in itself but a contradictory 'class fraction', composed of simultaneous yet divergent imperatives which divide members between the interests of labour and capital.[8] Groupings within the PMC, therefore, can take positions that align with bourgeois or working-class interests. One recent example in this vein is the battle over returns to in-person work in the Chicago Public Schools system, where teachers' refusals of unsafe working conditions were most forcefully opposed by other professionals working from home.

While most university workers form part of this contradictory grouping, conflicts deriving from differences within this group can create tensions in terms of formulating demands and priorities, and can introduce intra-group battles between the interests of labourers and reactionary positions that support the interests of capital. In addition, the potential for some members of this group to slip out of the professions entirely – to not obtain or retain positions as 'salaried mental workers' – must be included as part of the progression of downward mobility. One provocative argument, for instance, suggests that university labour functions as a two-tier system: secure staff with managerial roles vs. all insecure staff, including staff in 'professional' roles alongside e.g. cleaners and maintenance workers (so emphasising solidarity between these groups). Nevertheless, the likelihood that unemployed professional workers will find other work within the professions – and the persistence of a layer of elites who hold university jobs while not needing to make a living from them – suggests that an emphasis on shared precarity in university work has its limits.

Moreover, while university workers experience widening precarity across a range of uneven axes, it is not inevitable that these workers will become more radical or allied with working-class movements. Those who can afford to continue working in the sector may cling on to whatever vestiges of professional status remain available, perhaps buttressed by pre-existing privilege/wealth. The worse these conditions get, the more relevant the analysis of workers' contradictory positioning becomes.

Paid in pleasure

The conditions of casualised work in the sector (which both precarious and permanent staff increasingly experience) impact us psychologically, and this in turn affects our ability to collectively organise. On the one hand, we enjoy a high degree of autonomy and pleasure in our labour compared to most other forms of work, but we are downwardly mobile, insecurely employed, and undergoing deskilling (for example through the division of research and teaching). Consequently, and in keeping with larger trends under neoliberalism and the gig economy, we must spend a large amount of time marketing ourselves, managing our own social reproduction along the lines of the market, and competing with a reserve army of labour (including our own students, on whom universities are currently capitalising to further erode our pay, such as by getting undergraduates to do our administrative work during online seminars for free as 'virtual assistants'). These processes of self-management are all supposedly voluntary, which has pernicious effects on our sense of freedom, agency, (professional) identity, and intellectual life.

Accordingly, we find ourselves both driven to narcissism in order to self-promote and make ourselves employable (witness the dramatic rise in 'academic Twitter'), and inhibited in our ability to work, ridden with guilt and anxiety. We convince ourselves that our excessive working hours are either a result of personal insufficiency/inexpediency, or in service of personal development and therefore uncompensatable. Our actual vulnerability as workers on the market receives its inverse mirror image in superegoic fantasies of mastery and self-sufficiency, which inhibit our participation in egalitarian exchange. As Aimie Purser writes for the Nottingham UCU Mental Health campaign group, 'I (and my PhD) only have meaning inside the system. And inside that intensely demanding relationship, we are constantly told that however much we give of ourselves ... we are not enough'.[9] Moreover, the persecutory nature of capitalism inhibits our efficiency as we attempt to 'steal our time back' from the university, sometimes unconsciously and in a self-defeating way. Perhaps procrastination and writer's block (to say nothing of the more serious mental health crises and even suicides in the sector) are so endemic in part because, in the absence of a militant left, they are a form of protest towards the Other of capitalist time, redirected towards the self.

The university provides us with wages and to some extent with the fixed capital necessary to produce research outputs, degrees and services. While there is some mystification here, it is also true that we require facilities and accreditation to perform much of this work. Nevertheless, there is another side to our labour, our autonomous intellectual activity, which is not inherently confined to or dependent on the employer to operate. We lose sight of this when we understand our activity as something the university *gives us*, or makes possible, through its training, verification processes, library access, academic community, and most crucially, the university brand, rather than viewing our labour as something the university *purchases from us* for its own ends, and as power which we might be able to retain outside of its walls (for example, in public 'strike universities').

It is sometimes said that the enjoyable and enviable part of being an academic is that our work is not fully alienated. But it is precisely this promise of utopian unalienated labour within the traditional wage relation that prevents us from sufficiently opposing our employers, instead harbouring the fantasy that we are getting something uncompensatable out of the extra time worked, or that we should wait for a secure and rewarding job, when our time will be valued finally as full-time. The latter is, in Lacanian terms, an expression of obsessional neurosis wherein, rather than confronting the reality of our lack and charting our own path accordingly, we insist on the illusion that somebody *else* possesses wholeness (perhaps a senior permanent academic) and, stultified, hope for their death.[10]

For connected reasons, we also see the current debate over online education as really about the issue of compensation and recognition, rather than pedagogy. Arguments which raise the value of face-to-face teaching are terrorised by the potential of automation to intervene in the market value of the university and the role of the instructor as someone who artisanally sells his or her educational labour. We could alternately view automation as a labour-saving process with immense liberatory and pedagogical potential, from which we are barred under capitalism because it would also make our drudgery, and therefore us, obsolete. The reactionary but understandable impulse therefore emerges to protect even archaic forms of work as long as it preserves our jobs.

We should be suspicious of the pleasure we receive from our work, given that the university offers it instead of payment (even if this pleasure also points towards the potential of a socialist society where we may enjoy the free sharing of knowledge without worrying about payment). Thus while we are being paid in pleasure, we should firmly demand that we are paid for our hours.

Contradictory realignment

Despite all of these inhibiting dynamics, casualised staff have been at the forefront of recent university struggles internationally, in many cases in a dual capacity as postgraduate student teachers.[11] The two main features of our work that disempower and impoverish us – disposability and quantified time – also encourage our militant perspective. Universities are particularly dependent on us as among the most exploited workers relative to the value we produce, and this means we have the potential to be extremely disruptive if we act collectively.

First, if we withdraw our labour *en masse* this will have an immediate and decisive impact, since the number of hours we are contracted to work is flagrantly and systematically under-estimated (and this even before management used the pandemic to enforce massive increases in uncompensated workload). Some of the more dramatic and successful forms of industrial action have involved forms of working to contract or ASOS, led by casualised staff refusing to work beyond the meagre hours they are contracted for.[12] When casualised staff refuse marking in particular, as in recent boycotts, an entire course can collapse. As universities further stretch workloads and slash staffing budgets, this need for staff to plug the gaps will only increase. Second, as a disposable workforce, we are particularly sensitive to how shifts in the global economy directly affect our working conditions and future, because we are constantly on the labour market. Our awareness of how radically our lives could be reshaped even by modest improvements, and how little we have to lose, means that we can be determined fighters for our demands.

However, we also see a professional discourse emerging in our union, and in the broader political sphere, which no doubt resonates with what many workers believe. The idea is that we can come up with more rational management solutions, and that 'smart policy' is the solution to our economic problems. Inherent in these proposals is the idea that the contradictions of labour and capital can be held at arm's length, or even that university workers and management, despite conflicts over working conditions, may have an ultimately shared interest in keeping universities afloat. But as we have suggested already, this approach is fraught with significant contradictions, the most severe of which are practical ones.

One obvious line of critique is that a return to more professional autonomy and control by the most secure workers would not necessarily benefit anyone else. Professional autonomy is essentially a nostalgic fantasy unless it is tethered to a political project which would universalise this autonomy and not limit it to the professions. Intellectuals need to advocate for those aspects of our work that *are* important – namely, what autonomy remains in our work – to be generalised: the ability to decide what research projects we think are meaningful to pursue, for example, is equally something that workers in general deserve as part of the process of democratic ownership of the workplace. Similarly the participation of the public in knowledge-production is crucial. Sabbaticals, flexible hours, access to information and technology: we should not treat these as rewards that compensate for how hard we work but as rights that all people should fight for.

More saliently, as a group, professionals are unable to seize power because society as a whole does not depend on us; the more marketised and purely empty the education and research we pursue, the more this is true. In a capitalist society we cannot realistically fight for a set of specific professional interests and expect to win against the relentless incentives of profit-making. The impossibility of withstanding that onslaught suggests that university activism alone, however inspiring, cannot

deliver us past our current state. Without an alliance with the broader working class, of which we are a (contradictory) part, through organisations and coalitions that extend beyond our own workplaces, we will not succeed at turning the tide.

This does not mean that we should write off the university as such, despite its obvious limitations. Our professional training is valuable, which is why it extends beyond a commodity into concrete values in people's lives – for example, in the university-led scientific discovery of mRNA vaccines – and points towards what we could achieve under a planned economy.[13] Nevertheless, those 'abolitionist' currents which suggest that our objective interests as workers lie with the broader working class and not within the university, while questionable as regards their economic determinism, are essentially correct on the subjective level, in that struggle around our working conditions can enable a working-class realignment. Intellectuals and professional workers can, and should, see their ultimate interests as only being truly realisable through a struggle for the emancipation of society as a whole, which would inevitably transform universities.[14] Without awareness of our own contradictory position, we will remain a poorly defined set of peripheral actors within the university, though paradoxically essential to its functioning, on a pathway towards professionalisation that is constantly eroded. Yet we can observe some recent signs of heightened consciousness from the 'declassed fragments',[15] not least workers' willingness to put pressure on our workplaces, formulate demands, and operate under a collective banner.[16] The negative space we occupy within the university now has a name: casualised staff.[17]

Aimée Lê is a Vietnamese American writer. She is Associate Lecturer in Creative Writing at Exeter University and an associate member of the Royal Holloway Poetics Research Centre. Jordan Osserman is a Postdoctoral Researcher on the Waiting Times project, based in the Department of Psychosocial Studies at Birkbeck, and a clinical trainee with The Site for Contemporary Psychoanalysis.

Notes

1. Pope won the election over our own candidate Sam Morecroft, although he retracted his proposal following significant outcry.

2. University College Union, 'Counting the Costs of Casualisation in Higher Education', June 2019. https://www.ucu.org.uk/media/10336/Counting-the-costs-of-casualisation-in-higher-education-Jun-19/pdf/ucu_casualisation_in_HE_survey_report_Jun19.pdf. We do not know how many staff have lost their jobs during the current crisis, although our anecdotal experience (based on the auto-replies we receive from the CoronaContract mailing list) suggests the number is high; we have helped pass a motion for UCU to research this.

3. HESA, 'Higher Education Staff Statistics: UK, 2019/20', Accessed 15 April 2021, https://www.hesa.ac.uk/news/19-01-2021/sb259-higher-education-staff-statistics.

4. Trade Union Coalition, 'BME Women and Work', October 2020. https://www.tuc.org.uk/sites/default/files/2020-10/BMEwomenandwork.pdf.

5. Barbara and John Ehrenreich, 'The Professional-Managerial Class'. *Radical America* 11: 2 (April 1977): 7–32 and 'The New Left and the Professional-Managerial Class'. *Radical America* 11: 3 (June 1977): 7–24.

6. Barbara and John Ehrenreich, 'The New Left and the Professional-Managerial Class', 8.

7. See, for example, Catherine Liu, *Virtue Hoarders: The Case against the Professional Managerial Class.* (Minneapolis, MN: University of Minnesota Press, 2021); Amber A'Lee Frost, 'The Characterless Opportunism of the Managerial Class', *American Affairs* 3:4 (20 November 2019), https://americanaffairsjournal.org/2019/11/the-characterless-opportunism-of-the-managerial-class/.

8. See Gabriel Winant, 'Professional-Managerial Chasm', *N+1*, 10 October 2019, https://nplusonemag.com/online-only/online-only/professional-managerial-chasm/.

9. 'Solidarity: Journal of the UCU Mental Health Campaign Group' 4 (Autumn 2020), http://uonucu.org/wp-content/uploads/2020/11/Solidarity_UoN-UCU-Mental-Health-group_issue1.pdf

10. Of course, this same problem has been in place long before such widespread insecurity in the sector. In a marketised education system, even academics on permanent contracts – particularly those at the junior end of the spectrum – are not free to pursue their own interests, but are induced to offer ever more surplus value to the institution via the sentiment that their work, and the university they work for, is 'special'.

11. These include the 2020 Cost of Living ('COLA') graduate student struggle at the University of California; 2020 Michigan graduate students strike; 2021 Columbia University strike; 2020 Goldsmiths wildcat marking boycott; SOAS's Fractionals for Fair Play campaign; and the 2020 National Higher Education Action Network wildcat strike action across Australia.

12. See, for example, Carrie Benjamin, 'If You Fight You Can Win: Victory for Fractional Staff at SOAS'. *Counterfire*, 11 May 2017. https://www.counterfire.org/articles/opinion/18950-if-you-fight-you-can-win-victory-for-fractional-staff-at-soas

13. In this regard, Boris Johnson's recent claim, subsequently retracted, that 'greed' and 'capitalism' were responsible for the success of the UK's vaccination programme might be read as an anxious attempt to prevent popular awareness of the public planning and investment that underwrote the vaccines' discovery and distribution.

14. See Jordan Osserman and Aimée Lê, 'Waiting for Other People: A Psychoanalytic Interpretation of the Time for Action', *Wellcome Open Research* 5 (10 June 2020), 133.

15. Winant, 'Professional-Managerial Chasm'.

16. Salient examples of this consciousness among tech workers can be seen in the 2018 Google walkout and the 2019 Wayfair walkout. In both cases, these were not walkouts tied to the workers' direct economic demands but solidaristic protests of employers' complicity in sexual harassment and migrant detention camps, respectively. Workers in the professions might be especially sensitive to the realisation that the work one's company does is not socially beneficial (a recent Facebook internal survey showed that 49 percent of its employees thought that the company does not have a positive impact on the world). See Manik Berry, '49% Facebook Employees Don't Believe It Had Positive Impact On World', *Fossbytes*, 4 November 2020. https://fossbytes.com/49-facebook-employees-disagree-that-it-has-positive-impact-on-world/

17. Here we are drawing on ideas articulated in Alain Badiou, *Being and Event* trans. Oliver Feltham, (London: Bloomsbury, 2013). We can see the significance of this in the leaked minutes of the Russell Group (the employer body representing the UK's most prestigious universities) during our national strike action, which spoke of the need to address universities' 'reputational damage'. The Group placed the term casualisation in quotation marks, seeking to undermine its validity as a category, and referring to the various forms of casualised labour that universities employ (temporary research contracts, fixed-term, freelance, etc.) as reflecting the 'appropriate use of different contract types' that fulfil mutually beneficial needs. The reason for this is clear: by fragmenting us under spurious justifications, our employers attempt to undermine our ability to organise ourselves around shared demands.

On the subject of roots

The ancestor as institutional foundation

Roderick A. Ferguson

In 1983, Toni Morrison's classic interview-turned-essay 'Rootedness: The Ancestor as Foundation' was published in Mari Evans's anthology *Black Women Writers (1950-1980): A Critical Evaluation*.[1] In the piece, Morrison concerns herself with the figure of the ancestor in African American literature. For her, the ancestor is a 'distinctive element of African American writing', and because of this distinctiveness, the ancestor should be a central component of African American literary criticism.[2] She continues by saying, '[It] seems to me interesting to evaluate Black literature on what the writer does with the presence of an ancestor. Which is to say a grandfather as in Ralph Ellison, or a grandmother as in Toni Cade Bambara, or a healer as in Bambara or Henry Dumas. There is always an elder there.' This elder, according to Morrison, possesses a certain symbolic and hermeneutical weight. '[These] ancestors', she says, 'are not just parents, they are sort of timeless people whose relationships to the characters are benevolent, instructive, and protective, and they provide a certain kind of wisdom.'

In a period in which U.S. colleges and universities such as Harvard, Yale, Brown, Georgetown and Wake Forest are wrestling with their legacies in slavery, it would seem that our time is ripe for transporting Morrison's insights and those similar to hers beyond the terrain of literature and to the domain of the academy. Indeed, the former Trump administration's *The 1776 Report* – issued just before the inauguration of President Biden – acknowledged the ancestral stakes of conservative understandings of the U.S. university. The report stated, for instance, 'The founders insisted that universities should be at the core of preserving American republicanism by instructing students and future leaders of its true basis and instilling in them not just an understanding but a reverence for its principles and core documents.' In the report, the founders represent an ancestral ethos for compelling students to conform to state protocols.

We might say though that the kind of present-day reckoning with slavery and colonialism's role in producing the modern U.S. academy means that we must acknowledge that the founding fathers are not the only ancestors that haunt those institutions. The student protests and the institutional scrutiny that they inspire suggest a competing ancestral ethos, one that not only inspires us to 'get our history right' but to promote forms of knowledge and practice that are both critical of and alternative to the dominant ancestors' calls to identify with state and capital. Insisting on an alternative set of ancestors who need to be acknowledged, the recent record of protests on U.S. college campuses confirms the ancestral presence of the subjugated and our need to respond to that presence. In this way we can think of colleges and universities as contested ancestral grounds, ones in which dominant and subjugated ancestors vie for ideological authority.

Hence, the minoritised ancestor is not a discourse that's external to the university. Indeed, this essay engages the ancestor as both a figure of the unacknowledged labour that produced the modern academy and as an ethical interruption to the academy's normative operations, particularly in those moments when the ancestor's descendants reckon with the academy. In such a context, black intellectual cultural production emerges as an appropriate venue from which to theorise the minoritised ancestor as a catalyst for critical transformations. Put simply, turning to black cultural production allows us to converse with the minoritised ancestor in ways that the usual philosophical critique of the academy never could. However significant, the dominant philosophical registers have never addressed the minoritised ancestor as a figure of epistemological and institutional importance. Taking my cues from Morrison's essay, in particular, and black literary and intellectual production, in general, this essay alternatively takes some initial steps toward a hermeneutic that can analyse the various and contending ancestral discourses at work on our campuses and the struggles that they inspire.

The dominance of the European spirit in the western academy

An institutional criticism like the one that this essay calls for is not really foreign to the university. Indeed, the ancestor as a discursive figure has always had a particular function in the modern western academy and in classical social theory. In *The University in Ruins*, Bill Readings implicitly identified this function when he wrote, 'The reason it is necessary to reread Humboldt, Schiller, Schleiermacher, Fichte and Kant is that the vast majority of the contemporary "solutions" to the crisis of the university are, in fact, no more than the restatements of Humboldt or Newman, whose apparent aptness is the product of ignorance of these founding texts on the history of the institution.'[3] With this, Readings implies that the dominant ways in which we try to assess and attempt to fix the university betray the ways that we are possessed by a particular ancestral assemblage – that is, how we are the unwitting heirs of Humboldt, Schiller, Schleiermacher, Fichte and Kant. In the language that Avery Gordon gave us in her classic book *Ghostly Matters: Haunting and the Sociological Imagination*, we are haunted by the terms that these thinkers laid out for thinking and practicing the university.[4]

This assemblage of ancestors would set the grammar for the construction and continuation of the modern Western academy long after their deaths. Locating these thinkers within the tradition of German idealism, Readings argues, 'The achievement of the German idealists is a truly remarkable one: to have articulated and instituted an analysis of knowledge and its social function. [They] deduced not only the modern university but also the German nation.' For him, these thinkers who brought philosophy, aesthetics, and history together yielded 'an articulation of the ethnic nation, the rational state, and philosophical culture, which linked speculative philosophy to the reason of history itself (*for almost two centuries of imperial expansion*).' On the way to thinking the

terms of modern philosophy and aesthetics, these intellectuals conceived the modern nation-state, the modern academy, and modern national culture. These idealists may have wrongly presumed that ideas would change the world, as Marx would argue in *The German Ideology*, but their ideas did in fact bring institutions *into* the world.

Derrida reflected on this remarkable achievement through which thinking would birth institutions in his book *Eyes of the University*. He wrote, 'Every text, every element of a corpus reproduces or bequeaths, in a prescriptive or normative mode, one or several injunctions: come together according to this or that rule, this or that scenography, this or that topography of minds and bodies, form this or that type of institution so as to read me and write about me, organise this or that type of exchange and hierarchy to interpret me, evaluate me, preserve me, translate me, inherit from me, make me live on.'[5] This remarkable achievement gave birth to institutions that would train us to organise and evaluate the world, and in doing so, it would teach us to organise and evaluate ourselves and others. As they were implied through formulations such as 'the founding fathers' or 'founding texts', a dominant set of ancestors would direct us to come together according to certain rules, scenographies, typographies, exchanges and hierarchies.

This dominant set of ancestors arose out of the histories of imperialism. In terms of the American colonies, the historian Craig Steven Wilder has demonstrated that American colleges were central to expanding colonialism through the dispossession of native lands and extending slavery through the exploration of black labour. The dominant ancestral and therefore ideological foundations are rooted in colonial dispossession and enslavement. Those histories also helped to shape modern political and academic knowledge. To reiterate Readings, imperial expansion linked speculative philosophy, the academy, and the nation-state.

In *The Intimacies of Four Continents*, Lisa Lowe shows how modern liberalism and the colonial division of humanity gave birth to one another.[6] We see this explicitly in John Stuart Mill's *On Liberty*. In his chapter 'Of Individuality, as One of the Elements of Well-being' he argues, 'There is only too great a tendency in the best beliefs and practices to degenerate into the mechanical; and unless there were a succession of persons whose ever-recurring originality prevents the grounds of those beliefs and practices from becoming merely traditional, such dead matter would not resist the smallest shock from anything really alive, and there would be no reason why civilisation should not die out, as the Byzantine Empire.'[7] Worried that Western civilisation was getting too close to that of China, he said, 'We have a warning.'[8] Where progress was concerned, the Chinese, he argued, have become stationary – have remained so for thousands of years; and if they are to be farther improved, it must be by foreigners.' The Chinese, he continues, 'have succeeded beyond all hope ... in making a people all alike, all governing their thoughts and conducts by the same maxims and rules.' In contrast he asks,

> What has made the European family of nations an improving, instead of a stationary portion of mankind? Not any superior excellence in them, which, when it exists, exists as the effect, not as the cause; but their remarkable diversity of character and culture. Individuals, classes, nations, have been extremely unlike one another: they have struck out a great variety of paths, each leading to something valuable; and although at every period those who travelled in different paths have been intolerant of one another, and each would have thought it an excellent thing if all the rest could been compelled to travel his road, their attempts to thwart each other's development have rarely had any permanent success, and each has in time endured to receive the good which the others have offered.[9]

For Mill the European family of nations represents a long ancestral and racial line that moves toward progress. The modern Western academy would be born from and partake of this ancestral story. Those institutions, like the nations from which they came, would present themselves as the catalysts for and measurements of human development. In her interpretation of Mill, Lowe suggests that Mill understood Western originality to mean the unique combination of free trade, liberal democracy, and colonial government. Western Man would become the symbol of this originality, the sum total of an ancestral assemblage. In his own discussion of the figure of man, Foucault would argue, for instance, that Man was not a 'phenomenon of opinion but an event in the order of knowledge',[10] serving as the ground for modern thought since the nineteenth century, laying the foundation for the emergence of the human sciences.

At the heart of how the West has spoken about itself, its philosophy and its institutions, there has always been an argument about ancestors. Indeed, these particular ancestors have proposed ways to interpret the world according to their understandings of human development and knowledge formations. Moreover, they proposed institutions and disciplines that would facilitate and corroborate those interpretations. As the representative and enforcer of those interpretations, Western Man has operated as the ancestral sign of all that is supreme in human achievement. Part of his prerogative has always been to demand our identification. In her own discussion of the power and influence of this figure, Sylvia Wynter has argued, 'Our present arrangement of knowledge ... was put in place in the nineteenth century as a function of the epistemic/discursive constitution of the figure of Man ... [The] unifying goal of minority discourse ... will necessarily be to accelerate the conceptual 'erasing' of the figure of Man.'[11] With that goal in mind, let us now turn to those gone, forgotten and unfamed ancestors as the basis of a long-awaited hermeneutical and institutional enterprise.

The Post-WWII moment and the coming of the ancestors

Morrison's essay emphasises the presence of the ancestor as another characteristic of twentieth-century black literature. She states, 'What struck me in looking at some contemporary fiction was that whether the novel took place in the city or in the country, the presence or absence of that figure [of the ancestor] determined the success or the happiness of the character.'[12] Here, the ancestor becomes an interpretive device for the critic in both literary and social assessments – 'literary' in the sense that it becomes a way of evaluating the particularities of African American literature, 'social' in that the depictions allegorise one of the major transformations of African American history, the movement of a people from rural to urban settings. Morrison suggests that the black ancestor becomes a centre of gravity in the moment of social transformations and disruption.

It is significant that the literature that Morrison invokes arises in the post-WWII moment of minority insurgency through civil rights, anticolonial, and black power movements. *Invisible Man* was published in 1952, during the independence movements in Africa and the civil rights movement within the States. Toni Cade Bambara's

work arises at the end of the sixties when the civil rights movement begins to yield to the black power movement. The writer Henry Dumas's oeuvre was written during the period bookended by civil rights and black power as well.

Taken together, the anti-colonial, civil rights, and black power movements produced an ethos to revive those ancestors that the Western ancestor of Man attempted to overshadow and suppress. Touching on that revival, Stuart Hall would argue that you could not talk about the post-war world without also talking about the 'moment when the unspoken discovered that they had a history that they could speak.'[13] As he said, 'They had languages other than the language of the master, of the tribe. It is an enormous moment. The world begins to be decolonised at that moment.'[14] We might link Hall's and Morrison's arguments by saying that the minoritised ancestor becomes the metaphor for that discovery and the cultural production that this discovery would promote. We must say that neither this discovery nor this ancestor would be engaged as a relic of the past but as a

reconstruction for the present and the future. Hall said, for example, 'It is not just a fact that has been waiting to ground our identities. What emerges from this is nothing like an uncomplicated, dehistoricised, undynamic, uncontradictory past. Nothing like that is the image which is caught in the moment of return.' This was the moment for both invoking and reimagining the ancestor.

If the figure of Western man was designed to promote certain prescriptive norms, the minoritised ancestors were imagined to upset those norms. The function of the minoritised ancestors was to deliberate on how certain taken-for-granted institutions and forms might be alternatively inhabited. For instance, in her discussion of the institution of the novel, Morrison argued,

[When] the industrial revolution began, there emerged a new [middle] class of people who were neither peasants nor aristocrats. In large measure they had no art form to tell them how to behave in this new situation. So they produced an art form: we call it the novel of manners, an art form designed to tell people something they didn't know. That is, how to behave in this new world, how to distinguish between the good guys and the bad guys. How to get married. What a good living was. What would happen if you strayed from the fold.[15]

Morrison designates the novel as an inventor of and guide for an ethical formation suited for the new bourgeois class, a class that emerged in the wake of industrialisation.

The African American novel and the figure of the black ancestor, for her, were ways of guiding a social group transiting into predominantly white institutional and social settings. As she says,

[It] seems to me that the novel is needed by African-Americans now in a way that it was not needed before – and it is following along the lines of the function of novels everywhere. We don't live in places where we can hear those stories anymore; parents don't sit around and tell their children those classical, mythological archetypal stories that we heard years ago. But new information has got to get out, and there are several ways to do it. One is in the novel, I regard it as a way to accomplish certain very strong functions – one being the one I just described.[16]

This reinvented novel would be needed in the post-WII moment in which the opportunities of black advancement were expanding. This expansion would directly impact Morrison's sense of why the black novel was needed. As she said, 'the press toward upward social mobility would mean to get as far away from that kind of [ancestral] knowledge as possible.' Bourgeois ascendancy for blacks would potentially threaten those roots, but this jeopardy was in no way particular to black people. Recall that in *The Communist Manifesto*, Marx and Engels argued that part of what made the bourgeoisie a revolutionary historical force was its ability to end prior social relations.[17] For Morrison the novel was a means of intervening into a phenomenon that threatened the knowledge formations and cultural production of black communities.[18]

The ancestor was central to the black novel's efforts, she implies, because the ancestor was a force that could help black people negotiate the disruptions of these social transformations. Talking about the function of the ancestor within the novels, she writes, 'It was the absence of an ancestor that was frightening, that was threatening, and it caused huge destruction and disarray in the work itself.'[19] If the dominant ancestor, represented by the figure of Man, was designed by Humboldt, Schiller, Schleiermacher, Fichte and Kant to effect certain responsibilities for developing the self according to the reigning principles of Western institutions, then the ancestors that Morrison invokes in black literature represented the need for responsibilities that would compete with those of their dominant counterparts. Put plainly, the minoritised ancestors proposed ethical and ideological discourses created to problematise bourgeois subjective and institutional transformation, particularly their reliance upon and production of racial and colonial hierarchies. They also called for institutional practices suited for that task.

Slavery, race, and memory

If the ancestors made themselves visible in the post-WWII moment, as I've been arguing, we might think of the kind of reckoning with histories of slavery and colonialism happening throughout the global north, in general, and our universities, in particular, as the logical outcome of the ancestors' appearance. We might take inspiration from Morrison's engagement and call for a critical practice that asks how the figure of the minoritised ancestor can intervene into our academic institutions. In what ways can a critique developed for literature help us in the academy? We might imagine the ancestor asking, 'Consider all the ways that Western Man has asked you to inhabit this place, and ask yourselves, "What might be other modes of inhabitation?"'

In the introduction to *The Conflict of the Faculties*, Immanuel Kant notes how the university *intends* for us to inhabit it. He writes,

The university would have a certain autonomy (since only scholars can pass judgement on scholars as such), and accordingly it would be authorised to perform certain functions through its faculties (smaller societies, each comprising the university specialists in one main branch of learning): to admit to the university students seeking entrance from the lower schools and, having conducted examinations, by its own authority to grant degrees or confer the universally recognised status of 'doctor' on free teachers (that is, teachers who are not members of the university – in other words, *to create doctors*.[20]

The university *admits*; it *grants*, and it *creates*. The

sequence suggests that admission into these hallowed halls segues into the awarding of degrees and ends with the creation of people. The university not only certifies expertise; it bestows personhood.[21] It not only promises the recognition for work achieved. It also claims a brand new humanity for us. This is the ancient and dangerous seduction of that dominant ancestral norm known as Western Man, the one who mouths, 'We are here to show you that you fit within the established order of things. We've waited a long time for you. We've made a place for you at our table.'

Vincent Harding tried to impart this in his essay 'Responsibilities of the Black Scholar to the Community.' He wrote,

> Black scholars must remember their sources, and by this I mean no technically historical sources. I mean human sources. I mean they were not created as persons, as historians, as teachers, by Purdue University or UCLA or by the AHA or the OAH or any other set of letters. They are the products of their source – the great pained community of the Afro-Americans of this land. And they can forget their source only at great peril to their spirit, their work, and their souls.[22]

Here Harding uses the ancestral source to displace the university as the origin of personhood, particularly for black scholars. Rather than their intellection deriving from the procedures of the university, he argues that it springs from an extra-academic context. As such, their intellectual production and power – in a rebuttal to Western man – is not something the university can claim.

As Morrison suggested, the ancestors in Harding's essay emerge to guide people through a transition and an inclusion. The essay is situated in the 1986 volume *The State of Afro-American History: Past, Present and Future*, edited by Darlene Clark Hine. The volume came out of a 1983 conference held at Purdue University, a conference that was sponsored by the American Historical Association. The conference was designed to assess the innovative work in African American history that had just been produced in the mid-1970s, by the 'fourth generation of African American historians",[23] a group that arose as a result of the political achievements of civil rights and black power. That volume contains an essay by the dean of Black historians John Hope Franklin. He wrote, 'In the fourth generation [of historians of African American history], which began around 1970, there emerged the largest and perhaps the best-trained group of historians of Afro-America that had ever appeared. The Afro-Americans in the group were trained, as were the white historians, in graduate centres in every part of the country, in contrast to those of the third generation, who had been trained at three or four universities in the East and Midwest.'[24] Perhaps rebutting Franklin's argument, Harding's remarks are designed to complicate a narrative of progress, a narrative that posits the fourth generation and their work as the outcomes of the academy's procedures, a discourse that hails them as the children of a set of letters. An ancestral discourse emerges in Harding's text, offering a life-saving counsel to the fourth generation.

Granddaddy Willie Marvin – Daddy's daddy – gave me this counsel when I left home to go to college. A former sharecropper and grandchild of slaves, he – like so many other black parents in our rural Georgia community – had sent his children off to school and watched them return oftentimes as strangers. So after giving me a hug goodbye, he would grab me by the shoulders and say, 'Still stay Roderick'. Sitting on the yards of Morris Brown or Fort Valley State to see his daughters get their degrees was as far as Granddaddy got to any college. Even so, he knew something about the university and its imposition of personhood – enough to warn me about it.

Even with the gravitas of his message, I have always appreciated my grandfather's admonition that seemed filled with encouragement as well. *Be careful, but go and look at the work that awaits you*, his admonition seemed to say. Like Morrison, I am struck by how the ancestors come when encouragement is most often needed in black cultural production. There is a scene in Lorraine Hansberry's 'To Be Young, Gifted, and Black'. A black woman intellectual, no doubt modelled after Hansberry herself, is engaged in a spirited tete-a-tete with a white male intellectual. After hearing him go on and on about the guilt and racial megalomania of Negro intellectuals, she tunes him out and drifts into a reverie, and that's when the ancestors appear:

I could see his lips moving and knew he was talking, saying something. But I couldn't hear him anymore. I was patting my foot and singing my song. I was *happy*. I could see the bridge across the chasm. It was made up of a band of angels of art, hurling off the souls of twenty million. I saw Jimmy Baldwin and Leontyne, and Lena and Harry and Sammy. And then there was Charlie White and Nina Simone and Johnnie Killens and – Lord have mercy, Paul was back!

... Oh, yes, there they were, the band of angels, picking up numbers along the way, singing and painting and dancing and writing and acting up a storm![25]

At this moment, the ancestors make themselves manifest to declare that our simultaneously ethical, intellectual and institutional charge is to 'pick up numbers along the way'. This is an idiom of diversity that precedes and transcends any office within the academy. It is an idiom in which cultural and intellectual creation is both mass and minoritised production. And it is still our job to see and build that bridge across the chasm and to expose the institutional procedures that keep the bridge behind the veil.

Like Morrison, I am interested in the ways that a black ancestral presence manifests in the writing often at the very moment that the university asserts its claims on our work. For instance, Harding addresses what he believes to be the African American historian's relationship to the pained community of black people. He writes,

In this age of the fourth, fifth, sixth generation of historians, scholars must certainly say as loudly and clearly through their work and their lives that this people has not come through this pain in order to attain equal opportunity with the pain inflictors of this nation and this world. No, I think that our community's pain is meant to open it toward the light ... This is the responsibility: to keep remembering that to be human, to say nothing of scholarly, is to be constantly moving toward the light.[26]

Contrary to the claims of Western Man, Harding argues, a new responsibility is needed, a responsibility that sets as its campaign that of addressing historical trauma and developing a faculty that is learned in how not to carry the trauma on.

In her own essay in *Black Women Writers*, Toni Cade Bambara asks, 'Is it natural (sane, healthy, wholesome, in our interest) to violate the contracts/covenants we have with our ancestors...?'[27] Clarifying the way this question operates in her novel *The Salt Eaters*, she says, 'In *Salt* most particularly, in motive/content/structure design, the question is, do we intend to have a future as sane, whole, governing people?'[28] The ethical charge of the minoritised ancestors is the development of academic communities in which people own themselves and are not owned by the prescriptive norms of disciplinary or institutional belonging. Their work is marked by an imprimatur that does not belong to the stipulations of the academy.

Diverse as they are, what's significant in the discourse from these writers is that whether we're talking about Bambara, Hall, Hansberry, Harding or Morrison, none of them reduces the ancestor to a figure of authenticity or essentialism. Each one in their own way addresses the ancestor as a dynamic figure that instructs historically vulnerable people in how to adapt to and negotiate dangerous and alienating circumstances. In Morrison, the reader is presented with the ancestor as a teacherly figure that enlightens in the context of a social transition and upheaval. Bambara suggests an ancestor that inspires alternative and critical modes of governmentality and governance. Harding assumes an ancestor that calls for modes of identification that frustrate those offered by profession and discipline. Hall intimates an ancestor that inspires the creation of idioms that can deauthorise the master ideologies and narratives of Western modernity. Hansberry proposes an ancestor that promotes polymorphous cultural productions necessary for the survival of disfranchised communities. These formulations do not represent the hackneyed notion of the ancestor as the symbol of essence and identity. On the contrary, these writers and this essay promote the ancestor as a recombinant figure, rearticulating given idioms and social orders.

Just as there is Man, always there is an ancestor. In her book *The Difference that Aesthetics Makes: On the Humanities after Man*, Kandice Chuh calls for an 'illiberal humanities', one that '[bears] the promise of gathering a critical mass constituted in and by an undisciplined relationship to the university.'[29] The minoritised ancestors that I have imagined are endowed with this very demand, tasked with ushering into being modes of intellection and institutionality that are diverse and non-aligned, modes represented by as yet unimagined multiplicities and the most productive sovereignties. The question before us is – beyond the acknowledgements and apologies – how will knowledge and practice be reorganised after the ancestors have had their say?

Roderick Ferguson is Professor of Women's, Gender and Sexuality Studies and American Studies at Yale University.

Notes

1. The following is a revised version of a paper presented (online) at The Humanities Institute, Wake Forest University, 20 October 2020.
2. Toni Morrison, 'Rootedness: The Ancestor as Foundation', in Mari Evans, ed., *Black Women Writers (1950-1980): A Critical Evaluation* (New York: Doubleday, 1988), 342–43.
3. Bill Readings, *The University in Ruins* (Boston: Harvard University Press, 1999), 62.
4. Avery Gordon, *Ghostly Matters: Haunting and the Sociological Imagination* (Minneapolis: University of Minnesota Press), 2011.
5. Jacques Derrida, *Eyes of the University: Right to Philosophy 2*, trans. Jan Plug (Stanford: Stanford University Press, 2004), 101.
6. Lisa Lowe, *The Intimacies of Four Continents* (Durham, NC: Duke University Press, 2015).
7. John Stuart Mill, *On Liberty, Utilitarianism, and Other Essays* (Oxford: Oxford University Press, 2015), 63.
8. J.S.Mill, *On Liberty*, 70.
9. ibid.
10. Michel Foucault, *The Order of Things: An Archaeology of the Human Sciences* (New York: Vintage Books, 1970), 345.
11. Sylvia Wynter, 'On Disenchanting Discourse: "Minority" Literary Criticism and Beyond', *Cultural Critique* 7 (Autumn 1987), 208–09.
12. ibid.
13. Stuart Hall, 'The Local and the Global', in *Dangerous Liaisons: Gender, Nation, and Postcolonial Perspectives*, eds. Anne McClintock, Aamir Mufti and Ella Shohat (Minneapolis: University of Minnesota Press, 1997), 184.
14. S. Hall, 'The Local and the Global', 184.
15. T. Morrison, 'Rootedness', 340.
16. Mari Evans and Stephen Evangelist Henderson, *Black Women Writers (1950-1980): A Critical Evaluation* (New York: Doubleday, 1988), 340.
17. Karl Marx, *Communist Manifesto* (London: Verso, 2012).
18. Morrison saw the novel as a way of activating black cultural forms to assess the dangers of incorporation. To the extent that black cultural forms are being used in the contemporary moment to surrender to incorporation is the extent that those forms are being activated in contradistinction to what Morrison and this essay are describing. This essay is proposing the minoritised ancestor as a resource in the critique of power/knowledge and capitalist political economies.
19. Evans and Evangelist Henderson, *Black Women Writers*.
20. Immanuel Kant, *The Conflict of the Faculties – Der Streit Der Fakultäten*, trans. Mary J. Gregor (Lincoln: University of Nebraska Press, 1992), 23.
21. My thanks to Mery Concepción for this insight.
22. Vincent Harding, 'Responsibilities of the Black Scholar to the Community', *The State of Afro-American History: Past, Present, and Future*, ed. Darlene Clark Hine (Louisiana State Univ. Press, 1989), 279.
23. John Hope Franklin, 'On the Evolution of Scholarship in Afro-American History', in *The State of Afro-American History: Past, Present, and Future*, ed. Darlene Clark Hine (Louisiana State University Press, 1989), 18.
24. J. Hope Franklin, 'On the Evolution'.
25. Robert Nemiroff, *To Be Young, Gifted, and Black: Lorraine Hansberry in Her Own Words* (Hoboken, NJ: Prentice-Hall, 1969), 209.
26. Harding, 'Responsibilities', 281.
27. Toni Cade Bambara and Toni Morrison, *Deep Sightings and Rescue Missions* (London: Vintage, 1999), 139.
28. Toni Cade Bambara, 'Salvation is the Issue', in Evans and Evangelist Henderson, *Black Women Writers (1950-1980): A Critical Evaluation*, 47.
29. Kandice Chuh, *The Difference Aesthetics Makes: on the Humanities 'after Man'* (Durham: Duke University Press, 2019), 5.

Universities after neoliberalism

A tale of four futures

Christopher Newfield

We're used to one-way neoliberalism, regardless of party, in which we keep getting more of its familiar features: public budget austerity, marketisation, privatisation, selective cross-subsidies favouring business and technology, precarisation of professional labour, and structural racism. But under the pressure of international social forces, neoliberalism is increasingly breaking down. These forces include the Covid-19-induced public health crisis, the climate emergency, multiple modes of racism and neo-colonialism, and the grinding effects of economic inequality. Neoliberalism has fractured in places like Hungary and Turkey, where it is being replaced by an authoritarian form of national capitalism.[1] Something like that was happening in the US under Donald Trump, who sponsored a new round of tax cuts while denouncing trade liberalisation. At the same time, the liberal centre, incarnated by 'third way' New Democrat Joe Biden, has been backing away from the tradition that runs from Reagan and Thatcher through Clinton, Obama and Blair.

Biden's American Jobs Plan and American Families Plan are less interesting for content or size than as symbolic actions. They mark a clear paradigm shift away from a forty-year ruling consensus about rightful business sovereignty over the economy.[2] The AJP's 12,000-word 'Fact sheet' declares four decades of conservative economics a failure for national life. It casts Reaganomics as a mode of underdevelopment applied to the country's own working people and to its populations of colour, which resulted in a weakened society unable to rely on its decrepit public systems when it most needed them, as during the Covid-19 pandemic, and in the context of new great power rivalries. On the important level of paradigm framing, Biden's AJP aims not only to avoid the mistakes of Obama, Geithner and Summers but also of Roosevelt, Kennedy and Johnson: it is not colour blind but race conscious, and promises to distribute resources in a way that explicitly redresses racial disparities. For example, of the $40 billion that Biden requests for upgraded research infrastructure, half is to go to Historically Black Colleges and Universities and other Minority Serving Institutions. The US Senate will wreck this plan, of course. But the framework is out there: the owl of Minerva has flown in daylight.

The public critiques of austerity we've seen from Biden and also Boris Johnson won't go very far on their own. But in multiple domains – energy, policing, housing, banking and finance – the recent phase of 'punitive' neoliberalism is losing its political base.[3] A series of big reformist packages in the US, and bailouts for almost everything except universities and the arts in the UK, are opportunities for the higher education world to supplement its still-very-necessary critiques of the neoliberal, the racist and the settler-colonial university with plans for radical reconstruction.

At least four futures

My first point here is that the current situation puts higher learning up against a conflicted neoliberalism that is being forced to cede ground to opposing tendencies on both left and right, and my second is that multiple paths are now possible for the Anglo-American university in the 2020s. My third is that which paths universities follow depends not just on government policy but on the goals and actions of social movements outside but also inside of universities. I'll take these in order.

Universities are heading not only towards a familiar future but also toward three other futures that various

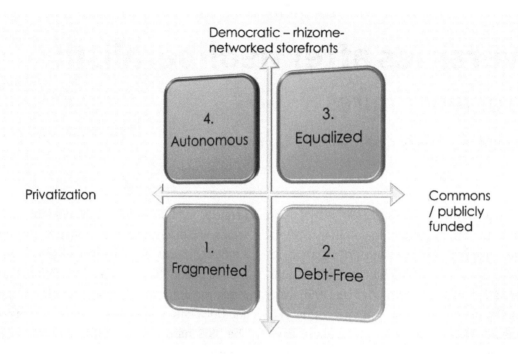

Fig. 1

people have been imagining. These are really four modes of future study. They aren't just abstract possibilities. The idea is that each can be generated by ratios of developments along the axes indicated there.

The first future might be called *Fragmented Decline* – made from the combination of privatisation (x axis) and platform (y-axis), replacing democratic deliberation with corporate managerialism. This is the business as usual track: the joyless storyline of 'decline foretold'. The conditions of this future were present before but were locked into place by policy and weak administrative responses in the 2010s, a decade that saw considerable increases in both privatisation in and managerial control of British universities. In the UK, David Willetts and the Coalition government cut central funding and replaced it with fees supported by student loans, producing an explosion of student debt. At the same time, managerial audit and direct control of teaching and research also increased, signalled by a proliferation of indicators, particularly the Teaching Excellence Framework (TEF) and the Longitudinal Educational Outcomes (LEO).

These indicators are regarded by professionals as deeply flawed – as measures of teaching quality or learning quantities. As techniques of induced compliance, on the other hand, they have been highly successful. As a measure, the LEO simply correlates an alumni's present income stream with their past course. It has no basis for making claims that participation in the course generated the income; more fundamentally, income is an effect of the way the job market prices vocations, not university instruction, so it is simply measuring something other than what is in its name. And yet, like the TEF, it has extended rankability and stratification among universities, forced the new 'losers' to scramble to increase the kinds of functions and behaviours for which the indicators select, and enhanced the authority of government to tell the sector what to do.[4] The main results have been fragmentation of the sector's purposes, increased resource inequality, greater poverty for the institutions most likely to educate the country's poorer students and students of colour, and decline in *net* educational resources for most if not all universities. *Fragmented decline* is a future we already know.

A second possible future is *Debt-Free College*. Although reformist, this future would require a major break with forty years of higher education policy. Here the Sanders-Warren tendency builds on Biden's opening to develop 'College for All' into a New Deal for Higher Education (to name a pair of US projects within this tendency). Labour's Corbyn-era National Education Service sketched a UK version, though after Corbyn any future version of this idea will likely need to be pushed by civil society groups. In this future, some kind of new New Deal would generate debt-free university for all students. This can only happen, as a practical matter, through tuition-free higher education.[5] The tax system would need a major adjustment to make this work, which would in turn require continuing high levels of popular organisation and escalating political pressure. However, free college, while keeping student costs low, would retain the current inequality of university resources – an inequality that is profoundly racialised. In this second future, college would become cheaper but also remain as unjust as it is today. Since lower tuition would, without major state intervention to compensate for it, also lower each university's revenues, the Debt-Free future for students might mean more institutional debt and insecurity for universities. That, in turn, would mean more educational inequality and mediocrity.

A third possible future is *Funding Equalised*. Here, various social movements might use the Biden opening to push College for All towards the overcoming of structural racism and class inequalities in educational resources. This would involve an entirely new political economy for higher education. It would distribute resources to achieve equality of economic inputs across different student populations, and invert those inputs according to need: less prepared students would get more instructional resources, not fewer as in the current state of affairs. The explicit goal here is equality of educational outcomes. It would use the tax system to redress injustices of income distribution, injustices that reflect the historical interaction of settler-colonial / imperial and neoliberal forms of accumulation. It would define educational needs and budget them accordingly, rather than today's reverse practice of establishing budget scarcity and then allotting educational opportunities accordingly.

A fourth possible future is abolitionist, and aims to dismantle the current university altogether, in order to replace it with fully non-capitalist and decolonised processes of higher learning. Ideas about how this system might work could be taken from existing Indigenous educational structures and epistemes, and would develop over the process of their construction. These processes would be inspired by varying combinations of Indigenous, decolonial and anti-racist thought, including their critiques of the epistemologies of the global North.

This fourth and most ambitious future rests on cri-

ticism of public-good theories of the social effects of higher education, as, among other things, being grounded in the land-grant and 'land grab' of settler-colonial appropriation.[6] The critique of neoliberalism has confirmed abolitionist insights into various abuses of the commons. In his new book *In the Shadow of the Ivory Tower*, for instance, Devarian Baldwin shows how public colleges have used their non-profit status to support private developer control of the city.[7] Given its concern about public funding as a crossroads of colonial and expropriative forces, this fourth future is unlikely to make claims on the resources of national or state tax systems. It may consist of local initiatives that reflect situated epistemologies and entangled identities. These might privilege self-organisation in quasi-permanent autonomous zones. These activities are likely to take place in civil society and would be private in that sense, although collectively and communally organised. They would have many models to draw on for organisation, including co-operatives, freedom schools, tribal colleges, related social systems and social movement services.

Much valuable work has been done to demarcate abolitionist from anti-neoliberal / anti-racist and public good transformations.[8] The lineages are distinct, as indicated in the four-quadrant graphic. The histories of Indigenous people, foregrounded in abolitionist futures, have developed in violent conflict with the public land-grant universities that grew out of settler-colonial expansion. Those memories and those differences must be respected and preserved. Neoliberal and neo-colonial logics also interacted in the past, and continue to interact. For example, techniques of privatisation deprive the descendants of British colonial subjects of the teaching grants and maintenance grants that were available to the overwhelmingly white student populations of the 1990s and 2000s expansion: both anti-neoliberal and decolonial critiques are relevant here. I'll discuss below a similar pattern in the University of California.

Elements of Futures three and four are likely to develop together. I put abolition on the private end of the private-public axis because it is grounded in part on a refusal of settler-descended public-good frameworks, and is likely to work with local contexts, differences and resources, at least in the beginning. However, I would like to see its autonomous institutions funded by the wider society through the tax mechanism, and increased in scope without reduction of independence or distinctiveness of values, epistemes and practices. I think we must do both. The same is true for the relations among other possible futures. *Debt-free* seems like a half-way measure, and it is, but would still require a massive upheaval in the political economy and group psychology of both the US and the UK to bring it about. The immense energy required to achieve it could itself lead to further things.

Critical university studies

The effects of the combination of managerialism and privatisation on students, instructors, researchers and frontline staff started to become clear to me in my workplace, the University of California, around the turn of the century, and by 2003 or so I set to work more systematically on their causes and effects. One goal was to figure out the effects of these shifts. The student debt boom was one, but there were less visible ones like the moving of research funding out of the humanities. Another was to identify the mechanisms that created these effects so that academics, including operations staff and students, could address them more effectively. We had to seek something like the truth behind the nonstop marketing that universities directed at politicians, executives, students and parents. For example, the marketing said that low-income students had a free ride at university, while the data showed they borrowed as much money as middle-income students: the latter needed to be demonstrated and then broadcast.[9] We needed to explain the mechanisms: *how* exactly did the 'high tuition – high aid' US model increase student debt? I saw the work as a materialist investigation of the university's political economy, building on previous landmarks like Slaughter and Leslie's *Academic Capitalism* (1997), working from the humanities rather than the social sciences or the science and technology business end of the university, and unearthing technical processes as well as undesirable educational and social effects. As the public university's non-recovery from the financial crisis got underway in the 2010s, I hoped this mixed study of culture, institutions and finance would increase workplace activism among my academic colleagues, including students. My aim was to transform existing universities rather than exit from or abolish them, though current practice is so entrenched and so discursively powerful that straight ab-

olition may ultimately prove more feasible. I will return to this point.

In 2012, Jeffrey Williams dubbed the interdiscipline of this kind of work 'critical university studies' (CUS), writing,

> A dominant tenor of postmodern theory was to look reflexively at the way knowledge is constructed; this new vein looks reflexively at 'the knowledge factory' itself (as the sociologist Stanley Aronowitz has called it), examining the university as both a discursive and a material phenomenon, one that extends through many facets of contemporary life. ... CUS turns a cold eye on higher education, typically considered a neutral institution for the public good, and foregrounds its politics, particularly how it is a site of struggle between private commercial interests and more public ones. ... [It] analyses how higher education is an instrument of its social structure, reinforcing class discrimination rather than alleviating it.

I'd insist too on the university's reinforcing racial discrimination, since the defunding of relatively accessible universities coincided with the increase of people of colour in the student population: the 1980s culture wars on anti-racist interventions were soon intertwined with budget wars that reduced the financial autonomy of public universities.[10]

CUS knowledge had to be activist knowledge since internal disruption is the only thing that will keep the default future of fragmented decline from continuing indefinitely. This is because the privatised-managerial model delivers an economically functional outcome. It's not the outcome that universities market, but it fits well with contemporary capitalism. Furthermore, no one explains to the public how the real and the marketed outcomes differ. This explanation became another CUS goal.

CUS sought to explain how the present model actually worked and show that its cures deepened the disease: tuition hikes, student debt, debt-funded capital projects, corporate research sponsorships were mostly net negative on revenues, with the major exception of student tuition, or required price-gouging of the university's own community, as with public-private partnerships for student housing.[11] The present model generates the first future as its default outcome. The high-tuition / financial aid model then continues as it is. Student debt rises, though more slowly. Institutional debt rises. Public funding remains stagnant and ripe for cuts at the first whiff of a fiscal downturn. The financial conditions of different types of universities continue to diverge. The more selective institutions with the largest private endowments are insulated from fiscal crisis, while all others struggle, compromise, often decline and sometimes close.

It's possible to assume that this is just how neoliberal capitalism works, so universities are inevitably mirroring larger economic forces. This implies that making universities less damaging must first wait for wider social change, or even a true revolution.[12] I understand the appeal of this view, and yet it underplays intermediating steps, internal variation and the partial or relative autonomy of all sectors in the economy. Universities have multiple simultaneous identities and contradictory effects. They are settler-colonial institutions in the US, and imperial or post-colonial institutions in the UK, that governments expect to deliver the technology for permanent military and economic supremacy on the world stage; at the same time, they sponsor autonomous research that is often anti-statist, anti-capitalist, anti-racist and anti-imperialist.

Just as fundamentally, they sponsor basic research pursued by people who are not primarily motivated by financial gain, meaning that, imperfect as their methods may be and biased as they individually are, the process and results are relatively independent of the economy and the state. Universities are widely regarded on the political right in both countries as a systemic menace to political and social order, and indeed sometimes they are. As I write, the Johnson administration is expanding a campaign to demonise critical race theory and to purge members of cultural boards perceived to be insufficiently anti-woke; it signals the seriousness with which conservatives regard university ideas in their everyday operations. The US culture wars were revived by Trump and are being amped up again as a weapon against Biden's movement towards economic and social inclusion: these crusades are too well known to need further explanation.

Reproducing inequalities

My corner of CUS has focused in particular on the intermediary steps through which the university generates a stratified graduate population that increases the concentration of accumulated wealth. The easiest way to show this is in the form of a devolutionary cycle, in which each apparently discrete effect, like student debt, is enabled and intensified by the one that came before.[13]

In brief, by the 1990s, senior university managers generally accepted the dominance of the view that higher education was like any other product marketed in a competitive economy: it would be most efficiently produced and delivered by private-sector methods, and should be treated, and paid for, as a private good. Even if they personally disagreed, and knew that even standard economics granted non-monetary and social benefits to higher education, they felt they had to get with the programme or suffer political ostracisation and fiscal decline. They committed themselves to pursuing private revenue streams – philanthropy, corporate contracts, real estate and other partnerships – as well as government contracts, whose net operating revenue results are negative (working through these accounts is an arena of technical labour that CUS often entails). The only good net positive private revenue source is student fees – in spite of the endless pitching of alternative revenue streams. This is a key point that needs to be taken on board by both critics and policymakers: the *only* reliable net positive private revenue is student tuition. This explains the fact that in the 2000s US public universities increased tuition charges at a multiple of the rate of inflation, or the fact that UK universities instantly tripled fees after the Cameron-Willetts Coalition government policy changes in 2011.

Next, the presence of student fee revenue encourages governments to cut tax-based state funding: Cameron-Willetts typically accompanied their increase in the fee cap with massive cuts in the teaching grant. This increases universities' resource dependency on students' private financial capacities. They offer students various loan mechanisms so they can pay tuition with money they don't actually have. Universities also pursue overseas students (and, in the US, students from other states) who pay double or triple the rate of 'home' fees. Public universities also create high-fee for-profit masters' programs for the same reason. The general outcome is that student debt becomes a personal hardship for many or most graduates, turns a bachelor's degree from career springboard to financial burden, and damages the university's standing with the general public, who increasingly see it as just another costly business to be watched out of the corner of their eye. Political blowback from debt, and the disappearance of the readily-available post-university job, induces continuous university cost-cutting in an atmosphere of political hostility. Managers often move money from the educational core to prospectively profitable auxiliaries, which reduces educational quality. The struggles of non-wealthy institutions lowers the degree attainment of their students and increases inequality across higher education.

This all leads to a graduate population whose unequal educational experiences generate unequal economic benefits (to say nothing of non-economic benefits). The advertised result of a B.A. degree is entrance to a good, fulfilling job and a stable financial future – in the US, it was the 'American dream' of a middle class life, supposedly still offered to a multi-racial student population.[14] The *actual* result of a B.A. degree is the limiting of this kind of affluence to a smaller elite – without expressly denying B.A. access to everyone else. We can refer to this as the US public university decline cycle.

Our default first future is one in which the current neoliberal political economy, using privatisation and managerial structures, creates a highly functional segmentation *within* the population of university graduates. In this system, wealthy super-premium private universities continue to do extremely well with global brands resting on endowment wealth that has benefitted from 40 years of financial asset price inflation, itself the result of systematic, bipartisan government policy. In the United States there are around 16 of these institutions. In the UK, there's Oxford, Cambridge, UCL, LSE, Imperial, and you could perhaps include Kings College London and Manchester among others, but probably not the entire Russell Group. In the US, you could throw in the 'Annapolis group' of liberal arts colleges (many not wealthy) and you have seats for 3-5% of college students. Another group of US universities that are selective to some degree, maybe 400 in total, tread water in this future, and keep their heads above it depending on regional and other factors. Mostly they can attract and retain students only by continually reducing their own net operating revenues. The third group of 'open access' colleges includes everyone else. In the US, they number about 3800. These will be funded as job training centres, or left to struggle, consolidate or close. The UK version is the sudden Tory re-discovery of further education, to be put in budgetary competition with higher education.

These three groups of colleges produce very different typical levels of learning (in spite of the heroic efforts of their instructors and students). Group I offers customised programmes with lots of individual feedback. Group III is, in the US, run on nearly 100% adjunct instruction and offers working conditions too poor to do anything but provide generic and increasingly automated feedback. As David Laurence discovered, in '[m]ore than 50%, or 2,188 institutions, deep in the universe of United States degree-granting colleges and universities, one has yet to encounter a single tenured or tenure-track faculty member.'[15]

Occupying the great middle ground of relatively selective institutions, Group II is closer to Group III than one might think. For example, at UC Santa Barbara (30% acceptance rate), in the department where I taught for three decades, perhaps 5% of English majors write a senior thesis. Thus only a small minority of a generally very bright population of UCSB English graduates are likely to be competitive in their academic skills with students from places like Princeton University or Reed College, where senior theses are required. To summarise roughly, gross resource inequality leads to inequality of student learning. In this status-quo future, *Fragmented Decline*, we have premium learning at the top, and limited learning in various gradations for everyone else – especially for a group I haven't even mentioned, the 50% of US college starters who leave without a degree.

The political economy of higher education is a clear example of racial capitalism in action. In a landmark study, 'Separate and Unequal' (2013), Anthony Carnevale and Jeff Stohl found that after 1995, most newly enrolled Black and Latinx students attended open-access institutions while their white contemporaries mostly went to selective colleges, which have much higher graduation rates. Crucially, the study correlated the racialised variation in graduation rates with large differences in (instructional) expenditures per student: 'The 82 most selective colleges spend almost five times as much and the most selective 468 colleges spend twice as much on instruction per student as the [3800-odd] open-access schools.'[16]

This data is already out of date: the trend of the past 15 years has been to extend resource scarcity into universities that previously had been spared. This is the story of the University of California as a whole, for instance, where the racial correlation is unmistakable. Figure 2

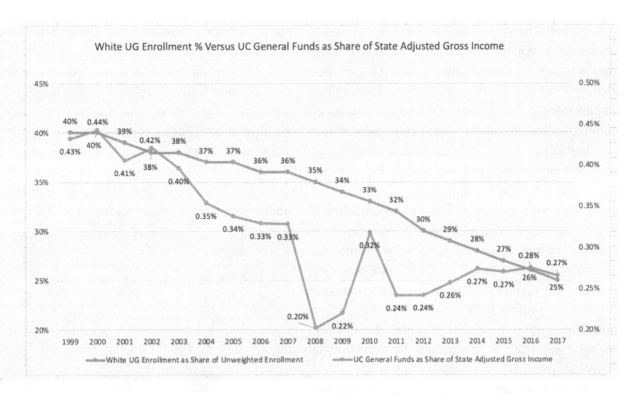

White UG Enrollment % Versus UC General Funds as Share of State Adjusted Gross Income

Fig. 2

shows a striking correlation: the share of state income going to the University fell in near-lockstep with the share of the student body that identifies as white.

This is a textbook definition of structural racism.

The University of California resembles nearly all universities in its official dedication to access, diversity and inclusion. It is increasingly comfortable denouncing anti-Blackness and opposing racism. So this racialised defunding conflicts with higher education's advertised goal of creating a racially inclusive form of capitalism based on knowledge, innovation and self-development rather than on exploitation, violence, segregation and war. It conflicts with the claimed outcome of equal opportunity for all university graduates regardless of race, gender, sexuality, immigration status and economic standing.

Let's return to CUS's contrast between the advertised and actual results of academia's political economy. The advertised outcome is cross-racial and cross-class equality of opportunity. The actual result is cross-racial and cross-class *in*equality of opportunity. But as long as it looks like universities *seek* equality of opportunity, they are free to generate actual inequality. In the process, they rationalise that inequality as meritocratic, which makes the resulting stratification much more difficult for regular members of the society to oppose. Mean-

while, economic decision makers – central bankers, national politicians, state legislatures, business lobbyists – can retain a particularly effective means of concentrating wealth, which is to reduce the share of national product that goes to labour. This was named a while back as 'plutonomy', and its advances have now been well documented. It means a smaller share of overall economic returns going to labour and a larger share going to capital, which Thomas Piketty has convincingly read as capitalism returning to its historic norm of growing returns to asset ownership faster than it grows the economy or returns to wages – as enabled by the absence of active state intervention.[17] By tying wage inequality to unequal educational outcomes, universities naturalise inequality that people would otherwise be more likely to trace to economic policies – like existing taxation rates – that are openly biased against wage labour. Universities complete the mystification by concealing the linkage CUS has sought to expose, between unequal educational outcomes and unequal material resources, particularly public funding.

The role of universities in intensifying this aspect of 'post-middle class' inequalities in the US encapsulates the last several decades of wage and employment degradation. The period from the 1950s and 60s reflects an

83

unusual social bargain between capital and labour. As workers became more productive during those decades, they were paid more money. Human capital theory came along to claim that they became more productive by becoming more educated. The motto was 'learning equals earning' – although factors such as union membership, racial exclusion and US economic dominance were arguably more important for pushing up wages for the mostly white male portion of the workforce.

This ended in the 1970s, first for blue-collar industrial workers during the deindustrialisation of what became the rust belt. Union busting is a big part of the story, offshoring is another part, and a third is race-based segmentation that allows the super-exploitation of some categories of workers, for example in the home care economy. But these methods of wage control don't work in the same way with college graduates. How could capital apply the same methods to college students?

The university business model provides a real solution to the goal that university marketing conceals: capital accumulation can be intensified by segmenting college graduates roughly into the three groups I mentioned before. Graduates of top colleges have a good chance of entering Elite Professional Services: consulting, corporate law, banking and finance, and the like.[18] The half of college starters who don't finish can do a lot of white-collar work from a position of employment precarity. Group III graduates are not much better off. The large group who graduate from a wide range of good but underfunded public and private colleges, Group II, who expect to enter a multi-racial middle class, get limited learning, which endows them with mid-level skills and which does not enable them to bargain effectively for high and increasing salaries. The benefit to Western capitalism (post-industrial, asset-ownership based, rent-seeking) is to shrink the entitled economic class of educated labour to about one-fifth of all university graduates, and perhaps even less.

In our default future's fragmented, stratified condition, the university system creates a cognotariat. It Uberises knowledge work. The university itself has pioneered economic precarity for professionals in the form of the contingent faculty system, who now form the majority of college instructors. It creates high-skill people, and links high-skills to middle-level and often precarious wages. It limits entitlements like pensions and health care to

specially trained and pedigreed white-collar workers, rather than spreading them widely as a sign of prosperity. If offshoring broke the wage-productivity bargain for blue-collar workers, higher education helped break it for white-collar workers. It accepted economic rule over political choices, pushed competition for scare premium places rather than egalitarian allocation of educational resources, and stratified educational quality. We talk quite a bit now about the gig economy. One of its enabling conditions is the gig academy.[19]

Elements of reinvention

That's our default future 1. As I noted, my CUS work has aimed to show that the current system isn't muddling through towards a bit more mobility and justice, but is instead tumbling down towards generalised precarity, post-democracy, professional decline and the permanent economic vulnerability of middle-income people with university degrees. A further aim is to show how the current system emerged from deliberate policy choices that academics didn't do enough to resist at the time, but which could still be rejected in favour of new and non-unitary structures. Escape from future 1 will require a large-scale rejection of its systemic effects and its economic model, starting with a rejection by academics.

I'll end by pointing out two distinct but synergistic modes of building the other futures in our post-Covid reality. The more fundamental of the two is beyond my scope here: we could reject the human capital theory version of the university, which means making the business world and the government responsible for both employment and incomes. HCT was a rationale of convenience that worked for higher education during a very specific time in history.[20] It was never correct as a general theory for all graduates, and it is now serving mainly as a way for governments to shift blame for bad jobs and poor wages onto the backs of universities that are not in fact responsible for them. It is a scapegoating mechanism that prevents governments and the private sector from facing the profound flaws in their models of capitalist affluence, and requiring them to change fundamentally. Until universities can convince society to hold employers responsible for employment, UK and US universities will stay trapped in the doom loop of future 1 I've described.

The second way of transforming the situation would be to define the universities that those working and studying in them actually want to have. The desired features would vary by country, region, social group and discipline (it's all quite different for bench sciences and professional schools). This means many more people actively defining the elements of reinvented universities that they think would work best. Here's my own list:

1. Replacing equality of opportunity with equality of outcomes across racial and socioeconomic status. If general graduation rates, presence across types of profession and so on vary by group, then inequality must be addressed with policy changes and additional resources. Does your country have 21,000 academic staff yet only 140 who identify as Black?[21] You need to bulldoze complaints about too much critical race theory and set goals and mechanisms and deadlines to achieve racial proportionality.

2. Achieving equality of educational outcomes across institutional types. This isn't a matter of TEF rankings, but of sending equal or greater funding to universities that admit more disadvantaged or underserved students until the academic results even out.

3. B.A. degrees that are debt-free. This will mean no fees and, in addition, rebuilt maintenance grants for a large percentage of students. The older members of the society should fund the educations of the younger through a progressive tax system that prevents low-income workers from subsidising high-income students.

4. B.A. degrees that reflect deep learning, which links personal identity, self-development, skills, field knowledge, and creative capabilities. This learning is labour intensive, mostly done in small groups, and expensive. Academics should articulate what this looks like in varying fields (not just learning objectives but full processes and methods), estimate its costs, and agitate for its funding. Funding for 'limited learning' under current conditions is completely vulnerable to cuts.[22] Academic staff and students should articulate the real thing and start forcing a triangulation with the diluted model.

5. Full funding of research, across all fields. No major problem has a solely technical solution, with Covid-19 providing a vivid example of how much we need social knowledge and public system development in addition to virology. When governments or universities fund STEM fields by sacrificing the arts, humanities and social sciences, they both discriminate against a large class of students and lower the public value of higher education. Arts and humanities fields have all but given up on asking for proper research funding, which ensures that they won't get it. That needs to change.

6. Just employment: reduce contingent employment until part-time and unprotected academic jobs are held only by those who want them. Universities should model the ethical workplace rather than its precarious alternatives.

7. Democratised academic governance. The first six features will not exist without this. Governing boards now primarily channel political forces into universities and norm their conduct to standards set by government or industry or powerful religious or other private interests.[23] They do not now offer distinctive expertise designed to curate their academic communities that cannot already be found in those communities themselves. The same is true for the many senior managers who have taken on an adversarial relation to academic staff. Democratisation can start small but it needs to start.

These features may seem impossible. One thing I am sure of is that they are affordable. They are also possible – if and only if academics make their methods and benefits concrete, and turn them into the goals of internal university movements that, through the visible effort of their pursuit, attract outside respect and support.

Christopher Newfield teaches in the English Department at the University of California, Santa Barbara. His books include Unmaking the Public University: The 40-Year Assault on the Middle Class *(2008) and* The Great Mistake: How We Wrecked Public Universities and How We Can Fix Them *(2016).*

Notes

1. On Hungary, see Gábor Scheiring, *The Retreat of Liberal Democracy: Authoritarian Capitalism and the Accumulative State in Hungary* (London: Palgrave Macmillan, 2020).

2. See, for example, Cédric Durand, '1979 in Reverse', *Sidecar* 1 June 2021, https://newleftreview.org/sidecar/posts/1979-in-reverse; Susan Watkins, 'Paradigm Shifts,' *New Left Review* II, 127 (March/April 2021), 5–12.

3. William Davies, 'The New Neoliberalism', *New Left Review* II, 101 (2016), 121–34.

4. See, for example, Rosemary Deem and Jo-Anne Baird, 'The English Teaching Excellence (and Student Outcomes) Framework: Intelligent Accountability in Higher Education?', *Journal of Educational Change* 21:1 (2020), 215–243; Stefan Collini, 'Universities and "Accountability": Lessons from the UK Experience?', in *Missions of Universities: Past, Present, Future* (New York: Springer, 2020), 55, 115.

5. See Christopher Newfield, *The Great Mistake: How We Wrecked Public Universities and How We Can Fix Them* (Baltimore: Johns Hopkins University Press, 2016), stage 5.

6. Robert Lee and Tristan Ahtone, 'Land-Grab Universities', *High Country News*, 30 March 2020, https://www.hcn.org/issues/52.4/indigenous-affairs-education-land-grab-universities.

7. Davarian L. Baldwin, *In the Shadow of the Ivory Tower: How Universities Are Plundering Our Cities* (New York: Bold Type Books, 2021).

8. Abigail Boggs et al., 'Abolitionist University Studies: An Invitation', *Abolition University* (blog), September 2019, https://abolition.university/invitation/; Sandy Grande, 'Refusing the University', in *Toward What Justice?: Describing Diverse Dreams of Justice in Education*, eds. Eve Tuck and K. Wayne Yang (New York: Routledge, 2018), 47–65; la paperson, *A Third University Is Possible* (Minneapolis: University of Minnesota Press, 2017); Sharon Stein, 'Navigating Different Theories of Change for Higher Education in Volatile Times', *Educational Studies* 55:6 (November 2, 2019), 667–88.

9. Anon, 'Trends in Student Aid 2020', College Board, 11 June 2019, https://research.collegeboard.org/trends/student-aid.

10. On the connections among attacks on racial equality, market ideology and technology transfer, see Christopher Newfield, *Unmaking the Public University: The Forty-Year Assault on the Middle Class* (Cambridge, MA: Harvard University Press, 2008).

11. Sofia Mejias Pascoe, 'UCSD Students, Faculty Push Back Against Steep Rent Hikes', *Voice of San Diego*, 22 March 2021.

12. Joshua Clover, 'Who Can Save the University?', *Public Books*, 12 June 2017, http://www.publicbooks.org/who-can-save-the-university/.

13. My account here is derived from Newfield, *The Great Mistake*.

14. Anglo-American economists have long identified a large university wage premium over the wages of high school graduates, and this average premium persists. This fact does not, however, conflict with the point I'm making here about stratification within the university graduate population. Economists generally treat each education level as a homogenous cohort, which lumps together graduates of wealthy elite universities with graduates of poor local public institutions to claim a generic causal link between learning and earning. But for an acknowledgement and discussion of the growing internal inequality that I discuss here from leading proponents of this mainstream economics of education, see David Autor, Claudia Goldin and Lawrence F. Katz, 'Extending the Race between Education and Technology', Working Paper Series (National Bureau of Economic Research, January 2020), https://doi.org/10.3386/w26705.

15. David Laurence, 'Tenure in 2017: A Per Institution View', Humanities Commons, https://hcommons.org/deposits/item/hc:27147/

16. Anthony P. Carnevale and Jeff Strohl, 'Separate & Unequal', Centre for Education and the Workforce, Georgetown University, July 2013, https://cew.georgetown.edu/cew-reports/separate-unequal/.

17. Thomas Piketty, *Capital in the Twenty First Century*, trans. Arthur Goldhammer (Cambridge, Mass.: Harvard University Press, 2014).

18. Lauren A. Rivera, *Pedigree: How Elite Students Get Elite Jobs* (Princeton: Princeton University Press, 2016).

19. Adrianna Kezar, Tom DePaola and Daniel T. Scott, *The Gig Academy: Mapping Labor in the Neoliberal University* (Baltimore: Johns Hopkins University Press, 2019).

20. Aashish Mehta and Christopher Newfield, review of Phillip Brown, Hugh Lauder and Sin Yi, *The Death of Human Capital?*, in *Los Angeles Review of Books*, forthcoming 2021.

21. Richard Adams, 'Fewer than 1% of UK University Professors Are Black, Figures Show', *The Guardian*, 27 February 2020.

22. Richard Arum and Josipa Roksa, *Academically Adrift: Limited Learning on College Campuses* (Chicago: University of Chicago Press, 2011).

23. See Lindsay Ellis, Jack Stripling and Dan Bauman, 'The New Order', *The Chronicle of Higher Education*, 25 September 2020.

Reviews

Solidarity to fraternity

Elleni Centime Zeleke, *Ethiopia in Theory: Revolution and Knowledge Production, 1964-2016* (Leiden and Boston: Brill/Haymarket, 2019/2020). 281pp., £135 hb., £20 pb., 978 9 00441 475 4 hb., 978 1 64259 341 9 pb.

One objective of Elleni Centime Zeleke's *Ethiopia in Theory: Revolution and Knowledge Production, 1964-2016* is to trace the contours of the nationalities question in Ethiopia today. First pronounced in the pages of literature produced by student movement activists mobilised against the government of Haile Selassie during the 1960s, the nationalities question concerns the terms of inclusion for different identities in the modern Ethiopian state. Ideas from that literature resurfaced in the 1995 constitution of the Federal Democratic Republic of Ethiopia. Under the stewardship of the Ethiopian People's Revolutionary Democratic Front (EPRDF) and following the overthrow of the Derg regime in 1991, the 1995 constitution forged a new system of regional federalism according to which control over land corresponded with designated national identities.

Just as *Ethiopia in Theory* appeared in print in November 2019, prime minister Abiy Ahmed inaugurated the Prosperity Party. The move broke a nearly three-decades long political consensus. At the time of writing, the country is embroiled in a civil war pitting Eritrean forces, Amhara militias and the apparatus of the state against various parties representing Oromo federalist interests and the former leaders of the Tigrayan People's Liberation Front (TPLF). The civil war would presumably end if the Tigrayan and Oromo leadership acquiesced to the dictates of individual citizenship regardless of identity, relinquishing claims to collective autonomy and land embedded in the 1995 constitution. The Prosperity Party, in other words, has sought to dismantle the country's federalist system in favour of a centralised state. Implicitly, the wager demands submission to a single national identity. As with all liberal states, aspirational or otherwise, abstract talk of universal equality and rule of law papers over enduring historical hierarchies.

Political theorists tend to address comparable events with recourse to the ninth chapter in Hannah Arendt's influential *The Origins of Totalitarianism*. Titled 'The Decline of the Nation-State and the End of the Rights of Man', Arendt's chapter deems nationalism an errant project. At best, she argues, it creates minorities forced to assimilate to the dominant identity of the state where they reside. Otherwise, nationalism fosters stateless populations, the condition that rendered possible mass atrocities and genocide during the Second World War. In response, Arendt champions rule of law and constitutionalism, calling for reconfiguration of the state form to preclude the violence inherent in different iterations of the national question.

But Arendt's assessment appears insufficient with regard to recent events in Ethiopia. On the one hand, Abiy's government posits a statist repudiation of seemingly undue privilege afforded disparate nationalities. On the other hand, the same government registers a nationalist repudiation of past technocratic statecraft. How, then, is Ethiopia navigating seemingly opposed precepts between the hyper-rationalism characteristic of technocratic statecraft and the irrationalism of national chauvinism? What histories shape the ongoing Ethiopian pursuit of modern nation-state ideals? What is the Ethiopian nation-state in its specificity? *Ethiopia in Theory* gives readers a method to think through these questions and to reassess the nationalities question as a question. This is its enduring contribution.

Consider an announcement from the Ethiopian Students Association in North America (also known as the Ethiopian Students Union in North America or ESUNA) directed toward the Iranian Students Association (ISA). I found the announcement in 2013, tucked among a cache of papers in the basement of a private home on the outskirts of Tehran. The documents were part of a collection that once belonged to Ahmad Shayegan, later preserved by his eldest son Ali. Ahmad's father, Ali's namesake, was a close friend and ally of Mohammad Mossadegh. He served as one of Mossadegh's lawyers when the prime minister appeared before the International Court of Justice and the United Nations in 1952 to defend the nationalisation of Iranian oil. An MI6 and CIA engineered coup toppled Mossadegh's government one year later, relegating the former prime minister to house arrest for the remainder of his life. The elder Ali Shayegan chose exile in the United States where he lived, raised a family, and helped organise a movement in opposition to the post-coup government.

That movement, spearheaded in the US by the Iranian Student Alliance (ISA), worked in collaboration with groups like the Ethiopia Student Union in North America (ESUNU). Ahmad Shayegan was one of the ISA's founding members and at some point served on its five-person secretariat, which included a seat to establish relations with external organisations. Iranian students' affiliations with Ethiopian students occurred through this channel. Ahmad was equally active in political organisations separate from the ISA but whose members attempted to recruit cadres and sympathetic followers from within the student group. These political organisations inherited and expanded the elder Shayegan's project of national liberation into a Marxist politics. The Organisation of the National Front of Iran Abroad (Middle East Branch) which would later become the Star Group [*Gurūh-i Sitārih*], the Communist Alliance Group [*Gurūh-i Ittihādīyih-yi Kumūnīstī*], and finally the Organisation of Communist Unity [*Sāzmān-i Vahdat-i Kumūnīstī*] pioneered transnational activism among Iranians. It seems appropriate that this document would be in Ahmad's personal collection.

The announcement employs two historically loaded terms for the relationship between Iranian and Ethiopian student activists. The first is 'solidarity': 'The ETHIOPIAN STUDENTS ASSOCIATION IN NORTH AMERICA fully supports this demonstration against the SHAH of IRAN; it expresses its solidarity with the IRANIAN STUDENTS ASSOCIATION IN THE U.S.' The second is 'fraternity':

> The Shah of Iran and Emperor Haile Selassie of Ethiopia are birds of the same feather. Both are heads of corrupt

and oppressive regimes; both are loyal servants of the American Empire. Iranian and Ethiopian students are thus committed to a common struggle against autocracy and imperialism. We are convinced that the bond of fraternity created between them during the initial phase of their struggles shall grow into a stronger revolutionary alliance linking the peoples of Iran and Ethiopia for the purpose of promoting the national liberation efforts of the THIRD WORLD.

Are solidarity and fraternity synonymous? Did the flyer's authors intentionally vary the language in question merely as a matter of style? Or does form – and hence the difference between these terms – matter for politics?

It would seem that solidarity and fraternity are distinct, the former limited to acts of articulation: 'the Ethiopian Students Association in North America ... *expresses* its solidarity with the Iranian Students Association in the US' (emphasis mine). One can express solidarity at little to no cost. Once upon a time, student activists held congresses where they read aloud solidarity statements from peer organisations to roaring applause. Nowadays multinational corporations, sports leagues and enterprising government officials (the leaders of the post-revolutionary state in Iran prominent among them) can declare that Black Lives Matter without making any substantial changes to prisons or policing. Substantial change requires more effort to cultivate shared affect: '... the bond of fraternity created between them during the initial phase of their struggles *shall grow* ...' One of the ideological pillars of the post-revolutionary French republic, this bond intimates an enduring process during which a new affiliation is formed. According to political philosopher and social theorist Andreas Esheté, in his 1981 essay 'On Fraternity' especially, fraternity is alive – experiential, social, relational. It concerns affective and sentimental bonds developed over time through shared experience. In the 'relationship of daily life and under ordinary conditions', one 'habitually recognises that the community is one's substantive groundwork and end.' Andreas, it should be noted, played a prominent role in the ESUNU during the 1960s and 1970s and later helped shape the 1995 post-Derg constitution.

His distinction between solidarity and fraternity maps neatly onto the distinction between content and form operating at the core of Elleni's *Ethiopia in Theory*. For positivist social scientists, conventionally speaking, form and method are a passive medium, a canvas on which to paint content and meaning. The scientists locate human life in *what* they say. *How* they say it is a dead letter, meant to vanish on arrival. For Elleni, form and method track the life of the knowledge producer, the social and historical lifeworld the researcher bears, the possessions they haul to every exchange. How do researchers come to know the past given the past lives among us in the present? How does the language of the social sciences obscure the truth, given that revolutions almost without exception are messy affairs? 'The task is not to predict the future based on an experience of the past', Elleni argues, 'but to re-open the future through confronting in theory and practice the unresolved contradictions of the past as it shapes the present'. *Ethiopia in Theory* does not just tell, it shows, eschewing pretensions to authorial independence and objectivity. The author places herself centre-stage for readers to observe universal theory grow from her embodied, situated knowledge.

The book enacts its argument, which is to say its method. Each page weaves together immanent critiques of Ethiopian revolutionary historiography and postcolonial theories of knowledge production. Elleni inhabits the interlocution; she listens and she layers. The resulting tapestry mirrors the sedimentation of experience, from the settling dust of upheaval into the illusion of time having moved on. But the book does not simply add another universalism alongside others. It digs into the specificity of knowledge production about the Ethiopian revolution, which includes the author's own vulnerabilities, to reach for a new universal.

Form matches content: as Elleni theorises, forlorn student movement activists appear as creative and generative political theorists. Beginning in the 1960s, these students debated in the pages of *Challenge*, a publication distributed in the US and Canada. Their debates would later (and quite remarkably) infiltrate the corridors of policy-making in the post-revolutionary state. Student movement activists created a notion of scientific progress specific to Ethiopia. To this day scientific discourse holds authority in the Horn of Africa, evidenced by the universalist technocratic pretensions of the current state. Abstract and ahistorical prescriptions for future policy fan the flames of ethnic conflict, bearing witness to the charge that the form of the students' initiatives endured even as they abandoned its original Marxist content after the Cold War. Like the immanent critiques of historiography and postcolonial theory performed throughout, Elleni reads these activist theorists generously, praising their creativity while pointing out flaws in their thinking. The students' Marxist intent remains, their commitment to scientism filtered away. *Ethiopia in Theory* searches for a method to embrace Marxism, instead of rejecting it because of what its proponents later engendered.

Just as Marx chastises classical political economy for exclusively focusing on content, Elleni repudiates the formal conventions of knowledge production. Her book does not recover Marxism as mere statement (an *expression* of solidarity), rather it embodies a Marxist spirit of creation (a phenomenological bond of fraternity). Returning to the Marxist theory at the root of contemporary Ethiopian politics accords with Elleni's understanding of Marxist theory at its core. If universal human nature is to construct and create (as Marx contends in his notion of species-being), then a return to Marx resists the ascription of primordial identity plaguing the nationalities question in contemporary Ethiopian politics. The endeavour requires Elleni echo her subjects' form. She too must be creative, but in her own right. *Ethiopia in Theory* shows how a mode of inquiry taken for granted as common sense transformed common sense by creating its own form.

What does this book, articulating this method, have to say about the nationalities question today? What can it offer those reflecting on events that took place since it was published? *Ethiopia in Theory* abjures predication as an enterprise and yet somehow manages to anticipate later events. The nationalities question, for Elleni, refers to the colonial and imperial effects of modern state formation in the Horn of Africa. This story invariably concerns knowledge produced about the state. A first wave of Ethiopian national historiography shaped by colonial institutions exalted centralisation, privileging the Abyssinian and Amharic-speaking region at the expense of other populations. A newer trend in historical writing, shaped by the student movement against Haile Selassie, aspired to counter unequal representations and attendant power imbalances. It comprised an inversion, fostering scholarship on the primordial identities of marginalised populations. Student movement-inspired scholarship was cast onto contemporary Ethiopian politics. Evoking Partha Chatterjee, Elleni shows how the resulting pluralisation of national identities in scholarship and politics alike preserved nationalism and colonial rule by perpetuating nationalist and colonial ways of thinking. She thus proposes to re-assess the nationalities question. Rejecting the premise of an internal debate between different ethnic groupings, *Ethiopia in Theory* recalls a history where the student movement first articulated nationalism to 'relate the Ethiopian nation-state to a capitalist world system'. How did this thought come to be internalised, she asks? And where was its internationalism lost?

Revolutions tend to exacerbate ruptures and contradictions. Positivist social scientists assume we can sew the tears together if equipped with precise classificatory schemas. Elleni is more inclined to revisit past wounds. To dwell in them, she claims, is to assemble alternatives that repudiate the convergence of science and politics. For instance, *Ethiopia in Theory* is concerned with the presumption that abstract policy prescriptions formulated in remote locales can helicopter into a place like Ethiopia without regard for local life.

Does this political goal require a wholesale rejection of positivism? Must authors writing about revolutions adopt a revolutionary disposition? Must their form necessarily match their content? We can write increasingly accurate and truthful accounts of social and political phenomena so long as we accept certain limits. Elleni asks a larger, and I believe, more courageous, question – what does it mean to be academic? She asks it of the Ethiopian student movement and its legacies, of the knowledge production shaping Ethiopian politics since the revolution, but also of herself and us. Historical writing presumes a separation between past and present sufficient to facilitate insights past actors themselves could not see. To say the present is haunted by the past is to propose that this imagined separation is in fact untruthful. Either our first step is blindness and everything thereafter an attempt to conceal our missteps or we grope about in the dark, open our other senses, acclimate to the dim light, inhabit.

Ethiopia in Theory does not conceal past mistakes. It layers. To perfunctory readers, the book may appear to be an extended literature review. It is and it is not: its object of study is social scientific literature. It is a literature review that does the work literature reviews conventionally occasion while reaching beyond the survey. To unreflective readers, the book may appear impressionistic. It is and it is not: it centres subjective experience as world historical. Paul Ricœur teaches that narrative is the human experience of time. Lived human experience does not neatly divide into past, present and future. In Elleni's narrative, the historian cannot in good faith stand aloof from the past.

For skeptics, the adoption of a revolutionary disposition to write about revolution, the matching of content with form, may look like historical writing 'out of joint with itself'. David Scott's *Conscripts of Modernity*, a book of consequence to Elleni's argument, argues that different generations pose different kinds of questions and answers. They inhabit different 'problem-spaces' because past, present and future are distinct. Historical writing falters, Scott concludes, when anticolonial questions-and-answers address our postcolonial predicament – when romantic narratives characteristic of past revolutionary endeavours propose final solutions in lieu of the tragically partial questions and answers suited to our present. The impulse to match form with content threatens to repeat the misstep against which Scott admonishes. How, after all, could the children of revolutions – people like Elleni and myself – occupy the same 'problem-space' as the generation of Andreas Esheté and Ahmad Shayegan? Elleni concedes that we do not. And yet, for her, the distinction Scott presumes between past and present is too neat – despite Scott's critique of positivist narrative arcs in historiography, his conception of historical time still too positivist. Taking her cue from *Conscripts of Modernity*, Elleni writes a tragic narrative but without presuming incommensurable differences between past, present and future. We may not share the same 'problem-space' as the generations that came before us, but we share the same structuring antagonisms. The passage of time alone does not resolve racial capitalism or colonial power. Our present is haunted.

And so, Elleni asks her own questions: How does the past live in *her* present and what does *she* need to do in order to liberate herself from it? To read these as strictly personal questions and thus reduce *Ethiopia in Theory* to memoir is to fall back into the policed designations of positivist social science, to think hauntings are individual phenomena. It is to lose sight of Elleni's argument. If a shared past haunts a shared present, memoir is theory.

Does Elleni's method – which is to say, her argument – travel? Five years after the Ethiopian revolution, while its former student activists were mired in an earlier civil war, the Iranians for whom they declared their support embarked upon an unanticipated revolutionary journey of their own. Can the children of Iran's revolution adopt Elleni's method to settle accounts with the past that haunts our present? Where does specificity give way to a new universal? What kind of knowledge production could forge bonds of fraternity between the children of the Ethiopian and Iranian revolutions?

Frantz Fanon – who celebrated internationalism in his writings and who endures as a magnet for international solidarity movements to this day – saw fraternity and solidarity otherwise. As Anuja Bose demonstrates, the Martinican psychiatrist and Algerian revolutionary, posthumously turned into the canonical scribe of race and decolonisation on the African continent, rejected fraternity as if shedding a straightjacket. The French tricolor championed fraternity but imposed restrictions on membership in its imagined national family: only white men could be brothers. The strictures inspired nausea in Fanon, a condition from which he sought relief in the felt experience of life and, inverting anti-Black racism, the affirmations afforded by the continued physical presence of his body. He discovered his humanity risking death alongside Algerians in their struggle for independence against French settler colonial rule. Solidarity bred life where fraternity denied his existence.

Describing *les damnés*, his heroic protagonist in 1961's *The Wretched of the Earth*, he writes:

> In this atmosphere of brotherly solidarity and armed struggle, men link arms with their former enemies. The national circle widens and every new ambush signals the entry of new tribes. Every village becomes a free agent and a relay point. Solidarity among tribes, among villages and at the national level is first discernible in the growing number of blows dealt to the enemy. Every new group, every new volley of cannon fire signals that everybody is hunting the enemy, everybody is taking a stand.

Les damnés stretched the revolutionary force of the French Third Estate and transformed it into a project for the Third World. According to Bose, he envisioned an 'international populism', uniting people across nation-state borders by virtue of like experiences of national solidarity forged in common struggles for independence: 'Iranian and Ethiopian students are thus committed to a common struggle against autocracy and imperialism.'

We are today experiencing a renewed commitment to decolonisation as protests against police murder in the U.S. spur solidarity marches across the globe. At times, these actions culminate in displays of symbolic power, from the renaming of a street to the toppling of a former colonial official enshrined in bronze and stone. Each defaced and dismembered statue in a postcolonial metropolis faintly recalls the acts of violence described in *The Wretched of the Earth*. The colonised, Fanon claimed, must perform acts of violence to sense their emerging independence. Now, the colonists' bodies are petrified symbols looming over the squares where daily life circulates. One symbol begets another. Movements demand and often readily receive expressions of solidarity. The ease with which those expressions are exchanged, however, threatens to undermine meaningful unity forged through shared, visceral experience. We are only beginning to confront 'in theory and practice' these 'unresolved contradictions'. We are yet 'to re-open the future' of our shared horizon. The spirit of Fanon's call to arms, dependent as it was on experience, may just require fraternity again.

Arash Davari

Troubled pleasures

Kate Soper, *Post Growth Living: For an Alternative Hedonism* (London: Verso, 2020). 240pp., £16.99 hb., 978 1 78873 887 3

Kate Soper has made some vitally important contributions to ecosocialist and feminist political theory over the last four decades and more. Her interventions around 'troubled pleasures', humanism and its discontents, realism/constructionism, and more, have often been seminal. Perhaps one of the most striking threads in her body of work has been the proposition that if a sane and progressive ecopolitics is to have any serious prospect of success, it needs to advance a compelling cultural politics of pleasure alongside a material and feminist politics of egalitarian redistribution. In this respect, her ecosocialist advocacy has been distinctive in its persistent push back against a certain kind of scolding miserabilism that has long fueled some of the worst aspects of environmentalism in the first world with unfortunate political results. The arrival of *Post-Growth Living* then is something to be celebrated.

The core arguments of *Post Growth Living* are made in concise fashion in the first few pages. *Contra* the claims of assorted ecomodernists and fully automated luxury communists, our climate and broader environmental crisis 'cannot be resolved by purely technical means.' Rather, it will require '... richer societies substantially to change their way of living, working and consuming.' Soper does not seek to ignore the importance of technology – 'Green technologies and interventions (renewable energy, rewilding, reforestation and so on) will prove essential tools for ecological renewal.' However, she maintains an eco-technical shift will only have a chance of success if it converges with 'a cultural revolution in thinking about prosperity'.

Perhaps the most interesting move in *Post Growth Living* is Soper's call for post carbon visionaries to go on the offensive. As she notes, '[t]he call to consume less is often presented as undesirable and authoritarian. Yet, the market itself has become an authoritarian force – commanding people to sacrifice or marginalise everything that is not commercially viable; condemning them to long hours of often very boring work to provide stuff that often isn't really needed; monopolising conceptions of the "good life"; and preparing children for a life of consumption'. We could do better. Alternative hedonism offers 'an opportunity to advance beyond a mode of life that is not just environmentally disastrous but also in many respects unpleasurable, self-denying and too puritanically fixated on work and money-making, at the expense of the enjoyment that comes with having more time, doing more things for oneself, travelling more slowly and consuming less stuff.'

Post Growth Living consists of seven chapters that make the case for not only alternative hedonism but a version of this political project that is grounded in Soper's broader commitments to ecohumanism and qualified realism, as articulated in her classic text *What is Nature?*. The argument centres around what Soper sees as the intersection between the narrow range of acceptable pleasures that consumer society allows and unfreedom in the capitalist workplace. It is these two self-re-enforcing features of high carbon capitalist living that are not only eco-destructive but, Soper argues, constraining of our liberty and our capacity for flourishing. The route forward is to stage a confrontation with work-and-spend culture around the question of pleasure.

This is an argument that does not place all the weight on naturalistic imperatives or crisis to cultivate eco or climate friendly behaviour. Nor does it follow the desire of more empirically orientated researchers to define an objective set of human needs and work back from this to consider the ways in which these needs might be satisfied by alternative institutional or cultural forms. Rather Soper outlines her argument as moving 'from expressions of concern to delineating an alternative structure of satisfactions, rather than presupposing unconscious needs for this alternative and then casting around in a theoretical void for consumers who might come to experience them'.

Alternative hedonism does not assume consumption will shift because of altruism or the desire to be 'responsible' or 'civic minded'. Rather, 'The hedonist aspect of this shift in consumption practice does not lie exclusively in the wish not to contribute to the unpleasant by-products of collective affluence, but also in the intrinsic personal pleasures of consuming differently.' As she observes in relation to making a choice to drive or cycle: 'The cyclist or walker enjoys sensual experiences, including those of greeting other cyclists and walkers, that the insulated driver cannot. But these different pleasures themselves require and thrive on alternative hedonist self-policing in car use and support for policies that restrain it'.

In terms of here and now politics, Soper casts alternative hedonism as a utopian longing for other ways of existing. She speaks of 'expressions of regret for pleasures we can no longer enjoy'. As such, alternative hedonism is also to be found in 'more subdued and private nostalgia over lost landscapes, communities and spaces for playing, socialising, loitering or communing with nature'. There are cultural sentiments which are somewhat elusive but may surface as:

> … a more generalised lament over commodification, as a yearning for a less harried existence or as an elegiac sense that, were it not for the dominance of the combustion engine, there would be much better provision for greener forms of transport, and both rural and city areas would look, feel, smell and sound entirely different. Or it may just figure as a vague and rather general malaise that descends in the shopping mall or supermarket: a sense of a world too cluttered and encumbered by material objects and sunk in waste, of priorities skewed through the focus on ever-more extensive provision and acquisition of stuff.

A further well-spring for alternative hedonism could arise from greater attention to the depth of alienation that is experienced in the contemporary workplace following four decades and more of neoliberalism. Here, Soper argues that the endless growth of 'bullshit jobs', precarious contracts and the expansive subordination that defines the information age workplace is ripe for transformation. Fuller recognition of the role that consumption plays in affluent societies as compensation for alienation at work and a suppressant of democratic citizenship outside work could bring into view a desire for other pleasures. As she notes:

> Time-scarcity and the sense of being dominated by the demands of work place a constraint on personal liberty: the more caught up you are in work, the less time you have to envisage, let alone act on, alternative ways of living, or to acquire insight upon or formulate political resistance to the existing system. Through its theft of time and energy, the work and spend culture deters development of free thinking and critical opposition.

Sustainable alternatives to this would have 'to provide for distinctively human forms of need, and meet our appetite for novelty, excitement, distraction, self-expression and the gratifications of what Rousseau called amour propre (the esteem and approval of others we respect).'

In more institutional forms, Soper presents alternative hedonism as minimally a call for a cultural politics that allies with and seeks to augment the practices of certain social movements such as aspects of fair trade, ethical shopping and investment but has a further, more expansive commitment to 'the various initiatives seeking to bypass mainstream market provision via alternative networks of sharing, recycling, exchange of goods and services and expertise (the Slow City, Slow Food movements, Buen Vivir, the New American Dream and now, most recently, and possibly most ambitiously, at least for the US, the Next System project).' But it is also a politics that seeks to link ecological downscaling to a politics committed to the fundamental reorganisation of work and an unravelling of the gendered division of labour.

Soper argues policies that strengthen unions and explore policy options for work time reduction all have their place here. Whilst rejecting techtopian accelerationism, she acknowledges automation of toil has a role to play in the reworking of work as long as it actually makes free time more available. The replacement of GDP with more humane and ecologically sane indicators and a universal basic income could, if properly designed, break down gendered divisions of labour. The focus of an alternative hedonism is not to eradicate work but to decentre a work-centred vision of prosperity with an engagement in intrinsically valuable activities: 'For some, this will mean doing less work, and thus having more free time; for others it may entail working in differing ways and to different rhythms'. More broadly, alternative hedonists need to be open 'to new forms of ownership and control over the means of provision for consumption, to more self-provisioning, mending and making do, to greener ways of travelling and, in general, to a less novelty-and fashion-driven way of meeting our material needs.' With less pressure derived from time scarcity, she argues that we could open up to slow, more sensuous travel, convivial lingering, a recovery of street life and communal mixing.

It is argued here that alternative hedonism with its focus on pleasures foreclosed and new pleasures that could be, might offer a more subtle and powerful policy framework through which more expansive public discussions could take place to guide sustainable transitions. Environmental policy battles, Soper argues, need to be bolstered by arguments that are premised on something more compelling than utilitarianism, nudge or cost/benefit, rational choice type arguments. A more democratic and deliberative mode of eco-social policy-making can appeal to citizenship but Soper maintains it ultimately needs to tap into much deeper latent desires for something different. Both suppressed pleasures, but again latent utopian 'structures of feeling', need to be mobilised to facilitate change. As she argues:

> As well as pointing to the benefits that will follow from new regulations and modes of provision (greater sustainability – but also improved health, richer sensual and aesthetic experience, more amenable public spaces), those pressing for their introduction must be able to appeal to some pre-existing disposition in their favour. Policy moves introduced on the basis of quite limited and low-

profile manifestations of public support can, through the positive effects of their implementation, prove educative in ways that overcome subjective prejudice against objectively good practice.

Soper's alternative hedonism is an attempt to unlock for environmental politics a thread of utopian desire for something different that runs from William Morris, the young Marx, Sartre and de Beauvoir to Mary Mellor, Juliet Schor and Murray Bookchin. It is, at root, an attempt to start a conversation about what human lives might be like if they were released from the law of value and it is a reflection on what the humanist Marxist and feminist traditions might offer to this project. These are important resources to deploy and this is why Soper's project is so valuable. However, the arguments in *Post Growth Living* are often more suggestive than definitive and some key moments in these arguments reveal several issues and limitations.

Alternative hedonism must be a big church politics if it is to have any chance of success. Yet, Soper offers in the first few chapters a set of fairly restrictive realist ontological demarcation strategies for who is philosophically in and out of the club. Notably, *Post Growth Living* commences with some quick critiques of various contemporary currents of post-humanism, new materialism, neo-animism, accelerationism and strong social constructionism, which clump together a fairly diverse group of thinkers as essentially saying the same thing. Here, Haraway's cyborg socialist feminism, Srnicek and William's left accelerationism, Latour's confused liberalism, Silicon Valley's neoliberal transhumanism and biologically reductionist currents of neuroscience are treated as more or less making the same moves and hence as needing to be regarded as politically suspect.

The general points that *Post Growth Living* makes in this regard, that some versions of hybrid or non-binary positions as political positions *can* be descriptive, self-defeating and incoherent in their attempt to unravel the human subject as political agent, and often decorative in their politics, are not without grounds. It was an argument that was well made in *What is Nature?* But the analysis in *Post Growth Living* often collapses together four different issues: (i) the value of entangled accounts of socio-ecological relations writ large; (ii) the coherence of the human/non-human continuum; (iii) the extent to which ecopolitical theory should accent non-human agencies; (iv) the ontological status of 'Nature' as an independent causal force separate from the social. These are issues which do not necessarily run together.

Different disciplines across the human/natural sciences often follow different ontological protocols because they are asking different questions in different contexts. Even within hybrid social theory, Latour's evasion of political economy and his anthropomorphic account of non-human agencies do not generate the same issues as the transhumanist preference for Promethean/Randian fantasies of everlasting life in the singularity. The technophilia/determinism of left accelerationism generates different kinds of political problems from neuro/bio-reductionism that can evolve in some parts of the life sciences and are then put to work in political discourse.

Post Growth Living sidesteps engagement with a vast body of applied work in feminist/queer/post-colonial and other kinds of political ecology, environmental history and human ecology that have found it important (and productive) to suspend nature-culture binaries to be able to investigate colonial landscapes, racialised and classed urbanscapes, gendered science or exploited socio-technical infrastructures. Much of this work has fairly conclusively demonstrated that when the socio-ecological histories of slavery, capital accumulation, and so on, are separated out from the social production of nature, bad, purist environmental politics often result.

Some of the most profound explorations of utopian longing and dystopian reflection are to be found in the work of contemporary afro-futurist, indigenous-futurist, queer, feminist and more-than-human science fiction where the grammar of cyborgs and nature-culture hybrids is now ubiquitous.

It could also be observed that many of the pleasures referred to in *Post Growth Living* have something of a high-minded Anglo-centric 'bracing country walks and listening to Mozart' feel to them. The elaboration of alternative hedonism does leave rather unexamined the possibility that pleasure and taste can be tools of differentiation, distinction and exclusion as much as they offer opportunities for joy and wonder. For example, as Julian Agyeman and Carolyn Finney have argued, a great deal of seemingly eco-friendly outdoor engagement in the US and the UK performs a certain kind of able-bodied white masculinity with its 'right' to occupy certain kinds of spaces. The 'wrong kind of people' walking through the countryside can lead to disaster. It would be interesting to consider how an alternative politics of pleasure found in what Stuart Hall called the popular cultural – sports, digital culture, street fashion/food/music – might expand the cultural project of *Post Growth Living*. De-centring an alternative hedonist analysis further to a more cosmopolitan, comparative and critical registrar could greatly enrich the conversation.

Whilst *Post Growth Living* is aware of the limits of a moralising liberal environmentalism, the relations between consumption, race and class are also left rather under-explored. Indeed, the analysis at times is oddly individualist. There are moments when the narrative of *Post Growth Living* slides from Sartrian humanism to an almost Blair-ite discourse of personal responsibility. A desire to tell 'uncomfortable home truths' presents a universally constructed 'western consumer' addicted to the purchase of white goods and cheap flights, resistant to energy taxes and traipsing around shopping malls. Yet this is the very same western consumer that Soper elsewhere acknowledges has been subject to four decades of wage stagnation, the vast expansion of healthcare and education funded debt, a massive housing affordability crisis and the unbounded expanse of elite consumption with public squalor.

This leads one to a further issue: the extent to which 'consumption' does the job as the pivotal organising concept of the book. *Post Growth Living* is cognisant of the ways in which what we call 'personal consumption' is situated more broadly in processes of accumulation and desire shaping. The analysis offered overstates the amount of agency that generic 'consumers' rather than producers have over patterns of industrial production and waste generation. We know from research in political ecology that certain kinds of high carbon consumption (say rural car dependency) are shaped by the spatial division of labour, built-in infrastructure, underinvestment, and historical racial, class and gender exclusions. Without access to a car, many people living in rural or ex-urban areas can't eat or work. A good deal of research by environmental justice scholars has suggested sustainable consumption movements can be deeply exclusionary and can end up promoting a politics of (white) upper-class virtue signalling and shaming which may not produce sustainable, let alone just outcomes. Modes of ecological analysis primarily focused on end-use behaviour can obscure the fact that the vast majority of waste, ecological damage and exploitation occurs much further up the chain at the point of extraction. A more systemic accounting of the socio-ecological consequences of *production-consumption relations* across the whole extraction-manufacturing-marketing-consumption-waste chain could open up the discussion. Locating alternative hedonism in a more global frame that outlined how commodity supply chains are further influenced by uneven exchange, militarism, imperialism, and so on, could expand the analysis here.

The criticisms outlined above should not detract from the virtues of this text. Whatever its sociological and geographical limits, there are many moments when *Post Growth Living* provides an important normative attempt to think about a pleasure-based politics that can facilitate more humane, less alienating and less carbon intensive modes of being in the world. Working time reduction and plant rich diets, a political challenge to work and spend culture, and attempts to validate more convivial, ecological, egalitarian and pleasurable ways of being in the world are important moves for getting us to a more-sane future.

Yet, blind spots in *Post Growth Living* – particularly in relation to racialised uneven development – also point to certain political limits to the insights of the largely white, middle class environmental movements that defined the small is beautiful/limits to growth 1970s moment (and their utopian socialist offshoots).

Rapid and just decarbonisations are going to have to operate at scales proximate to the crisis we face. This will involve finding multiple leverage points and policies at scales that can shift whole sectors of the global economy towards just transitions and decarbonisation whilst also improving the lot of the multi-racial working people in the developed North and vastly improving quality of life for people living in the Global South. This is a politics that will have to constantly and iteratively adapt to and design for life on a warming planet. We will have to deal with a world marked by further challenges posed to coastal cities by rising sea levels, waves of people movements escaping worst effected areas, a possible upscaling of regional and geopolitical challenges, and very possibly new patterns of conflict: between the 'carbon entrenched' and the 'carbon transitioners', the political ecological 'winners' who benefit from a warming world and the flooded losers, the lucky and the unlucky.

Politically, this is not an easy circle to square. History reminds us that past eras of major transitions have often been bloody and chaotic. There are good reasons to believe though that for a progressive post-carbon politics to have any chance of success, it will have to be highly differentiated, attentive to context and contain both productivist *and* anti-productivist moments. It will have to master a practical politics that can address the communities that have been historically and structurally locked into high carbon production by necessity, the communities that have never been included in the consumer society, and offer a fairly compelling account of the material gains *and* the pleasures that could allow just transitions that open up other pathways. In short, in almost all conceivable circumstances, decarbonisation is going to involve a highly complicated and messy set of moves which will surely involve *degrowing* some areas, sectors and activities and *ecomodernising* others. More bike paths, yoga studios and charity shops alone are not going to cut it. This is perhaps where the Green New Deal might offer some hope and offer space for regrounding Soper's project in a sturdier institutional frame.

Despite its many flaws, the Green New Deal is a practical political project that is attempting to think about scale, trade-offs, alliance building and messy complexities in ways that have never really been accomplished by decades of anti-productivist utopian ecosocialist thinking. Nevertheless, there could be many convergent points between Green New Dealers and alternative hedonists. A technocratic focus on energy transition dominates much of the public discussion of the Green New Deal. Yet, Soper is correct to suggest that changes in living, working and consuming will have to become part of this discussion. A Green New Deal over the long term will have to move from addressing energy, infrastructure and investment to consider ways in which further shifts could occur in material culture, from 'more' to 'better', from disposable design to emotionally and physically durable design, from object production to post carbon service provision to meet a range of needs for transportation and entertainment, pleasure and leisure. Here the kind of vision of the Green New Deal recently articulated by Kate Aronoff, Alyssa Battistoni, Daniel Aldana Cohen and Thea Riofrancos, with their focus on *decommodification* of the essentials of life and public investment to provide low carbon *communal luxury* for all, provides one potential bridging moment with Soper's project. An individualist and consumer-driven alternative hedonism focused on equitable downscaling and centring the eco-virtues of the upper middles classes is not going to win any elections and is not ultimately going to go anywhere. An investment, regulation and justice orientated Green New Deal that is further focused on a cultural politics of pleasure might just have a fighting chance.

Damian White

Contingent contagions

Angela Mitropoulos, *Pandemonium: Proliferating Borders of Capital and the Pandemic Swerve* (London: Pluto Press, 2020). 132pp., £14.99 pb., 978 0 74534 330 3

'When every home becomes a quarantine zone, and every epidemiological map is mistaken for an accurate representation of molecular spread, the convergence of neoliberalism and fascism around an oikonomic understanding of health and disease is all but complete.' Posting these words on her website on 12 March 2020, Sydney-based scholar and activist Angela Mitropoulos remarked forcefully on the biopolitical measures undertaken as the inexorable unfolding of Covid-19 was beginning to take shape. For anyone familiar with Mitropoulos' work prior to *Pandemonium*, these words, tagged as a 'postscript' to her earlier book-length publication *Contract and Contagion: From Biopolitics To Oikonomia* (Minor Compositions, 2012), could not but elicit the uncanny feeling of historical *déjà vu*. For *Pandemonium* can be said to appear 'after' *Contract and Contagion* only in the crudest, chronological sense one might experience historical time. Much like its predecessor, *Pandemonium* is an indispensable intervention that exposes the dangers of the culturalisation of the biopolitical and the biologisation of the geopolitical. While shorter and more journalistic in tone than *Contract and Contagion*, this publication continues the significant critical work that Mitropoulos has been developing through a number of journal articles, interviews and blog posts. Because of this pre-Covid 'pre-history', as a theoretical contribution, *Pandemonium* is best-read in the context of queer-feminist, autonomist conversations on precarious labour, risk and indebtedness, and on the constitutive role of the household in upholding the values and borders of the capitalist nation-state – before, during and, no doubt, 'after' Covid.

Over the past decade, Mitropoulos has been one of the many post-Foucauldian voices to insist that the moral logics of economic liberalism and political authoritarianism, and of financial speculation and securitisation, are co-constitutive modes of governance. More singularly, Mitropoulos has astutely diagnosed the ever-present fascist undercurrents within (neo)liberalism and presented a trenchant critique of policies and discourses firmly rooted in the imaginaries of purity, origin and the restoration of legal and natural order. Yet unlike other voices on the left who can only conceive of the 'not-privatised' through the lens of 'the nationalised' (healthcare provision being an obvious case in point), Mitropoulos cautions against forgetting the murderous distinction between citizen and non-citizen, and between (political) *demos* and (economic) populations.

Mitropoulos' key analytical framework of *oikonomia* rests on her refusal of a politics that is bounded by the national, and its autonomist reconfiguration of the relationship between nation and household renders it helpful for making sense of the political reality of Covid-19. *Oikonomia* incisively cuts through the pernicious ways in which the legal has historically been conflated with the natural – and the pivotal role of the 'home' in such an ideological move. As Mitropoulos elaborates in *Contract and Contagion*, the *nomos* of the hearth is founded on the invisible, coerced labour of subjects: from the classical *oikos* of ancient Athens as the management of women, children, slaves and animals to the neoliberal management that governs the Thatcherite nuclear family. *Oikos* is more than the home. It is the privatised care and duty-of-care, it is the unwaged and devalued labour of those who are not 'masters', it is the non-porous entity of the bio-family established by the blood ties of procreation and of genetic and material inheritance. In its foregrounding of the labour-value of affective work within the intimate sphere, *oikonomia* could perhaps be mistaken for social reproduction theory. Yet Mitropoulos' framework is distinct from social reproduction approaches in that it foregrounds the bounded character of the domestic in relation to the national (via Melinda Cooper, Lauren Berlant and Elizabeth A. Povinelli). Unlike a Marxist-feminist emphasis that seeks to identify a domestic mode of production, *oikonomia* centres instead on how the labour-value extracted from unwaged and unfree workers in the hetero-patriarchal household is always already implicated in the biopolitical management of populations. As Mitropoulos puts it in a pithy neologism that appropriates the idea of GDP: 'what it takes to live, to be healthy and flourish, vividly clashes with the capitalist mystique of economic productivity, of the idealized household and the metrics of the Gross National Product'. The thought of post-*operaisti* figures such as Paolo Virno, Maurizio Lazzarato or Franco 'Bifo' Berardi is here relevant only insofar as their analyses of labour pertain to post-Fordist social relations. When it comes to giving flesh and blood to the precarious subject, it is the livelihood (and the very life) of the undocumented migrant that is at stake for Mitropoulos, not the working conditions of the nomadic cognitariat.

Another key epistemic divergence, which has recently been made explicit through the critiques Mitropoulos has waged against Jean-Luc Nancy and Giorgio Agamben, in 'The pandemic, and the pandemonium of European philosophy' (*Political Geography*, January 2021), pertains to the concept of property. Although *oikonomia* is not an intersectional concept, strictly speaking, Mitropoulos' indebtedness to property law and Cheryl I. Harris's foundational 'Whiteness as Property' (1993) enables her to operate at the nexus of race and gender and attend to the ways in which the moral-economic logic of household management exposes the property relation as constitutive of legal and political personhood. This is a process that is inextricable from what Mitropoulos calls 'naturalisation', to involve not only processes of a racialised, sexed subject's reduction to biology but also forms of depoliticisation and de-temporalisation that point to theologically-inflected imaginaries of providence, eternal taxonomy and restoration of order. As such, when in February 2020 Mitropoulos published a piece in *The New Inquiry* entitled 'Against Quarantine', she was far from adopting a position close to Agamben's. Whereas Agamben's much-discussed statements against statist restrictions on freedom of movement are premised on the state of exception's infringement on personal liberty (with personhood here classically conceived in terms of civic rights originating in property law), Mitropoulos' questioning of quarantine's efficacy interrogates the distinction between an epidemic and a pandemic (the latter crossing national borders); between physical distancing, case isolation and quarantine; and between measures based on epidemiological evidence and measures based on racialised and territorial speculation. In Mitropoulos' own words, 'the assumption that political rights and citizenship are varieties of inherited entitlement rests on a naturalized analogy between private property and political representation'.

This nexus of property *as/of* personhood is further bolstered by Mitropoulos' analysis of contingency. Through her tactical deployment of ideas from Lucretius' long didactic poem *De Rerum Natura*, and the incalculable and unpredictable singularising atomic modification that occurs through a *clinamen* or swerve, Mitropoulos aligns herself with a Negrian Spinozism, thereby forging her *oikonomic* critique against Aristotelian taxonomy, Malthusian population theory and, implicitly, Leninist historicity. In *Pandemonium* and the context

of the historical reality of Covid-19 especially, the *oiko-nomic* measurement and management of contingency is exemplified by the functions and operations of the so-called 'cat bond' (short for 'catastrophe bond'), a type of financial investment that only pays out nation-states when sufficient numbers of populations have first died. Mitropoulos compellingly establishes the philosophico-political connection between the future-perfect temporality of pandemic bonds and the racial necropolitics of herd immunity. What is less compelling, regrettably, is the manner in which individual thinkers are fleetingly mobilised in doing so (Plato, Aristotle, Nietzsche, Derrida, Marx, Hobbes), their names deployed effectively as synecdoches for competing ideological standpoints. While such a simplified schema may be apposite insofar as *Pandemonium* seeks to galvanise a non-academic audience in the form of a short, radical handbook, the insertion of names-as-ideologies into what is an otherwise subtle and sophisticated analysis of the chronobiopolitics of contingency does seem to move Mitropoulos in the opposite direction of abstraction, and towards a reified de-historicisation of philosophical thought.

In its opening pages, *Pandemonium* declares its intention to address the question of 'how and whether the pandemic presents a turning point or swerve, and toward what'. Mitropoulos certainly makes a convincing case about the pandemic's endogenous relation to necropolitical capitalism, *contra* liberal accounts that have been positing a historicity of crisis and suspension. Less indication is given about the swerve's direction of travel. Nor is the question about 'how and whether the pandemic presents a turning point' answered anywhere in the text. One would expect Mitropoulos' recalcitrant account to culminate in a call-to-arms that, at the very least, rhetorically invokes a post-capitalist, post-nation, post-family horizon. Curiously, *Pandemonium* ends on an unexpectedly modest and sober note, offering tentative suggestions of wildcat strikes amidst corporatist trade unionism and not much else besides. Perhaps this resistance to a feel-good ending marks Mitropoulos' suspicion of any predictable turn or *telos*, especially when the latter is couched in all-too-familiar leftist tropes of post-insurrectionary redemption. Nevertheless, key questions that are broached but not explicitly addressed require attention and – for those of us who are allies in this struggle – unfinished work to-be-done.

One such question pertains to the material unit of the couple-form and its relationship to the hetero-patriarchal, nationalist nexus of *oikonomia*. In articulating the centrality of household management in the constitution of the nation-state, Mitropoulos does not explicitly draw on the discursive formation of the couple-form. Rather, it is the institution of the (biological) family and (heterosexual) marriage that provide the ground for exposing all that is wrong with racialised, propertarian social relations. Although modes of queer kinning are mobilised, there remains a tacit assumption that the institutions of family and marriage are always already heterosexual, leaving little room for an analysis of the social reproduction of capitalism within gay marriage and, even more pressingly, for an *oikonomic* analysis of homonationalism. As stay-at-home measures have painfully exposed, mononormativity, too, is alive and well and it remains to be seen how far couples of reproductive capacity have made the most of the pandemic by making babies (and not kin).

Staying with this expanded *oikonomic* analysis, we might also consider two further vectors that would continue *Pandemonium*'s trajectory. This would place us in conversation with Mitropoulos' own interlocutors and fellow-travellers: the Out of the Woods collective. Out of the Woods share Mitropoulos' anti-nationalist, anti-racist political programme and have themselves offered astute critical responses to the Malthusian turn within contemporary environmental movements. Mitropoulos is eager to stress the etymological common root between 'economy' [*oikonomia*] and 'ecology' [*oikologia*] – arguably a curious move for someone so alert to the dangers of originary epistemologies. More pertinently though, Mitropoulos' *oikonomic* analysis demonstrates that it is at this very point of convergence between inherited property (land, housing, assets) and inherited properties (genes) where nature becomes naturalised. Lastly, if state regulation of privatised risk-management is to be eschewed as a strategy, it is worth probing what role communisation might play in either eliminating or radically altering the organisation of risk post-Covid. Parliamentary politics is rightly pronounced as limited but, beyond the fleeting mention of 'debt as an acknowledgment of the interdependent conditions of survival and care', Mitropoulos refrains from offering tactical toolkits or political prognoses. And yet *Pandemonium* remains resolute in its affect and convictions. The publication's very final words – 'that everything can be reckoned otherwise' – gracefully capture how the intersecting point where calculation, evaluation of worth and punishment currently resides could find a different source, one that does not stem from natural law but from a moral economy we have yet to practise.

Chrys Papaioannou

Between speculation and discipline

Christopher Tomlins, *In the Matter of Nat Turner: A Speculative History* (Princeton: Princeton University Press, 2020). 376pp., £25.00 hb., 978 0 69119 866 8

Christopher Tomlins is not the first historian to have focused on the Nat Turner rebellion. In 1831, the slave Nat Turner led a group of blacks in an insurrection in St. Luke's Parish, Southampton County, Virginia that resulted in the brutal killing of fifty-five white men, women and children. Although Turner was apprehended, tried and executed, the insurrection struck terror in the hearts of the South's slave-owning classes. It played a critical role in the hardening of pro- and anti-slavery positions that would, following many twists and turns, culminate in the American Civil War. Given the Turner rebellion's scale and seriousness, it is not surprising that many historians should have focused on it. Non-historians have been drawn to it as well. In 1967, the American novelist William Styron published a celebrated fictionalised treatment – *The Confessions of Nat Turner* (1967) – in which he attempted to give voice to Turner. In light of all this, one might well ask: What else might there be to learn about Nat Turner? What might Nat Turner teach us about ourselves?

As it turns out, a great deal. Christopher Tomlins' *In the Matter of Nat Turner: A Speculative History* offers new insights into the thinking of Nat Turner and then employs those insights to meditate upon the discipline of history itself. Through his searching study of the actors and events of 1831, Tomlins interrogates contemporary historians' own thinking and practice, their blind spots and erasures, their commitment to a disciplinary machine that yields often crushingly familiar answers. For these reasons, *In the Matter of Nat Turner* deserves a readership not only among historians of the antebellum South, but also among all interested in history as a modern knowledge form.

In the Matter of Nat Turner ends on an arresting note: 'We who are readers of texts, who are historians, if we are to read as true historians, we must always be ready to read what was never written. Always.' Coming from a contemporary historian, this is an intriguing exhortation. After all, the modern discipline of history traces its origins to the Rankean injunction that history be written 'wie es eigentlich gewesen' (as it really was), an injunction that accompanied the nineteenth-century opening of German state archives to the prying eyes of scholars. Historians have ever since been obsessed with talking and writing and judging in terms of what *was written*. The historian's craft is still all too often imagined as mastery of an archive. Historians frequently dazzle one another by displaying the range of sources they have consulted. Professional criticism takes the form of urging scholars to look at yet another source. Contextualising – that most unshakeable of the historian's disciplinary commitments – takes the form of joining bits of writing to one another to produce the ensemble effect (the thicker, the better) of the 'social', the 'political', the 'cultural', and so on. In light of this disciplinary leaning towards adding more and more of what was written, it is worth interrogating Tomlins' assertion that the 'true historian must always be ready to read what was *never* written.' How precisely does one read what was 'never written'? How does reading what was 'never written' make one a 'true historian'?

To get at what was 'never written', it turns out, Tomlins turns his gaze precisely to what *was written*. In the first instance, *In the Matter of Nat Turner* is a book in which Tomlins shows historians how to take seriously what has been before them all along, how to attend scrupulously to an existing archive that they have averted their gaze from, how to read carefully. This involves multiple unearthings on Tomlins' part, each involving what was written, each mirroring the other.

Tomlins takes to task historians who have been suspicious of the *Confessions of Nat Turner*, the brief text (not to be confused with Styron's fictionalised account) that circulated in the immediate aftermath of Nat Turner's trial and execution. For many historians, the *Confessions* is a text too heavily compromised by the biases of the entrepreneurial white lawyer, Thomas Ruffin Gray, who obtained access to Nat Turner in his prison cell, was present at Turner's trial, compiled an account of the events, and then profited from the text's publication. For others, Gray's *Confessions* is altogether too well-known: there is simply nothing more to be gained from it. Arranging the conventional dominos of social history in a familiar pattern around the text gives us better access to Turner, such historians might argue, than the text itself. But Tomlins categorically rejects this position. As he puts it: '[M]y own impression is that … we actually know very little about Turner and his motives, that throughout its long history the original *Confessions* has not so much been thoroughly drained of all possible knowledge as read without sufficient care or curiosity'. Here we have our first act of unearthing, the unearthing of the written text of Gray's *Confessions* from the disciplinary conventions of contemporary history that have failed to take the text seriously on its own terms.

This unearthing is followed by a second. Employing the devices of literary theory to reexamine Gray's *Confessions*, as a physical object and as a text, Tomlins seeks to extract Turner's voice from the numerous textual devices and conventions that frame it, obscure it, or overwhelm it. In so doing, Tomlins distinguishes between Gray's *Confessions*' account of Turner's experiences before the rebellion (which Tomlins reads as Turner's own voice) and – separated by a crucial break in the text – an account of the actual events of the rebellion (which Tomlins reads as Gray's voice).

This second unearthing is succeeded by a third: the revealing of Turner as a profoundly religious man. Upon isolating Turner's voice, Tomlins insists that we attend seriously to Turner's religiosity on its own terms. Too often, for scholars who write about religion, the religious scholar Robert Orsi (whom Tomlins quotes approvingly) states: 'Religious practice and imagination [are] about something other than what they are to practitioners. This something else may be human powerlessness, false consciousness, ignorance, hysteria, or neurosis. It may be the social group's shared identity of itself. Whatever it is, religion is not about itself.' In making Turner's religiosity 'about itself', which demands an excursus into eighteenth- and nineteenth-century religious texts, Tomlins gives us a picture of a man driven by God himself to do the religious work of killing whites. As Tomlins puts it: 'When the time came for [Turner] to explain what had happened, and why, he had resort not to a language of revenge, or revolution, or self-expiation, or guilt, but to an eschatological cosmology of revelation and judgement'.

Careful attention to what was written brings us face to face, then, with an individual driven by religious eschatology, by what was 'not written' in any sense the historian might grasp. How can the contemporary historian write about such a man? What does such a man have to tell the contemporary historian? The gift of Tomlins' book, for me, is its ability to force the contemporary historian to confront a subject (Nat Turner) who is profoundly alien (even destabilising) to him or her, a subject beset by divine visitation who understands the world, and work, and time in ways that resist our own disciplinary ways of making sense of the world, work and time. So what does Tomlins do with Turner once – through careful attention to what was written – Turner is retrieved from the rubble of close to two centuries of contextualisation?

Tomlins has recourse to the philosophy of history of Walter Benjamin. As he puts it: '[R]esort to one species of messianic philosophy of history to help unravel another may be worthwhile'. Indeed, it may be 'worthwhile', but this, to put it mildly, understates how Tomlins understands the import of the enterprise. Using Walter Benjamin to make sense of Turner, Tomlins reads Turner's refusal to admit guilt in the mass killing as a radical break from capitalism/reformed Protestantism's endless deferrals of guilt and debt, which is how Tomlins reads the Virginia debates over the political economy of slavery in the aftermath of the Nat Turner rebellion. Given the imbrication of slavery, debt and guilt that marks the Virginia debates, there is much to support Tomlins' reading of Turner's rebellion as an 'event' that breaks radically with (or that blasts open) the endlessly deferred progression of capitalist history. In his ability to take the plunge into divine violence, Tomlins suggests, Turner had taken a 'decision' – something to be distinguished from mere 'choice' – which, for Walter Benjamin, 'is an index of human freedom in the realm of faith'. Turner's turn to divine violence and his refusal to expiate his guilt forces a break in the endless cycle of debt and guilt in terms of which slavery/capitalism would have surrounded him.

It might be 'worthwhile', to borrow Tomlins' understated tone, to wonder what all of this might mean for the contemporary historian. As stated above, for all his labour in reading what was written, Tomlins urges the 'true historian' to look beyond, to 'read what was never written'. While the more conventional Benjaminian understanding of this urging might be the exhortation that the historian realise his present moment in the past, one wonders whether reading what was 'never written' is not precisely what Nat Turner himself did as he violently broke free from the overdetermined world of capitalism/reformed Protestantism that threatened to engulf him. Is Turner our 'true historian'? Is Turner the model that Tomlins (via Benjamin) wants us to set for ourselves? Is Tomlins' retrieval of the religious Turner from the endless disciplinary contextualisation of contemporary history – precisely through a breaking of the text of Gray's Confessions through tools of literary criticism foreign to most historians – a Turnerian rebellion of sorts?

Tomlins is much too careful a historian to rely entirely upon a Benjaminian Turner as a model for his own professional and disciplinary practice. At various critical moments in Tomlins' book, the confrontation with what was 'never written' becomes not the pretext for a 'decision' to break free of context, but a more sober reflection on the limits of historical knowledge. Here, Tomlins suggests, what cannot be read simply cannot be known. I want to attend to two such instances, both of which suggest that Turner's eschatology might not in fact 'explain' the rebellion.

As suggested earlier, Tomlins argues that Gray's Confessions contains a crucial break. There is Turner's account of his own religiosity (which Tomlins takes to be

Turner's own voice) and then an account of the killings (which Tomlins takes to be Gray's voice). A break, then, between Turner's 'decision' and the actual killings, which involved not just Turner but a growing group of mostly enslaved blacks in the community who joined the rebellion. How does one lead to another? Turner might have been (in Tomlins' rendering) a Kierkegaardian 'lonely knight of faith', but how did he enter the secular world to mobilise others to join him? How did Turner cross, as it were, that break? Here, Tomlins confesses: we simply do not know. As Tomlins puts it: 'We cannot know the precise content of the politics [Turner] invented for that moment, but we do know that Turner's politics enabled their collective, violent defiance'. Here is a break in meaning caused by an absence of writing, one that brings us to the limits of our (and Tomlins') knowledge, the edge of our ability to produce meaning.

We confront the same limit to knowledge caused by a lack of writing when we talk about the actual killings. Tomlins rejects the historian Eugene Genovese's view that the Turner rebellion was 'mindless slaughter'. The killings make sense, Tomlins insists. But at the same time that Tomlins insists on the possibility of meaning, his own text reveals that that meaning dissolves into a series of unanswered (and unanswerable) questions. We might perhaps know what drove Turner, but we have ab-solutely no way of knowing what drove the other rebels. As Tomlins puts it: 'The killings were not indiscriminate, but purposeful. They followed a logic. But what was their logic? Was it instrumental – revenge? Was killing incidental to some overriding purpose, such as flight or revolution? Or was it in in itself a central and essential redemptive act?'

In Tomlins' book, then, we confront two different ways of responding to 'what was never written'. On the one hand, Nat Turner emerges as a model for the 'true historian' who reads 'what was never written' to blast open 'self-contained facticity'. Tomlins himself adopts this model when he forces disciplinary history to confront a Turner that it cannot contain. On the other hand, at various crucial points in Tomlins' account, in what is a very different model for a 'true historian', Tomlins also reads 'what was never written' – the nitty gritty of winning others over to join the rebellion, the hidden logics of the real work of killing – in terms of the limits of our abilities as historians, the realisation that we simply do not and cannot know. The former points to a surfeit of meaning, the latter to its breakdown. How do we decide? What is the relationship between the two? In Tomlins' reaching beyond and yet cleaving to his disciplinary training as a historian, the answers reside.

Kunal Parker

Moribund elegance

Philipp Ekardt, *Benjamin on Fashion* (London: Bloomsbury, 2020), 256pp., £74.59 hb., 978 1 35007 599 3

In Daniel Mourenza's *Walter Benjamin and the Aesthetics of Film* (2020), we learn that Walter Benjamin, in the summer of 1938, went to see a Katharine Hepburn film at the cinema – it might have been *Holiday*, it might have been *Bringing Up Baby*. In Philipp Ekardt's *Benjamin on Fashion* (also published last year) we learn of the 'hardly acknowledged if not entirely ignored fact that in his Parisian exile during the 1930s, Walter Benjamin must have visited fashion shows.' This is evidenced in a letter written in July 1935 to Gretel Karplus, wife of Adorno and one-time manager of a family leather business (something I also learnt from the Ekardt's book). 'If all goes well', Benjamin writes, 'I will be able to treat myself again with one or two fashion shows.' This anecdote frames Ekardt's monograph on Benjamin's work on fashion – only the second on such a topic, since Ulrich Lehmann's *Tigersprung: Fashion in Modernity* (2000) – which functions not just to reconstruct Benjamin's esoteric and unsynthesised writings on fashion, but to do so through the textures, cuts and silhouettes of the time, as if to reassemble a 1935 runway show as the runway might have been viewed at that time. In this vast Warburgian panorama, history finds new patterns and transformations.

Benjamin on Fashion is divided into two parts. The

first half addresses fashion's temporality and historiography. Fashion is held as a 'measure of time' (*Zeitmass*), ruled not just by continuity but a continuity of discontinuity: a repetition or eternal return of the eversame, where the old appears in ultra-modern get up. Drawing on Georg Simmel's 1905 essay 'Philosophy of Fashion', Ekardt shows how fashion is forever becoming through its unbecoming: cancelling itself in its realisation, charting its rise and its demise simultaneously. To fulfil its own promise, fashion must continuously destroy itself, and fail to escape its own temporal logic. Ekardt provides two models: the revolutionary, which leaps tiger-like into the past, to arrest the present from the eternal churn of homogeneous empty time; and *apocatastasis* where the entire past is condensed into the present. The result is uncertain, hard to establish: a *mode* that abolishes time and ignites history, or one that breaks with the deathly charm of the commodity form, even one that abolishes the dull treadmill of fashion's seasonality.

The second part turns to Benjamin's relation to fashion's textured history, and Ekardt evokes a chorus of designers, cutters, photographers, journalists, spectators and socialites. The most central figure is Helen Grund, who most likely would have accompanied Benjamin to the 1935 show. Interestingly, Grund only gets a footnote in Lehmann's *Tigersprung: Fashion in Modernity*, but with her married name. 'Frau Hessel' was married, we are told, to Benjamin's co-translator of Proust, Franz Hessel. In 1935, Grund (her maiden name that she always used for writing) published *The Essence of Fashion* in a limited run of 1,000 copies by the German College of Fashion in Munich, which is extensively quoted in the *Arcades Project*. Ekardt shows how Benjamin's writing is indebted to Grund's work, and how to exclude this would replicate the detachment of his 'genius mind' from the work of those around him. Ekardt not only seeks to acknowledge Grund's work in all its expertise and elegance, but to expand on it, to fill in the gaps that Benjamin also left vacant or unacknowledged (helped along the way by fashion scholars such as Caroline Evans and Judith Clark).

This work of reconstruction has already begun, but largely in German. In 2014, Mila Ganeva edited *Ich schreibe aus Paris: Über die Mode, das Leben und die Liebe* [*I write from Paris: on fashion, life and love*], which collects Grund's writings together in a glossy single volume for

the first time, including articles on sports apparel, organdie and hairdressing, In 2018, the magazine-periodical *Mode and Mode*, edited by Laura Gardner, devoted eighty pages to a couple of translations of these *feuilleton* articles, an interview with Ganeva, alongside facsimiles of Grund's correspondence with Henri-Pierre Roché (the writer of *Jules et Jim*, a novel that depicts his polyamorous entanglement with Grund, the basis for François Truffaut's 1962 film of the same name).

Helen Hessel photographed in Paris, c.1929 (Nimbus Books /Manfred Flügge)

A theory of elegance is a significant product of Ekardt's engagement with Grund's work, refracted back through Benjamin. This, the second part of the book, is based on a previously unpublished eight-page fragment held in the Benjamin Archive in Berlin, thought to be the transcript of a lecture delivered to Grund's fashion students in Munich, which somehow fell into Benjamin's hands. For Grund, elegance is the production of something beyond mere dress. It refers to materials but is 'a surplus in relation to the mere textile and its materiality'. It relates to how the body animates matter, beyond a concept of beauty. It is a form of confidence, fused into grace through gesture and movement, enabled by clothes that would otherwise appear dead or inert.

From here, Ekardt explicates a theory of the model (alongside the mannequin), on the runway or in the studio, who embodies elegance through the animation of material, rather than the mere presentation of dead, inert matter. This is what Benjamin extracts most from Grund's work: the development of what Ekardt names as 'obdurate fashion', an interest in the morbid, the hard-edged, the inorganic. To animate matter is to vivify the deadly, to shock, subvert and ironise. Here we find the book's first reversal of reification, in which the garment and (by implication) the subject becomes 'thing' in order to become 'subject' again. Elegance teases death. Ekardt mobilises the example of the designer Elsa Schiaparelli, whose models walked as drawers and cabinets, with door handles for nipples. The same can be seen also with Schiaparelli's other famous construction: the shoe that becomes a hat. One can add another example. In 1968 the designer and union activist Elizabeth Hawes designed a jumper that might most demonstrate obduracy. In the knit was included what looks like a US phone number: 382-5968. Dial it up. The threads of the knit speak back: FUC-KOFF. Ekhardt argues that 'stuff' doesn't move; in this case, 'stuff' obdurately speaks back.

Elizabeth Hawes, Sweater, 1968 (Collection: The Metropolitan Museum of Art)

For Ekardt, elegance is tied up with the rejection of the androgynous looks of the 1920s, in favour of gender-dimorphous silhouettes of the 1930s. At this point, historiography becomes important. The classicism of the 1930s look – lower hems, higher waists and more typically gendered silhouettes – points to a counter-revolutionary turn in which the imperialist or neo-classicist tendencies of the 1930s were dressed in the garb of the imperialist past. Ekhart shows us stark silhouettes of models, shot by the likes of Horst, George Hoyningen-Huene or Cecil Beaton, who appear as if petrified in Munich's Glyptothek, as if to prefigure Leni Riefenstahl's opening of *Olympia* (1938). Here the famous trope of Marx's *Eighteenth Brumaire of Louis Napoleon* (1852) remains true in its reversal: counter-revolutions as much as revolutions find their expression in the garments of the past.

Sex, sexuality and subversion also come to play a significant part in the text. Ekhardt reads Grund's work through an essay by George H. Darwin (Charles Darwin's son), 'Development in Dress' (1872), which argues that fashion permits 'the ability to recompose one's appearance (i.e., the difference and variation in comparison to a panorama of earlier looks) which sparks sexual attraction'. What can be understood as a 'heterosexual naturalism', whereby fashion's display functions to signal or encourage procreation, also leads to a surrealistic morphology where augmentation, modification and elaboration transform the body, through the dissolution between the boundaries of the organic and inorganic. The bride who closes the fashion show, now appears wedded, not to a groom, but to a deadened and transformed nature. Fashion here entices sexuality to recognise its relation to the inorganic world: to sequins, shells and whale bone. Such obscure references in Benjamin's work, particularly in convolute B of the *Arcades Project* find their historical underpinning in Ekhardt's work.

Ekhardt takes the argument further, to the point where fashion does not *reflect* sexuality but *substitutes* it. The claim is that fashion exists because there isn't enough sex, whether out of the necessity of repression or, perhaps, as Brecht has it elsewhere, because 'the bourgeoisie has contrived to ruin even sexuality' to the point where it will die out. Ekhardt finds this explicitly in the history of contemporaneous fashion, through Schiaparelli's 'genital millinery', which Benjamin refers to in the *Arcades*, a reference that would otherwise be lost on the reader, as it was on me. A history can be told of hats that, at some point, were phallic and hats that, at other points, were yonic. This, for Ekhardt, represents a shift from the androgyny of the 1920s to a biorphication of the body in the 1930s: rendered classically, with exaggerated sexualities. The connection to a fascist aesthetic could be elaborated further here, as it is in Irene Guenther's *Nazi Chic: Fashioning Women in the Third Reich* (2004) and Eugenia Paulicelli's *Fashion Under Fascism: Beyond the Black Shirt* (2004).

For Benjamin, as for Ekardt (bar a brief discussion of textile manufacture), production remains a neglected part of the analysis, which does not mean that they think it unimportant, even foundational. Marx began the first volume of *Capital* in a similar place, with the commodity and its transfigurations, but he fell back quickly to a discussion of linen and its quantities and the conditions of its making. Étienne Balibar has claimed that one should start by reading the final chapter of *Capital*, so that the first element of capital's accumulation – i.e. primitive accumulation – is at the start when (spoiler alert) it isn't. But if capital is a whirling circuit of imminent disaster and exploitation, it does seem strange to ignore the sweatshops, the monopsonies, the mythical factory ships that combine production with circulation, the industrial disputes and disasters, the wage relation, the environmental extractions and disasters, the way in which racism and gendered violence structure all moments of the circuit. After all, if elegance is teased by death, isn't this because, as commodities, the elegant things of fashion contain the dead labour of their production, and, as such, like all other commodities, they drip with the tragedy of their production?

Fashion is a corpse. Benjamin knew that, but fashion too animates the body in new ways, against (or through) the objectification of subjects in capital. But it does so insufficiently and incompletely. Of Benjamin's famous image, in which the hems of the dresses expand with the territorial expansion of French Empire, one wonders what could happen to our dresses, our hems, our touch, our relation to materials after empire's total abolition. Only at this point, the tiger jumps backwards, into another world. Ekardt, through Grund and Benjamin, points the way.

Sam Dolbear

The doctor's knife

Silvia Federici, *Beyond the Periphery of the Skin: Rethinking, Remaking, and Reclaiming the Body in Contemporary Capitalism* (Oakland, CA: PM Press, 2020). 145pp., £11.55 hb., 978 1 62963 706 8

Silvia Federici is one of contemporary feminism's celebrity thinkers, and with good reason. Her work since the 1970s on capitalism and gender has been of fundamental importance in developing theories of social reproduction. She is known as both a scholar and an activist, as a founding member of the Wages for Housework campaign. Her writings have reached a new audience in recent years through a series of essay collections published by PM Press, helping to galvanise a popular revival of Marxist feminism that offers a valuable counterpoint to the shallow neoliberal individualism that has underlaid much of feminism's mainstream resurgence. Federici remains distinctive in Anglophone feminism for her attention to environmental issues and to feminist justice on a global scale; her concern with elder care and ageing is similarly unusual and praiseworthy. Her work on social reproduction has taken on a renewed urgency in light of the Covid-19 pandemic, with women disproportionately bearing the burden of homeschooling and increased demands for unpaid care.

Federici's latest book consists of ten short chapters on familiar themes. These include the historical context for the disciplining of the body under capitalism (the subject of her earlier work *Caliban and the Witch* (2004)); the body in second wave feminist thought and activism; theories of gender performativity, with which Federici takes issue; and the feminist politics of surrogacy and of sex work. The book collects a number of essays mostly published in the last ten years, along with new material developed from lectures delivered in 2015.

Beyond the Periphery of the Skin will be of most interest for its promise to address a tension in Federici's work. That is, how can her theorisations of social reproduction, which typically rely on a narrow and cisnormative model of the female body, accommodate the more diverse understandings of womanhood that characterise contemporary feminism? In her Introduction, she asks: 'is "women" still a necessary category for feminist politics, considering the diversities of histories and experiences covered under this label, or should we discard it, as Butler and other poststructuralist theorists have proposed that we do?' Her further questions concern 'new reproductive technologies' and their capacity to heighten our agency or 'turn our bodies into objects of experimentation and profit-making at the service of the capitalist market and the medical profession'. Federici's framing of the latter question makes her answer clear. This slide from considering the feasibility of the category of 'woman' to casting doubt on technologies that 'remake our bodies in ways that better conform to our desires' raises concerns that the book does not sufficiently assuage.

A key target of Federici's critique is a perceived shift in feminist thought from an engagement with '"biological" factors' to an understanding of the body as primarily textual and discursive. For Federici, the latter fails to adequately explain the social origins of ideas about the body and their roles within systems of exploitation, while also lacking sufficient sense of the coercive power of actual and threatened punishment, and of historical and ongoing struggles for change. These ideas are largely not attributed to a specific author, but Federici's target appears to be Judith Butler, particularly in their 1990s incarnation as a postmodernist bogeyman, a model latterly revived by the right.

Federici's account of Butler's work is fuzzy. She writes that Butler calls gender a 'performance', criticising what she calls 'performance theory'. For Butler, gender is instead 'performative', or brought into being through the repetition of socially prescribed acts. The distinction is important: while 'performance' suggests that a subject chooses their gendered presentation, 'performativity' identifies these acts as bringing gender into being and sustaining the social fiction of its naturalness, and, in turn, the naturalness of binary sex and heterosexuality. It is also worth noting that Butler is well aware of the social sanctions and physical risks attendant on an 'incorrect' gendered embodiment (as they write in their 1988 essay 'Performative Acts and Gender Constitution', 'those who fail to do their gender right are regularly punished'). Federici is on stronger ground when alluding to Butler's ahistorical mode of argumentation, an issue previously noted by Nancy Fraser. (Federici might have productively engaged with the 1998 Butler-Fraser debate in *New Left Review*.) Later, Federici notes that she is concerned less with Butler's work than with 'the popular version circulating among feminists'. While this is worthy of attention, Federici's reluctance to concretely identify the body of ideas with which she takes issue and engage fully and accurately with its texts leaves the feeling that she has constructed something of a straw man.

Federici's critique of what she sees as feminism's retreat from the body forms the basis of a broader argument about the hazards of 'remaking' the body with new technologies. Her thesis, broadly construed, is that contemporary feminism, informed by Butlerian notions of gender as merely 'performed', has uncritically adopted a dominant tendency of our age to 'promote remaking our bodies as a path to social empowerment and self-determination'. This shift threatens to entrench capitalist social relations, with 'body remakes' (only ever loosely defined) likely to intensify the mechanisation of the human body that she identifies here and elsewhere as a key driver of capitalist accumulation. Federici argues that the increasing power of technology to alter the human body may ultimately just enable capitalists to create the bodies they need.

Federici is further concerned that changes to individual bodies do not alter overall social and economic conditions, noting that elective procedures are primarily accessible to wealthy people and, for this reason, sharpen social hierarchies. Yet her claim that 'the trans and intersex movements' are insufficiently concerned with these issues neglects activism and scholarship that indicate the opposite. Federici's hope for 'the development of an egalitarian society where appearance no longer matters' is not ill-intentioned, but her remarks feel culpably insensitive to the realities of trans people's experiences and needs in the present.

As in her earlier work, notably *Caliban and the Witch*, Federici is sharply critical of the role of doctors in this process. She doubts the likelihood that a profession that has 'sterilized us, lobotomized us, ridiculed us when we cried in pain giving birth' can offer a route to liberation. Many of her broader claims about medicine, particularly in its privatised form in the United States, are true, if not especially remarkable. She rightly takes aim at the emphasis on 'personal responsibility' as a cause of illness over social and environmental factors, the insurance industry, and the history of medical experimentation on African Americans. Her preferred approach to bodies and health is less persuasive. She argues for 'the power and wisdom of the body as we know it' and for attention to modes of knowledge that have 'formed over a long period of time, in constant interaction with the formation of the earth, in ways that are tampered with at great risk to our wellbeing'.

Federici's concern for nonhuman nature has long been a strength of her work. However, the connections between women and nature in her writing have not always been entirely clear, often leaning towards an essentialism that is neither fully endorsed nor fully eschewed. This lack of clarity invites troubling conclusions, an issue that is compounded by her stylistic tendencies. Her habit of moving between topics, geographies and time periods can be exhilarating and provocative. Here, a slide from

a discussion of the 'magic' of cis women's bodies giving birth to the ways that '[n]ature too is magical' leaves unanswered questions. Her typically vivid descriptive language, which causes her to describe 'body remakes' as 'experimentation' and 'dismemberment', might have been toned down to avoid evoking tropes of trans monstrosity. Reviews of the book have unsurprisingly concentrated on its trans politics. Nevertheless, it is worth noting that Federici's account of cis women's bodies, focused on wombs, birth, and sceptical of elective caesareans, leaves much to be desired. The vagueness of the notion of 'body remakes' leaves it unclear on what grounds Federici would exclude other, less eye-catching health procedures and aids from her critique. At present, pacemakers, hip replacements and glasses seem captured by her concerns over the blending of bodies and machines. She might have productively considered the relationship between her comments here on the body, technology and capitalism and her work elsewhere on ageing, to give an account of the disability implications of her claims.

Reconnecting our bodies with nature is part of Federici's project of moving 'beyond the periphery of the skin'. She portrays the body as coextensive with the world, in 'a magical continuity with the other living organisms that populate the earth: the bodies of humans and not-humans, the trees, the rivers, the sea, the stars'. This evokes work in material feminism, notably Stacy Alaimo's notion of 'trans-corporeality' (2010) and Astrida Neimanis' work on 'bodies of water' (2017). Yet *Beyond the Periphery of the Skin* sits in strange self-isolation from much recent feminist theory. Most notably, Federici's recuperation of the 'natural' and opposition to body modification sits in sharp contrast to the 'technomaterialist, anti-naturalist, and gender abolitionist' philosophy of Xenofeminism. Even so, Federici recalls Xenofeminist ideas in her brief demand for the sharing of medical knowledge within communities to enable greater agency in medical decision-making and accessing care, echoing Helen Hester's discussion of DIY abortion technologies (2018). Her lack of engagement with the most prominent recent feminist theorisations of nature, the body and technology, is a missed opportunity.

Federici's latest book is a frustrating read. It largely fails to deal with pressing questions for her version of social reproduction theory, including whether and how it can avoid gender essentialism, and the possibility of squaring it with a gender abolitionist position. As has been widely noted in reviews, her (at best) confused approach to trans lives is disappointing at a time at which feminist solidarity with trans people, particularly from figures of her stature, is acutely needed. Nevertheless, the book does offer – perhaps in spite of itself – starting points for answering these questions within Federici's model. Her emphasis on 'a *common terrain of struggle for women*, even if it is one in which contrasting strategies may develop', suggests a broader and more inclusive approach to identity and strategy, as does the claim that "'woman" is not a static, monolithic term but one that has simultaneously different, even opposite and always changing significations'. Federici's efforts to resignify the meanings of body parts seem as applicable to trans and gender-nonconforming people as to the cisgender women who are Federici's primary concern. At times Federici makes claims for the resistant potential of trans lives. While her comment that trans and intersex people offer a way to 'recognize the broad range of possibilities

that "nature" provides' derives from her antagonism to modifying bodies, we might also read this line as congruent with queer ecology's challenge to any notion of 'natural' sexual dimorphism. Her description of trans people as offering a model of the body that is 'nondependent on our capacity to function as labour power' similarly points towards a potential trans-inclusive reorientation of Federici's work.

The most promising part of the book is the Afterword. Federici argues for 'joyful militancy', or the principle that 'either our politics are liberating, either they change our life in a way that is positive, that make us grow, give us joy, or there's something wrong with them'. Joyful militancy rejects a notion of activism as heroic self-sacrifice in service of the future, prioritising instead 'the reproductive side of political work' that transforms our lives and our selves in the present. This final chapter, which is evocative, illuminating and strategically astute, is a reminder of what Federici, at her best, can do.

Hannah Boast

Precarious euphoria

Tina Managhan, *Unknowing the 'War on Terror': The Pleasures of Risk* (London: Routledge, 2020). 132pp., £120.00 hb., 978 1 35104 860 6

It is a wild adventure we are on. Here, as we are rushing along through the darkness, with the cold from the river seeming to rise up and strike us; with all the mysterious voices of the night around us, it all comes home. We seem to be drifting into unknown places and unknown ways; into a whole world of dark and dreadful things.

Bram Stoker, *Dracula*

Dracula may seem like a strange place to start a review of a work primarily concerned with the global War on Terror. But, in the same way Tina Managhan walks us through the 'excesses and uncanniness of this war', so Bram Stoker's novel lays bare the libidinal urges haunting imperial Britain. Stoker tells a tale about the eternal return of the supernatural (racialised) 'other' embodied in Dracula and his voluptuous undead ladies, whose nightly visitations and seductions of virtuous Victorians serve only to reveal the impotence of 'science' in the face of

other-worldly attacks. While conventional accounts of Dracula focus on the fight between good and evil, science, superstition and female sexuality, it is the unbridled *enjoyment* or *jouissance* experienced by Van Helsing and his cohort in battling the Count which drives the novel forward. From illicit sexual encounters and amateur detective work, to the joy of driving a stake into the heart of one's enemy and, most of all, the sheer thrill of the pursuit of Dracula, an obscene light is shed upon characters we are invited to think of as the pinnacle of civilisation and modernity.

If dominant ways of theorising the War on Terror have been rooted in ideas of precautionary risk logics or the understanding that 'we act *not* on the basis of knowledge, but on the basis of "catastrophic contingency" – on the basis that the slightest conceivable risk of the absolute worst that could happen', then Managhan implores us to heed the pleasures we take in such risks. Drawing on Lacan, psychoanalysis, phenomenology and affect theory, the book points to the anxieties, fears and desires which animate and circulate notions of risk and the practices which ostensibly seek to manage these: 'The repressed of precautionary risk logics is the pleasure of risk – the pleasures of a world inhabited by monsters and ghosts and, with them, all the archaic passions that have always haunted Enlightenment reason'. It is precisely these *pleasures of risk* with which Managhan is concerned and which in their uncanny fashion echo the spirit of Dracula. The book details how the War on Terror is littered with phantoms, monsters and ghosts who offer an insight into what makes 'the West' tick.

The two spectacular contexts that are subjected to sustained analysis are the 2012 Olympic Games in London and the hunt for the Boston Bombers. Managhan situates the London Olympic Games in a longer imperial history of World Exhibitions and Expos, whose staging served to produce narratives about Western progress vis-à-vis the 'backwardness' of colonised subjects whose presence was the source of fetishised titillation. What would the 2012 Olympics Games 'tell' about Britain today? The games unfolded in a wider context of the

2011 London riots, the austerity-induced immiseration of working class populations and the ongoing War on Terror. The Prime Minister at the time (the cataclysmic David Cameron) had pronounced the death of multiculturalism in the UK, as in his view it was akin to ethnic and racial separatism and the excesses of cultural difference, and its accommodation by the state was causing terrorism. Although all was clearly not well in this green and pleasant land, the news that London was awarded the Olympic Games on 6 July 2005 was met with celebration across the capital. The following day on the 7th of July, however, London was the scene of multiple suicide attacks which targeted the transport system. The breakneck shift in public mood from jubilation to horror in those two days served to underscore the tension between the harmonious imagery of multicultural youth exemplified in London's Olympic bid and the deep fault lines rippling under the surface.

Managhan explores how in this context of overarching security risks and crisis, the Olympics Games offered an opportunity for the enjoyment of 'precarious euphoria'. The heightened sense of risk served to deepen the pleasures of the games which included awesome displays of sovereign power embodied in the triumphant militarisation of the Olympic Games. Even Danny Boyle's production of the opening ceremony – which ostensibly offered an inclusive vision of Britain where the NHS, factory workers, women and immigrants featured heavily – 'worked to consolidate hegemonic power relations'. Boyle's potted history of Britain as the home of harmonious race relations, tolerance and fairness was premised on the 'absent present' British Empire whose afterlives are central to making the inequalities experienced by the very same black and brown bodies vaunted in the opening ceremony. Furthermore, the spectacles of military force, of missiles placed on rooftops and snipers in helicopters circling events under the aegis of the War on Terror, revealed Britain's undimmed appetite for violence and the 'exaltation of community' formed through this: 'Under the auspices of risk and the Olympic Games, the British public could enjoy the transgressive pleasures of Empire while officially leaving Empire, racism and "the island story" of Little England behind'. Ultimately, the Olympic Games in London offered an opportunity to retell the story of Britain in which Empire was formally disavowed but reared its head through awesome displays of nationalistic military power ushered in by the War on Terror.

An analysis of the hunt for the Boston Bombers – the two young men responsible for killing 3 and injuring a further 260 people at the Boston Marathon on Patriot's day in 2013 – offers insight into the context of US politics and its risky indulgences in the War on Terror. In light of the mobilisation of overwhelming militarised state power in pursuit of the 26 year-old Tamerlan Tsarnaev and 19 year-old Dzhokhar Tsarnaev, Managhan demonstrates how the blurring of fantasy and reality generated a surplus *jouissance* culminating in the death of the former and capture of the latter. The cinematic quality of the hunt itself is thrown into sharp relief through the countless pre-existing imaginings offered by film and literature about what the hunt would look like and how it would be felt. Ultimately, attention to the uncanny yields something which should have stayed out of view: the hunt itself echoed the historical lineages of (racial) violence which have been integral to the formation of the United States. Managhan argues that nation-states are more than simply vessels for the provision of security or public goods, and that they are made and sustained through a politics of *jouissance*. Moving from the transgressive pleasures of risk, to the wider question of the libidinal investments which inform and direct ideas of who 'we' are in opposition to who 'we' are not, the politics of *jouissance* is a window into the rewards of being part of a nation. Drawing on Lacan and Žižek, it is the constitutive lack which generates desire manifest in the form of questions like, 'who am I' and 'what do you want from me?' The fantasy of the nation generated by the constitutive lack provides answers to these questions. Through the hunt for the Boston bombers, the American nation found itself through a combination of the pain of the violence directed at fellow Americans and the pleasure generated by the hunt itself.

Managhan details the pleasures taken in punishing the transgressor and his subversion of 'our' way of life. She notes that had the bombers been white their pursuit and punishment would not have carried the same pain or the same pleasure. This is where mapping the 'racialised contours of jouissance' allows us to grasp a much bigger argument about the relationship between nations as fantasy and the violence directed at 'outsiders'. Namely, that in this US context, Managhan is able to draw a convincing line from the lynching of African Americans to the torture of Iraqi prisoners in Abu Ghraib and white nationalist marches in Charlottesville. All these 'hunts' allowed for the consolidation of white community fully backed by the power of the law and the sovereign power lurking therein. The War on Terror and its many and shifting faces rest on this one disavowed premise: that of white superiority.

In this present moment, the book contributes to an ongoing critique of the complicated disavowal of 'race' and racism as constitutive forces in global politics plaguing the discipline of International Relations (IR). While there is a wider disciplinary critique emerging along these lines from scholars such as Meera Sabaratnam, Robbie Shilliam and Robert Vitalis, there is something similar happening in what we can loosely describe as the sub-field of critical security studies. Critiques of critical security studies have focused on the way in which this scholarship inadequately, if at all, engages with (racialised) imperial and colonial histories and consequently with what Derek Gregory has dubbed 'the colonial present'. *Unknowing the War on Terror* shows us how the 'precautionary risk logics' literature evacuates the concept of risk from its racialised historical provenance and from its neo-colonial present, thereby unwittingly reproducing 'the West' and what it calculates to be risky as logical and rational. This scholarship more or less elides any meaningful engagement with the racial animus haunting the risk society. Racism is not an unfortunate by-product of risk, a matter of 'stereotypes' or 'bias' or generic 'othering' but a constitutive, foundational aspect of what is considered to be 'risky' and 'at risk' in the War on Terror. In my view, this is Managhan's most powerful move not least because this point of departure allows her to develop a reinvigorated engagement with the idea of risk – via Foucault, Lacan and Žižek – and invites us to take race seriously when exploring the underside of the War on Terror and the manifold pleasures it has afforded those who have been living in it and with it.

Nadya Ali

Border abolitionism as method

Alison Mountz, *The Death of Asylum: Hidden Geographies of the Enforcement Archipelago* (Minneapolis: University of Minnesota Press, 2020). 304pp., £81.00 hb., £20.27 pb., 978 0 81669 710 6 hb., 978 0 81669 711 3 pb.

The implementation of the EU Pact on Migration in September 2020 has marked a further step in the sheer politics of migration containment that the European Union has been enforcing for two decades: accelerated asylum procedures, migrants' detention upon landing, multiplication of bilateral agreements with third-countries and 'solidarity in deportation procedures' among member states are some of the legal stratagems that the Pact envisions to render migrants' journeys more dangerous and to obstruct their access to asylum. And yet, this is far from being only a European history. As Alison Mountz poignantly illustrates in her new book *The Death of Asylum*, the history of the exclusionary politics of migration is a global history and therefore needs to be investigated by intertwining different geographies of containment and beginning from multiple starting points. In the book, Mountz traces back border offshoring politics to the late 1970s, going against the grain of the presentism which characterises discourses on the 'refugee crisis'.

Such a genealogy of externalisation and containment enables also a foregrounding of partial continuities between different forms of confinement, which have targeted not only those racialised as 'migrants' but also other unruly subjectivities. This genealogy is intertwined with the history of the deterioration of asylum and of its externalisation: indeed, this latter 'began at sea in the Caribbean in the early 1980s, when the United States intercepted, detained and returned Haitian and Cuban nationals'. In fact, asylum offshoring is constitutive of the broader politics of border externalisation. The US interceptions of Haitians in the late 1970s; the Golden Venture vessel in 1993, which rescued close to New York with 286 Chinese migrants on board; the Australian Tampa incident in 2001 and the subsequent Pacific Solution adopted by the Australian government; Frontex deployment on the Canary Islands to block African migrants and vessels that was pushed-back to Libya by the Italian authorities in 2007-2009 – these episodes that Mountz takes into account are landmarks of what today has been consolidated as a politics of migration containment.

Retracing this scattered genealogy enables constructing a collective memory of the politics of containment whose structural violence tends to get lost in the timeframe of 'the crisis'. Maintaining a memory of the heterogenous biopolitical and spatial tactics deployed by states for pushing back, diverting and disrupting migrations, might also help in tracing the political legacies of migrant struggles. There is no archive of the collective struggles for movement and practices of solidarity that occurred in response to the structural violence of what international agencies and states defined as 'migration management': the temporariness of these struggles and their exposure to states' evictions contribute to their invisibilisation. In fact, they are the object of a proactive politics of neglect that tries to erase traces of emergent collective formations. Thus, building an archive of migrant struggles starting from what Ann Laura Stoler terms their 'piecemeal partiality' is a key epistemic-political task for countering the violent erasures of racialising bordering practices. Migrants' presence cannot be fully erased, and they keep 'haunting the international state system as ghostly figures out of place'. Nevertheless, the story of the border regime and of what Vicki Squire has described as the 'exclusionary politics of asylum' is also a story of their repeated permutations: borders, Mountz interestingly notices, today function as islands and, we could add, as hotspots. That is, borders are mobile and multiply far beyond the national frontiers, following migrants everywhere to the point that 'migrants are detained en route'. Arguing that the border works as an island means also highlighting that its function is not only to divide and create barriers, but also to contain, confine and isolate migrants and, together, to preventively illegalise those who are deemed to be ineligible for international protection.

The progressive deterioration of asylum, according to Mountz, is culminating today in the social, political and ontological death of asylum. In this regard, it might be added that the shrinking of international protection goes together with the shrinking of the figure of the refugee: if in 2015 Syrian migrants represented (as I have discussed elsewhere) the 'yardstick of humanitarianism' and were depicted as the 'good refugees', five years later even 'genuine refugees' are hampered from accessing rights and are criminalised as 'undeserving'. More broadly, migration policies and laws are now oriented to preventing migrants who can become refugees. Yet, at the same time it is worth noticing that the politics of asylum has been exclusionary since its inception, predicated upon hierarchies of violence and driven by racialising criteria.

The current blatant politics of containment is not (only) made of negative operations, which consist in states' inaction and in the withdrawal of humanitarian support: it is enacted through multiple interventions on the part of both state and non-state actors which deploy political technologies that work to obstruct migrants' access to the refugee system. Hence, more than just taking stock of the death of asylum as such, there is a need to scrutinise the multifarious legal, biopolitical and spatial tactics devised for harming migrants, and undoing their infrastructures of liveability (as Jasbir Puar has shown).

In other words, what Mountz defines as the death of asylum is ultimately symptomatic of the political and legal architecture of the border regime which is pro-actively oriented to hinder migrants' access to international protection, rights and humanitarian support. In this sense, we can turn from an analysis of the death of asylum towards an inquiry into the what I call the dismantling of asylum and of the spaces of refuge. Mobile infrastructures of deterrence have been put in place to prevent migrants from reaching Europe, from building living spaces and from pursuing their desires. Migrants are injured and hampered through spatial confinement and temporal borders: the stolen life of migration that Shahram Khosravi has identified is one of the most harmful effects that migration laws and policies generate for people seeking asylum.

The Death of Asylum pushes us to reflect on which political spaces can be built and opened up in the face of such a politics of containment and of the destitution of refugees it creates. The book invites us not to stop the laborious work of critique by documenting the shrinking of the asylum system. Nor, I add, can we limit our analyt-ical work to reporting that, despite everything, migrants resist and engage in acts of refusal. Which transformative political-epistemological approach to the politics of migration can we envision? And how can we tackle border violence, even in its most invisible forms, without reifying 'migration' as a self-standing field of analysis? Mountz's insights into migrants' carceral archipelago and the heterogenous modes of confinement can be a starting point for gesturing towards border abolitionism as a method. Ruth Gilmore's conception of an abolitionist geography 'as an antagonistic contradiction of carceral geographies' can be productively put to work as an analytical lens for rethinking a critique of migration governmentality. Border abolitionist as a method pays attention to the interlocking racialising mechanisms that sustain modes of differential confinement and exploitation. Unlike NoBorders perspectives that assume the image of borders as discrete sites and as the main targets of action, an abolitionist approach challenges the very distinction between deserving and undeserving refugees, dismantling the very logics of racialised confinement and captivity.

Martina Tazzioli

Return of the conjuncture

Vittorio Morfino and Peter D. Thomas, eds, *The Government of Time: Theories of Multiple Temporality in the Marxist Tradition* (Leiden and Boston: Brill, 2017). 306pp., £91.00 hb., 978 9 00429 119 5

A sense of impending collapse is a fixture of the present. Signs abound of the limits of a worldview of infinite accumulation in a finite world. These contradictions are not only apparent in economic and epidemiological charts; they can be felt viscerally in quotidian life. In this illuminating volume, Vittorio Morfino and Peter D. Thomas bring together voices that explore temporality and the under-appreciated prospect of its multiplicity. The chapters challenge the monolithic time of the neoliberal present, shedding light on fractures along its surface. *The Government of Time* deserves praise as a compendium of theories of multiple temporality, serving as a primer as well as a series of provocative interventions that could rejuvenate historical materialist theory and politics. These interventions substantiate the ontological contemporaneity of times in the plural, precariously woven together in a *conjuncture*, over and against a taken-for-granted static temporal background.

Historical materialism embodies the effort to develop a methodology of persuasively scientific and grounded social analysis. Marx and historical materialists after him have therefore refined the theoretical armoury of critical political economy in line with this aim. This could be why, as Massimiliano Tomba observes, Marx did not draw up a 'passe-partout historical philosophical theory' at a level of abstraction, and devoted more attention to political economy. We can nevertheless observe intimations towards such a theory across Marx's invocations of the temporal rifts dotting the European social landscape. Following these reflections, we find a Marx that did not neglect temporal multiplicity. His explorations are scattered across political writings such as those on the social 'backwardness' and philosophical 'forwardness' of Germany, reflections on the unfolding temporality of the collective subject in the French Revolution, along with his widely overlooked reflections on the Russian rural commune *mir*. Apart from these local observations, Stefano Bracaletti presents a latticework of temporalities moving through *Capital*, showing how Marx attended to interweaving processes and transpositions of cause and effect in this work.

Such divergent explorations indicate the potentials of problematised temporality and its incorporation into critical theory and social science. In addition, these chapters serve as reminders that Marx was not the founder of an ecumenical body of thought with inviolable laws. On the contrary, historical materialism is a constitutionally incomplete and expansive 'philosophy of praxis' and this openness allows it to reflexively revisit, refine and complement its categories (following Gramsci). Reading Marx with an underexplored notion such as temporality in mind helps bring to life a thinker that periodically rethought his concepts and combed through various themes simultaneously, with innovative outcomes at every turn.

Aside from accounts of Marx's multiple temporalities, the volume leaves ample space for other historical materialists, covering wide reaches of Western Marxist thought. Ernst Bloch, Antonio Gramsci and Louis Althusser are brought under particular scrutiny. These readings reveal, due partially to the multilingualism of the contributors, notions that have heretofore evaded sweeping accounts and translations of major works. Morfino invokes *multiversum*, Bloch's outline of a temporally and geographically diverse global history against a Eurocentric fundamental time, and an articulation of historical change that can avoid the twin threats of linear modernism and incredulous postmodernism. As Morfino recounts, Bloch reappropriates progress from its condescending and imperialist connotations, presenting a continual and multifocal unfolding captured in the metaphor of a 'chariot with many horses'. Non-European historical civilisations find respective places across a grand humanity without a particular *telos* or retroactive narrative of modernisation. Disposing of this delimited notion of progress allows for a deeper appreciation of the particular elements across

a tapestry of the myriad contours of human civilisations. Over a topography of cosmopolitan steps towards the (re)foundation of a classless society and points of darkness, this 'expansion' of the conceptual content of history is at once heartening and humbling.

The imputation to history of a Hegelian endpoint, as we can deduce from Bloch's rich philosophical vocabulary, is a crude materialist reproduction of a monolithic and self-contained notion of history. Any given present, from this perspective, is a self-referential culmination of a linear process, conceptually barring the non-contemporaneous from its substantial content. Hence, as Althusser states and Thomas underlines, it is not without reason that there has not been, nor can there be, a transformative politics in a Hegelian register; once an 'essential section' is taken as an immediate reflection of a historical essence, those elements that sit uneasily with its unifying temporal frame are glossed over. In other words, there is nothing that can escape the essential determinations of this totalising backdrop. Thomas' chapter counterposes an interweaving of times that profoundly blurs the 'present'. In this light, the term has analytic utility as a shorthand for an otherwise irreducibly complex real temporality. An etymologically informed return to the notion of *conjuncture*, once prominent in post-war French theory, is a requisite for a cogent elaboration of multiple temporality. Following Althusser and Gramsci, two thinkers often superficially and wrongly seen as lying at opposite poles, Thomas argues that the apparent unity of the present is retrospectively imposed as 'accomplished fact', and hegemonically sustained as a flat, inevitable moment.

Thomas goes further than other conceptualisations of the present (including mine) that subject it to temporally diverse inflections. This treatment disputes the ontological and theoretical autonomy of the present from the multiple times that constitute it. Heterodox approaches to historical time can be organised under 'archaeological' and 'cartographical' approaches. According to the former, the present houses longitudinally diverse layers of temporality, at least some of which continue to permeate its texture. And according to the latter, its spatial undulations and heterogeneity are emphasised. Both of these conceptions are more sophisticated than a facile localisation of the present as a point on a straight line. This would amount to an uncritical espousal of *chronos*: time as a quantitative, uniform flow, over the rough and choppy temporality of *kairos*: the qualitatively distinct time in which, for Walter Benjamin, messianic and redemptive moments were manifested. In sum, the 'present' of the singular point on a line can be described as (x). Its archaeological and cartographical expansions facilitate a more robust appreciation of its depth and breadth, identified now as a set of coordinates (x, y, z). However, Thomas maintains that these perspectives still maintain the 'essential section' of a self-same present, no matter how uneven. The present as *kampfplatz*, a terrain of political contestation, falls short of illuminating a revolutionary political line; it reproduces a 'structural spatialisation' of a given object – the present – and competing contemplative subjects, a notion which would raise the ire of Althusser, who had always protested against his structuralist characterisation.

For Thomas, Althusser and Gramsci have composed the groundwork for an alternative to the autonomous present. Social reproduction takes place along relatively discrete levels with 'times' of their own, and the assumption of an 'objective' reference time is a figment of ideological misrecognition. In its place, it is apt to take up these times within the 'articulation, displacement and torsion' that harmonises them, at the *clinamen* where discrete elements conjoin for a precarious moment (which, in the historical scale, may last decades or ages). Such articulations may take on a formidable stability, as a juridico-politically imposed temporal order can establish itself for long stretches of time. However, their unity in a present is always tied together as a *fait accompli*, and their *givenness* is in itself an ideological ruse wherein the powerful conjure up a self-image of their inevitable permanence. Taking this correspondence between the empirical social formation and conceptual models presupposes a structure, or in Thomas' terms, a 'totalised hierarchy of elements whose relation is fixed prior to their relation with the totality itself'.

The continual unwinding implicated in processes of articulation finds expression in the *conjuncture*, a term that comes up in both Althusser and Gramsci's works in remarkably similar ways. Referring to the fleeting yet forceful synchronisations of various temporalities, the conjuncture is the particular moment of the interweaving and conjoining of relational elements. As opposed to the objective *kampfplatz*, this relativisation of the present has significant political consequences. Political subjects with transitional goals are no longer only a side on the objective political chessboard. Temporal relationality also comes into focus. The task of transformative politics is not solely to promote an alternative 'present', but to radically engage in a defiant non-identitarianism with the dominant temporal order by relating to the conjuncture in ways that can unravel it while binding together novel articulations. In this way, revolutionary politics cuts through essential sections of all sorts, and tethers the struggles of the past to the becoming of future societies. This inquiry into the multiple temporalities of Althusser and Gramsci underlines their points of contact and possibilities of mutual translation in terms of strategy, as the political task described above can also be expressed in terms inspired by the conceptual repositories of both thinkers: multi-temporal hegemonic activity can bind together new lines of ruptural fusion.

Morfino explains how atemporal politics is far from a concern solely entertained by democratic thinkers: Nietzsche, in fact, had proposed that the 'masses' blindly lived in the present, and only the 'great individual' could experience, purvey and handle the untimely. This elitist perspective on the untimely, non-conformist attitude to the present is undoubtedly politically objectionable, but it could be observed today in the exaltation of neo-fascist figures and heads of government at the cost of the erosion of already battered liberal democratic norms. As neoliberalism has laid waste to our economic and cultural lives, and we continue to bear the burden of its decimation of social welfare systems, 'anti-establishment' sentiment is only likely to increase. Its appropriation by the right is neither acceptable nor inevitable, but requires a rejuvenated political imaginary. The fundamentals necessary for a radical non-identity with the status quo come through in the interventions across *The Government of Time*. As the temporal cohesion of the present has lately been shattered, what better place to chart ways to overcome it than a radical critique of the conjuncture?

Onur Acaroglu

The human mask

Asad Haider

> All the characters in this misunderstanding are on stage here, each playing the part ascribed to it by the effect expected of this theatre.
>
> Louis Althusser, Reading Capital

> You too, my friend, should have come here in disguise – as a respectable doctor of scholastic philosophy. It's my mask that allows me a little freedom tonight.
>
> Bertolt Brecht, Life of Galileo

In *Reading Capital* Louis Althusser made note of an 'obvious' presupposition: that 'the "actors" of history are the authors of its text, the subjects of its production.' This strange theatre, in which 'the stage-director has been spirited away' and the actors have written their own roles, illustrated the ideologies of 'humanism' and 'historicism', which Althusser provoked international controversy by criticising.[1] This controversy continues, as Kyle Baasch shows with 'The Theatre of Economic Categories' (*RP* 2.08), which has the great merit of revisiting French and German readings of *Capital* in the 1960s.* However, despite its scope and erudition, Baasch's argument is undermined by a surprisingly chauvinistic insistence on the superiority of German over French thought – clashing sharply with the young Karl Marx, who in a letter to Ludwig Feuerbach before he left for Paris called for a 'Franco-German scientific alliance.'[2]

'It is essential to read *Capital* not only in its French translation', Althusser proclaimed, 'but also in the German original.'[3] Baasch inverts scholarly conscientiousness into 'philological irresponsibility', which he believes is 'illustrated by the almost ideographic presence of the italicised German word *Träger*' (20). Those who feel inclined to check will find that in the texts of Althusser and Étienne Balibar *Träger* appears no more than five times, but Baasch is right that they use it to present an interpretation of Marx which views individuals as the 'bearers' of social relations rather than their subjects.[4]

In response Baasch gives Balibar a vocabulary lesson on the word *Charaktermaske*. Balibar uses it in his argument that 'things are transformed in the hands of the agents of production without their being aware of it, without it being possible for them to be aware of it if the production process is taken for the acts of individuals.' These individuals 'really are only class representatives', but classes cannot be understood as 'sums of individuals': 'it is impossible to make a class by adding individuals together on whatever scale.' Rather, 'classes are functions of the process of production as a whole', and therefore 'they are not its subjects', but 'are determined by its form.' 'Character mask' illustrates 'the mode of existence of the agents of the production process as the *bearers* (*Träger*) of the structure': individuals '*are nothing more than masks*.'[5]

Initially Baasch aims to correct Balibar's usage of 'mode of existence': 'only social categories have modes of existence', while 'concrete individuals simply exist' (21). However, this is not an error but the point of Balibar's argument: 'concrete individuals' do not 'simply exist'. When Balibar speaks of 'agents of the production process', he is not referring to an expression of already existing 'concrete individuals', but to abstract categories,

---

* Kyle Baasch, 'The Theatre of Economic Categories: Rediscovering *Capital* in the Late 1960s', *Radical Philosophy* 2.08 (Autumn 2020), 18–32. Subsequent references given as page numbers in the text.

corresponding to social relations that produce forms of individuality as their effects.[6] For Baasch we cannot claim that individuals are nothing more than bearers of social relations, because there has to be an underlying person who *wears* a mask. Accordingly, as a 'concrete individual', I am made to bear the economic determinations of capitalist society, but I am not reducible to them.

These days we cannot fail to 'recognise' ourselves behind masks. It seems 'obvious', one of the '"simplest" acts of existence'.[7] As an already existing person, I put a mask endowed with its own autonomous existence on my already existing face, to work, purchase commodities, or perform in a play. No one can be blamed for a desire, in our historical moment, to drop the mask – but an unsettling aspect of our 'lived experience' is shock or disgust at the sight of a human face.

Centuries earlier, and not in German, Hobbes defined 'person' as 'he, *whose words or actions are considered, either as his own, or as representing the words or actions of an other man*.' To explain the curious role of representation Hobbes takes us to the theatre: 'The word Person is latine: ... the *disguise*, or *outward appearance* of a man, counterfeited on the Stage; and sometimes more particularly that part of it, which disguiseth the face, as a Mask or Visard.' Yet in the theatre – *and* the courtroom – 'a *Person*, is the same that an *Actor* is', and 'to *Personate*, is to *Act*, or *Represent* himselfe, or an other; and he that acteth another, is said to beare his Person.' A person may be an *author*, 'he that owneth his words and actions' – but in this case 'the Actor acteth by Authority.' *Even the author is an actor*, who must 'personate' or 'represent' himself with the mask of a character or a legal personality.[8] Hobbes dismantles our common sense that empirical individuals adopt discrete masks: as 'persons', or their 'bearers', our faces are already masks.

Eighteenth-century 'French theory' extended the theatrical metaphor beyond Hobbes's account of political representation to social life, and a self formed behind the mask. For Rousseau masks represented the falsity of the society of spectacle and spectatorship, and theatre demonstrated that this alienation was inherent in representation. Actors become adept in deceit, unlike the orator who appears in public to speak rather than to make a spectacle of himself, who 'represents only himself' and plays his own role. The self of the actor is cancelled by the character.[9] Diderot used masks to satirise the self-interested performance of social roles, and suggested that breaking with social conventions and acknowledging the theatricality of everyday life 'unmasks scoundrels'.[10] But Rousseau also sought to overcome representation with transparency: 'So far I have seen many masks; when shall I see men's faces?'[11]

Hegel declared that 'to describe an individual as a "person" is an expression of contempt.'[12] Ancient Greece made no distinction between individuals and their social roles, while Roman law granted individuals the status of personhood. Yet this reduced individuals to the abstract right of property ownership – *persons* who are *literally* 'nothing more than masks'. Hegel too takes us to the theatre. Tragedy represented the subordination of human will to fate, but moved towards self-consciousness as actors behind the masks asserted their wills, speaking before the spectators and impersonating their characters. Comedy developed self-consciousness by dropping the mask, acknowledging its theatricality, showing there was no distinction between the self, the actor and the spectator. The French Enlightenment had demonstrated the theatricality of social life, but for Hegel its project of unmasking had to be superseded: the moral judgment of hypocrisy was predicated on abstaining from the action that could itself be judged, and retreating behind theatricality to natural innocence would mean giving up the 'spiritually developed consciousness' it had made possible.[13]

In Baasch's account this history becomes a synchronic binary opposition. French theory 'transfigures the radical stereotypicality of everyday life into yet another act in a trans-historical theatrical production' (27). German theory alone can transform 'the grim sociological consciousness of what it means to bear a character mask in an economic drama into the implacable longing for the unrealised individuality' (29). Note that Hegel found the longing for unrealised individuality in bearing the mask, while dropping the mask made a mockery of the subject. The binary opposition makes it difficult to interpret even the German theory. Robyn Marasco suggests that 'both Althusser and the first generation of Frankfurt School critical theorists cast "critique" in opposition to idealism and hypostatized subjectivity', following Marx in 'rejecting the myth of authorship as an absolute origin.'[14] Whether one emphasises divergences or affinities, the new readings of *Capital* emerged in an international context. At the 1967 conference in which Alfred Schmidt debated with Nicos Poulantzas, he wrote in his own paper that 'at the present position of international discussion', an 'accurate understanding of Marx's method' depended on 'the concept of "presentation"' – the relation between the order of categories and historical development. The footnote, before referring the reader to his own article, cited 'the publications of the Althusser school in Paris'.[15]

The effort Schmidt subsequently dedicated to criticising *Reading Capital* indicates his awareness of its significance, and in *History and Structure* he explained the historical basis of the international discussion. The Second International orthodoxy understood the 'constitutive role of history' in *Capital*, but did not grasp 'how historical and structural-analytic elements were related to one another.' The 'indisputable service that the Althusser school has performed' was to point to 'the philosophical content of *Capital*' and the difficulty of historical method, going beyond what Schmidt called 'the empty cult of the "young Marx"' that had previously limited the response to the orthodoxy.[16] 'Historicism', Schmidt wrote, was 'decisive for differentiating the Marxist from the Hegelian dialectic.' He defined it succinctly as the notion that 'knowledge simply coincides with the historiography of its subject matter.'[17] In agreement with Althusser, Schmidt wrote that 'Marx advocates anything but an unreflected historicism, in which knowledge runs directly parallel to the chronological course of events.' It was the problem of 'presentation' that he had already noted in *Reading Capital*: one of 'Marx's insights' that 'Althusser also repeatedly stresses' is that the logical order of categories does not reflect their historical appearance.[18]

For Althusser, what differentiates the Marxian from the Hegelian dialectic is the conception of historical time, which determines the relation between knowledge and the course of events. Althusser takes us yet again to the theatre: at the centre of *For Marx*, an essay on the play *El Nost Milan* and Bertolt Brecht's dramaturgy presents a theatrical critique of Hegel's 'dialectic of consciousness'. This dialectic remains within the *tragic*, the temporality of classical theatre 'induced by its internal contradiction to produce its development and result', and it is 'completely reflected in the speculative consciousness of a central character.'[19] But alongside this heroic time *El Nost Milan* staged the 'non-dialectical time' of the labouring masses, indifferent to heroic consciousness, the time of 'everyday life' in which history does not take place. The coexistence of these two temporalities was the 'latent structure' of the play, which could not be exhausted in the self-consciousness of any 'character'.[20]

In the first edition of *Reading Capital*, Althusser recalled this essay and the term 'latent structure'. But he excised it in future editions, to eliminate any resemblance to a *structuralist* conception of a structure that determines its elements. Althusser conceived of a structure that only exists *in* and *as* its elements – 'structural causality' – to produce a concept of history adequate to Marx's discoveries.[21] For the idealist dialectic history is a linear and continuous progression of the origin towards its end, divided into periods corresponding to a succession of totalities. Every phenomenon expresses the essence of the totality, and historical knowledge becomes self-consciousness of the present: contradictions already inscribed in the origins of history finally become visible in capitalist society.[22] The materialist dialectic rejects this 'expressive causality': historical knowledge is not an expression of the historical process. Marx had to *produce* a different conception of historical time – not a structuralist schema, but a theory of dislocations between temporalities: 'the present of the *conjuncture*'.[23]

In Baasch's argument the directional character of the capitalist mode of production itself renders Hegel's teleology valid. This is a kind of hyper-historicism, in which historicism is validated by presupposing an underlying historicism which makes historicism historical. Here the dialectical veers near the tautological. The pre-Hegelian, quasi-Rousseauian notion of dropping the mask in Baasch's article derives from this historicist reading of the *Phenomenology* 'as a kind of self-development of hell', and *Capital* as a 'parodic recapitulation of a Hegelian theodicy of world-spirit', a 'phenomenology of anti-spirit' whose 'teleological narrative' is one in which the 'reconciliation between the individual and the universal takes place at the expense of the individual' (32n44, 28). It is not clear why what Baasch acknowledges is an 'idiosyncratic understanding of Hegel' should be accepted as more accurate or convincing than Althusser's far more delimited reading, which even at its most polemical sought neither to reject nor transmogrify apparently Hegelian categories like the 'dialectic' or 'process', but rather to distinguish them from the Hegelian teleology

in order to specify Marx's conception of history. *Capital*, on this reading, is not a literary adaptation of the *Phenomenology*, but an analysis of the capitalist mode of production, and its standpoint is not that of a uniquely German and 'unmistakably Christian eschatological discourse of reconciliation and salvation' (26), but the international political project of abolishing the capitalist mode of production.

Althusser's philosophical strategy was to move through the Hegelian dialectic to the anomaly it claimed to surpass: Spinoza's critique of consciousness and teleology. Though he notes this influence, Baasch's criticisms consist of very general opinions about the history of philosophy. Baasch says Althusser was inspired by the 'trans-historical model' of 'rationalist metaphysics' to apply the 'critique of social domination to spheres beyond the specifically economic' (19).[24] But Althusser theorised the specifically economic with Spinoza's conception of substance which exists in its attributes: structural causality is 'the key epistemological concept of the whole Marxist theory of value, the concept whose object is precisely to designate the mode of *presence* of the structure in its *effects*.'[25]

While Baasch suggests Althusser did not understand the theory of value, he anticipated many points later central to the German discussion, to the point that John Milios speaks of a 'harmonious merger' between 'the Althusserian theoretical intervention' and 'an approach drawing on Marx's value-form analysis'.[26] Althusser clearly established that *Capital* was not 'a continuation or even culmination of classical political economy', the starting point of Hans-Georg Backhaus's article inaugurating the German 'new reading' of Marx four years later.[27] 'Marxist political economy' presents 'substantialist' theories of value, granting abstract labour a natural and physiological reality inherent in individual commodities and measurable in units of labour-time. But for Marx's *critique* of political economy, labour is abstract insofar as it is socially validated through exchange of its products, and value is not measurable prior to money. Structural causality demolishes the idea that the substance of value

has an independent and prior existence.

Much of this has been obscured by pitting a thesis of 'continuity' between Marx's early and late works, often associated with the initial German new reading, against Althusser's concept of the 'epistemological break'.[28] Properly understood, the epistemological break bears out Michael Heinrich's argument in his recent Marx biography that neither continuity nor discontinuity explains Marx's theoretical development.[29] As Balibar points out, the break is not an event or empirical date, but a tendential and internally contradictory process, which actually has nothing to do with continuity or discontinuity.[30] The target of Althusser's critique was a reading of Marx in the 'future anterior' – or in Heinrich's terms, 'a novel of personal development' with a 'teleological tendency', 'narrating history as a constantly progressing maturation and convergence upon a goal.'[31] Althusser's proposition that 'history is a process without a subject or goal(s)' – subject to as many scandalised distortions as the epistemological break – takes on a very practical relevance.[32]

Althusser's theory of ideology is also a critique of teleology, as his use of Spinoza's concept of the imaginary indicates. Baasch precludes engagement with this theory in advance with the historicist and nationalist claim that 'in Frankfurt, it was recognised that the antinomy of agency and structure' – to which French philosophy is apparently reducible – was 'merely the re-emergence' of an earlier 'sociological problematic that pits structure against agency' (19). We are far from Frankfurt principles of 'immanent critique', and there is a 'performative contradiction' between the emphasis on human agency and a structural-functionalist reduction of French consciousness to this supposed antinomy. Consequently Baasch criticises Althusser's theory of ideology as presuming that freedom is a 'narcotic doled out to the masses, rather than a lived experience conditioned by legally non-coercive individual economic transactions' (23). However, Althusser differs from most Marxist theories of ideology by arguing that it is *not* a 'narcotic', implying false consciousness or a capitalist ploy. As with Balibar on 'concrete individuals', this is not an error but the point of his argument: 'lived experience' is an effect of social relations, not an independent and prior substance they modify. When Althusser says that the 'lived' is 'imaginary', he is elaborating Spinoza's point that due to the limits of our perception, we attribute phenomena to our will or desire without understanding their real causes. His claim that ideology will continue to exist in communist society simply means that we will never apprehend in our consciousness all the real relations that constitute us. This is only disturbing if we equate any opacity of social relations with false consciousness and social domination.

Yet Spinoza's entire exposition is directed towards human freedom. The imaginary leads to inadequate ideas as an effect of our corporeal limits, but through reason we can arrive at more adequate knowledge of the causes that affect us, to overcome the tyranny of superstition and organise our relations to increase our powers of acting.[33] If we are unwilling to let go of the fantasy of the transparency of social relations, identifying freedom with the hope that the world is ordered and meaningful, we remain servile to fear. What is at stake is a conception of freedom that does not rely on the sovereign will of the author. We are back in the theatre. Near the end of his paper for *Reading Capital* Althusser gives the following illustration of structural causality:

> the mode of existence of the stage direction (*mise en scène*) of the theatre which is simultaneously its own stage, its own script, its own actors, the theatre whose spectators can, on occasion, be spectators only because they are first of all forced to be its actors, caught by the constraints of a script and parts whose authors they cannot be, since it is in essence *an authorless theatre*.[34]

The resistance to theoretical anti-humanism is a yearning for authorship, ownership of words and actions as property and authority over representation. But in the authorless theatre, there are no authentic faces obscured by masks – concrete individuals, human subjects, disfigured by a malignant author whose place we seek to occupy – and we cannot rewrite the script by imagining ourselves to be the original authors of social relations.

As spectators we are united with the actors in the authorless theatre; our consciousness is the play itself. We recognise ourselves in the theatre of ideology, and perform our roles every time the curtains are raised. But every play is incomplete, restaged again and again, and

its contingency opens to the dislocation of ideology. In his essay on theatre in *For Marx*, Althusser is a spectator. But as he leaves the theatre, he is able to think of 'the production of a new spectator, an actor who starts where the performance ends' – the emergence, within an apparent passivity, of the power of acting which is politics.[35]

Asad Haider is a founding Editor of Viewpoint Magazine and author of Mistaken Identity: Race and Class in the Age of Trump *(2018).*

Notes

1. Louis Althusser et al., *Reading Capital*, trans. Ben Brewster and David Fernbach (New York: Verso, 2015), 291. I would like to thank Robyn Marasco, Warren Montag, Teddy Paikin, Panagiotis Sotiris and Gavin Walker for their helpful comments.
2. Karl Marx, 'To Ludwig Feuerbach in Bruckberg', in *Collected Works*, vol. 3 (London: Lawrence and Wishart, 1975), 349.
3. *Reading Capital*, 11.
4. In *Reading Capital*, see Althusser, 40, 260, 335, and Balibar, 418, 435.
5. *Reading Capital*, 435.
6. As Balibar writes: 'Men do not appear in the theory except in the form of bearers of the connections implied by the structure, and the forms of their individuality as determinate effects of the structure.' *Reading Capital*, 418.
7. *Reading Capital*, 13.
8. Thomas Hobbes, *Leviathan*, ed. Richard Tuck (Cambridge: Harvard University Press, 1999), 111-2. Baasch cites a passage at the beginning of the second chapter of *Capital* in which Marx uses the words *Charaktermaske* and *Träger*, though it adduces no evidence to support his interpretation; the purpose of citing it seems mainly to imply that Balibar did not read this chapter and was not good at German. But this passage shows that Marx is specifying the content of the 'juridical relation, whose form is the contract': 'The persons [*Die Personen*] exist for one another merely as representatives and hence owners, of commodities.' Karl Marx, *Capital*, vol. 1, trans. Ben Fowkes (New York: Penguin Books, 1990), 178-9. See also the course on Hobbes in Louis Althusser, *Politique et histoire, de Machiavel à Marx*, ed. François Matheron (Paris: Seuil, 2006). I am indebted here to Ross Poole, who provides a more comprehensive historical account in his 'On Being a Person', *Australasian Journal of Philosophy* 74:1 (March 1996), 38-56.
9. Jean-Jacques Rousseau, *Politics and the Arts: Letter to M. D'Alembert on the Theatre*, trans. Alan Bloom (Ithaca: Cornell University Press, 1968), 81. Consider Althusser's account of Rousseau's 'discrepancies' in *Politics and History*, trans. Ben Brewster (London: New Left Books, 1972), and his *Lessons on Rousseau*, trans. G. M. Goshgarian (New York: Verso, 2019).
10. Denis Diderot, *Rameau's Nephew and First Satire*, trans. Margaret Mauldon (Oxford: Oxford University Press, 2006), 4.
11. Jean-Jacques Rousseau, *Julie, or the New Heloise*, trans. Philip Stewart and Jean Vaché (Hanover: Dartmouth College Press,

1997), 194.

12. G.W.F. Hegel, *Phenomenology of Spirit*, trans. A.V. Miller (Oxford: Oxford University Press, 1977), 292.

13. Hegel, *Phenomenology of Spirit*, 444, 450, 401–2, 319. See Allen Speight, *Hegel, Literature, and the Problem of Agency* (Cambridge: Cambridge University Press, 2001).

14. Robyn Marasco, 'Althusser's Gramscian Debt: On Reading Out Loud', *Rethinking Marxism* 31:3 (2019), 343.

15. Alfred Schmidt, 'On the Concept of Knowledge in the Criticism of Political Economy', in *Karl Marx 1918/1968* (Bad Godesberg: Inter Nationes, 1968), 96, 238n173. Baasch dramatises the debate between Schmidt and Poulantzas as a confrontation between the German and French readings. Schmidt's student Hermann Kocyba situates it instead in Schmidt's evolving engagement with French theorists – to the point that his initial critiques of Althusser and 'structuralism' drew mostly on the critiques already made in France by Goldmann, Lefebvre and Sartre. 'Alfred Schmidt: On the Critique of Social Nature', trans. Jacob Blumenfeld, in *The Sage Handbook of Frankfurt School Critical Theory*, eds. Best, Bonefeld and O'Kane (London: Sage, 2018), 310.

16. Alfred Schmidt, *History and Structure*, trans. Jeffrey Herf (Cambridge: MIT Press, 1981), 84, 109. I emphasise Schmidt's agreements with Althusser to demonstrate that he engaged with it seriously, rather than reducing it to a national stereotype. Nevertheless, the goal of *History and Structure* is a critique of Althusser, so agreement is noted in the context of substantial criticisms, some of which concern theoretical disagreement, while others are marred by conflations and omissions; compare Schmidt's points on the reading of Hegel to Louis Althusser, 'Marx's Relation to Hegel', in *Politics and History*.

17. Schmidt, *History and Structure*, 31. See *Reading Capital*, 40–9. Baasch describes anti-historicism in passing as a 'conception of history as an entirely impersonal process', but this is more precisely a description of anti-humanism. 'Theatre', 24.

18. Schmidt, *History and Structure*, 61. In 'On the Concept of Knowledge', Schmidt repeats this point about presentation, but he argues that the 'logical order' is exactly the reverse of the 'historical order' (98). Althusser rejects this view, instead arguing that there is no one-to-one correspondence, even in reverse. See *Reading Capital*, 264.

19. Louis Althusser, 'The "Piccolo Teatro": Bertolazzi and Brecht. Notes on a Materialist Theatre', in *For Marx*, trans. Ben Brewster (New York: Verso, 2005), 138, 143–4. On this essay's role in Althusser's theory of history, see Vittorio Morfino 'Eschatology à la Cantonade: Althusser beyond Derrida', in *Althusser and Theology*, ed. Agon Hamza (Leiden: Brill, 2016), 115–28. A dossier responding to Étienne Balibar's 'Althusser's Dramaturgy and the Critique of Ideology' in *differences* 26:3 (2015) elaborates many themes I touch on here.

20. Althusser, 'The "Piccolo Teatro"', 145.

21. *Reading Capital*, 271–6. This revision is reviewed in Warren Montag, *Althusser and his Contemporaries: Philosophy's Perpetual War* (Durham, NC: Duke University Press, 2013), chapter 5. Baasch cites this book in his article, yet consistently labels Althusser as a structuralist, a characterisation whose inaccuracy Montag's book demonstrates in detail.

22. Althusser, *Reading Capital*, 241–2.

23. Althusser argues that the structuralist turn to the synchronic still relies on the homogeneous and linear diachronic time at the core of both the Hegelian and the Second International philosophies of history. See *Reading Capital*, 242–3. When Schmidt writes that Althusser accords 'methodological priority' to 'the synchronic over the diachronic', his criticism is rather wide of the mark. See *History and Structure*, 5.

24. Baasch conflates 'structuralism' with a rationalism influenced by Spinoza, though it is once again a book in his own footnotes which shows us the greater complexity of this intellectual history: Knox Peden, *Spinoza Contra Phenomenology* (Stanford: Stanford University Press, 2014).

25. *Reading Capital*, 342–4.

26. John Milios, 'Rethinking Marx's Value-Form Analysis from an Althusserian Perspective', *Rethinking Marxism* 21:2 (April 2009), 269–70, 261.

27. *Reading Capital*, 13, 310. Hans-Georg Backhaus, 'On the Dialectics of the Value-Form', *Thesis Eleven* 1 (1980), 99. For an overview of the German new reading, see Riccardo Bellofiore and Tommaso Redolfi Riva, 'The *Neue Marx-Lektüre*: Putting the Critique of Political Economy Back into the Critique of Society', *Radical Philosophy* 189 (Jan/Feb 2015), 24–36.

28. See Althusser's criticisms of the categories of continuity and discontinuity and the practice of periodisation in *Reading Capital*, 251.

29. Michael Heinrich, *Karl Marx and the Birth of Modern Society*, vol. 1, trans. Alexander Locascio (New York: Monthly Review Press, 2019), 27–8.

30. Étienne Balibar, 'From Bachelard to Althusser: The Concept of "Epistemological Break"', *Economy and Society* 7:3 (1978), 207–37, and 'Structural Causality, Overdetermination and Antagonism', in *Postmodern Materialism and the Future of Marxist Theory*, eds. Antonio Callari and David F. Ruccio (Middletown: Wesleyan University Press, 1996), 109–19.

31. Heinrich, *Karl Marx*, 336. It is important to consult Althusser's first 'classic' essay, 'On the Young Marx' in *For Marx*, which presents no periodising schema.

32. See Louis Althusser, 'Marx's Relation to Hegel' and 'Remark on the Category: "Process without a Subject or Goal(s)"', in *Essays in Self-Criticism* (London: New Left Books, 1976).

33. Here we encounter the question of the subject, which, contrary to popular belief, Althusser dealt with directly by tracing a line from Machiavelli to Lenin. See Louis Althusser, *Machiavelli and Us*, ed. François Matheron, trans. Gregory Elliott (New York: Verso, 2000) and 'Contradiction and Overdetermination' in *For Marx*. See also Panagiotis Sotiris, *A Philosophy for Communism* (Leiden: Brill, 2020).

34. Althusser, *Reading Capital*, 349. See Montag, 'Althusser's Authorless Theatre', *differences* 26:3 (2015), 46.

35. Althusser, 'The "Piccolo Teatro"', 151. This essay is another primary site in Althusser's work for the encounter with the subject; see the contributions to the dossier in *differences* 26:3 (2015) by Judith Butler, 'Theatrical Machines', and Banu Bargu, 'Althusser's Materialist Theater: Ideology and Its Aporias'. In July 1962 Althusser is completing 'Contradiction and Overdetermination' just as he goes to see the 'Piccolo Teatro'.

Dramatic differences

Kyle Baasch

It is a privilege to read Asad Haider's critical response to my article, 'The Theatre of Economic Categories: Rediscovering *Capital* in the late 1960s' in *Radical Philosophy* 2.08).[1] His enthusiastic defence of Althusser's theoretical innovation allows one to witness the impact of *Reading Capital* on a disciple who takes its practical implications seriously. However, the central intention of my essay was to enumerate the dramatic differences between *Reading Capital* and *Capital* itself, and my convictions are only confirmed by Haider's lack of reference to any of Marx's writings beyond a solitary passing mention in a footnote. *Reading Capital* may be internally coherent and inspiring – Haider's arguments testify to this – but that alone does not make it a reading of *Capital*. In reply, I will offer a close analysis of some of Althusser's specific interpretations of Marx's writings which will allow the reader to appreciate the questionable theoretical foundations upon which Haider's energetic advocacy for Althusser's project ultimately rests.

But it is first necessary to briefly address two tangentially related arguments in Haider's response before turning to Marx. The first is his bombastic opening sally. He avers that my 'argument is undermined by a surprisingly chauvinistic insistence on the superiority of German over French thought'. Haider does not substantiate this damning thesis with any specific passages from my article, but he presumably has in mind my remark that French and English interpretations of Marx in the 1960s 'fail to appreciate the relation of freedom and necessity that is insisted upon in Marx's work', which is rooted in the 'German philosophical tradition' (19). Or perhaps he is thinking of my assertion that the 'German interpretation of Marx' – in the context of the article, the Frankfurt School – is more capable of understanding the links that bind Marx's work with 'the nation's philosophical history' (26). The point of these passing remarks is to underscore the fact that the philosophers trained in the specifically and profoundly German context of Marx's

works are better equipped to understand their theoretical orientation than a philosopher trained in an environment in which Hegel's writings were imported the day before yesterday and subjected to famously tendentious interpretations. Haider curiously suggests that such a claim 'clash[es] dramatically with the young Karl Marx' simply because in 1843 Marx wanted to publish French and German articles in the same journal.[2] More representative is Marx's famous 1858 letter to Ferdinand Lasalle, in which he describes his work as 'economics as a science [*Wissenschaft*] in the German sense of the word.'[3] Like every other European philosopher of the nineteenth century, he took the distinction between French and German intellectual traditions for granted.

The second point concerns Haider's elaborate and distracting justification of the use of theatrical motifs in *Reading Capital*. As Haider observes, the focal point of my critique is Étienne Balibar's claim that Marx presents 'individuals' as *'nothing more than masks'*.[4] I argued that this elides the systematic distinction that Marx makes between concrete individuals and forms of appearance, and thereby obfuscates the critical import of Marx's theatrical metaphor. When Marx uses the term 'character mask' in *Capital*, the distinction between the concrete human being and the mask that it bears is grammatically unambiguous: 'Humans confront each other ... *in* character masks'; 'The economic character masks cling to [*festhängen*] a human'; they 'stick to' [*ankleben*] their bearer.[5] Marx even lampoons the narrow-mindedness of bourgeois ideologues who are unable to differentiate the character mask from its bearer.[6] I therefore described Balibar's conflation of the concrete individual with its form of appearance as a misinterpretation, an error. Haider states that 'this is not an error but the point of Balibar's argument', and then shows how the identity of existence and appearance plays a fundamental role in Balibar's social theory. That may be so, but this claim appears as part of the general attempt in *Reading Capital* to rescue Marx's writings from a century of misinterpretation. Unless it is textually substantiated, it deserves to be called an error.

Haider then provides an illuminating conceptual history of the 'mask'. There is much sleight of hand in this section of his argument. His intention is to establish the philological connection between 'person' and 'mask' in order to undermine my claim that 'there has to be an underlying person who *wears* a mask.' This would be persuasive if this were my claim. However, I state, 'it is as wearers of masks that *individuals* confront one another on a market, which suggests that *individuals* are not identical with these masks' (21; emphasis added). Crucially, my entire paper rests upon this distinction between the concrete individual and its mask, not the person and the mask, rendering much of Haider's argument irrelevant. Furthermore, his philological illustrations are oddly chosen. He notes, for example, that Thomas Hobbes developed a theory of the 'person' as a representative who acts on behalf of another. This, according to Haider, 'dismantles our common sense that empirical individuals adopt discrete masks ... our faces are already masks.' But Hobbes' point is precisely the opposite: his theory of representation is built upon the distinction between the 'natural person' – the empirical individual who is the author of their own words – and the 'artificial person', who represents others. Hobbes' social contract theory would not make any sense if it were not possible to distinguish between these two kinds of persons.

It is a mistake to try to map these early modern political categories onto Marx's work, since it encourages one to assume that the central question animating academic discussions of Marx today concerns whether or not individuals who carry out modern social processes are the 'authors' of the latter. No serious reader of Marx would argue this. The fact that individuals are *not* the authors of society, that modern society develops through what Marx calls natural-spontaneous [*naturwüchsige*] processes, was a methodological point of departure for the Frankfurt interpretation of Marx in the 1960s. As Marx makes clear in the *Grundrisse*, the capitalist social totality arises out of 'the mutual influence of conscious individuals on one another', and yet these interactions 'produce an *alien* social power standing above them, produce their mutual interaction as a process and power independent of them.'[7] Bourgeois society as an organic totality has a life

of its own, as it were; it exercises explanatory priority over the individuals who paradoxically bring it into existence through their conscious practical activity. This distinction between the efficient and final causes of social action is already common in Scottish Enlightenment philosophy and Hegel's social theory.

The question that distinguishes the Frankfurt and Parisian interpretations of Marx is whether a society that unfolds independently of individuals, who are conditioned by society to recognise themselves as the cause of their actions, should be seen as an immanent contradiction or an insoluble disparity between 'the imaginary' and 'the real'. This is a dramatic difference, and Marx's own position is unambiguous. He describes bourgeois society as 'a social formation in which the process of production has mastery over men, instead of the opposite.'[8] The 'alien and independent character' that society assumes in relation to individuals proves that they 'are still engaged in the creation of the conditions of their social life' and have thus 'not yet begun ... to live it.'[9] Marx laments that the 'point of departure' in modern society is a 'power over the individuals which has become autonomous' instead of the 'free social individual'.[10] When the latter is the point of departure, 'the shape of the social labour process casts off its mystical veil of fog.' The relations between individuals become 'transparent in their simplicity'.[11]

Althusser consistently rejects these remarks found on every other page of the mature Marx as naïve, ideological, unscientific. In Haider's words, these remarks endorse a 'fantasy of the transparency of social relations', or a 'pre-Hegelian, quasi-Rousseauian notion'. On the contrary, this recurrent tension between the social structure and the broken promise it conditions is what constitutes Marx's critique of political economy as an 'immanent critique', whose formula, as Rahel Jaeggi explicates it in her recent work, 'takes as its starting point the claims and conditions posited together with a form of life; it responds to the problems and crises that arise in this context, and it derives from this in particular the transformative potential that goes beyond the practices in question and seeks to transform them.'[12]

The transformative potential in Marx's work consists in the fact that it treats the 'alien social power' that confronts the individuals in bourgeois society as something that is both conditioned by the forms of interaction

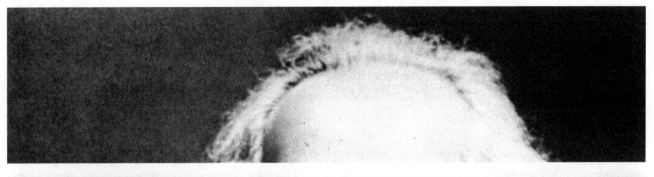

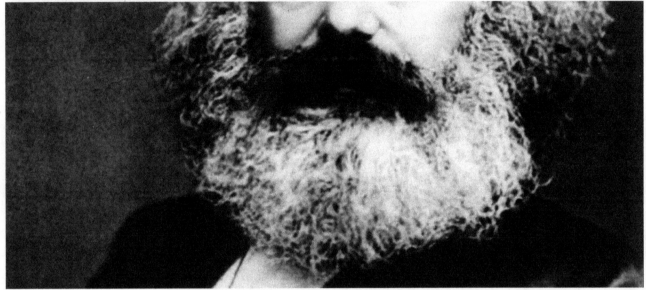

within this society – namely, a society organised around free commodity exchange – *as well as* an impediment to the realisation of the robust criterion of freedom with which this society justifies its own existence. When freedom as a norm in bourgeois society is confronted with the illumination its own structural impossibility, the attendant dissatisfaction becomes a potential ferment of social transformation.

Haider is right to draw attention to Althusser's novel conception of historical time and structural causality, which are not given careful consideration in my essay, for this is where the chasm that separates *Reading Capital* from Marx's writings is most obvious. Althusser substantiates these ideas with the assistance of quotations from Marx's introduction to the *Grundrisse*, and it is thus worth examining these passages in detail in order to further determine why the 'idiosyncratic understanding of Hegel' that I attribute to the Frankfurt School 'should be accepted as more legitimate than Althusser's far more delimited reading.'

In the section of this introduction titled 'The Method of Political Economy', Marx addresses the distinction between the scientific investigation of economic categories [*Forschung*] and the logical presentation of the latter [*Darstellung*]. The import of this distinction arises from the fact that the complex categories that the researcher encounters at the end of a process of progressive conceptual abstraction are in fact logical presuppositions of the seemingly more basic categories encountered at the outset of research. The result of this process, the 'thought-totality' [*Gedankentotalität*], or the intellectual grasp of the whole of society, 'appears in the process of thinking, therefore, as a process of concentration, as a result, not as a point of departure, even though it is the point of departure in reality and hence also the point of departure for observation and conception.'[13] This entire section of the *Grundrisse* is clearly modelled on the introduction to Hegel's *Philosophy of Right*, in which Hegel justifies his phenomenological presentation of categories: 'What is actual, the shape which the concept assumes, is ... from our point of view only the subsequent and further stage, even if it should itself come first in actuality.'[14] For Marx as for Hegel, the goal is to understand all of the 'inner connections' of the social organism so that it 'appears as if we have before us an *a priori* construction'.[15] Despite this affinity, Marx criticises Hegel's overestimation of thought as such – hyperbolically, but that is neither here nor there – and emphasises that in his own method, 'the real subject [*das reale Subjekt*]', namely society as self-developing organic whole, 'retains its autonomous existence outside the head just as before', and 'must be kept in mind as a presupposition'.[16]

This point is banal. It was a commonplace in nineteenth-century German historiography to foreground the *hiatus irrationalis* that separates the historical entity as it is in-itself from the researcher's conceptual reconstruction of the latter. One thinks of Max Weber's later definition of an 'ideal-type' as a 'thought construct' [*Gedankenbild*] which 'cannot be found empirically anywhere in reality'.[17] But Althusser, interpreting this page of the *Grundrisse*, has hallucinations of Spinoza, and calls upon this vision as evidence for the lack of continuity between Hegel and Marx. 'Spinoza warned us that the *object* of knowledge or essence was in itself absolutely distinct from the *real object*', Althusser writes, astonishingly and inexplicably mistranslating Marx's 'the real subject' as 'the real object' [*l'objet réel*] and thus misunderstanding the entire point of Marx's critique of Hegel.[18] Althusser continues: 'for, to repeat [Spinoza's] famous aphorism, the two objects must not be confused: the *idea* of a circle, which is the *object* of knowledge, must not be confused with the circle, which is the *real object*'.[19] Althusser has in mind a scholium in the *Ethics* in which Spinoza develops his theory of attributes. It states:

> Thinking substance and extended substance are one and the same substance, comprehended now under this attribute, now under that. ... For example, a circle existing in Nature and the idea of the existing circle—which is also in God—are one and the same thing, explicated through different attributes.[20]

It appears that Althusser does not understand the basic principles of Spinoza's metaphysics. Spinoza does not claim that things comprehended under the attribute of extension are more 'real' than things comprehended under the attribute of thought; the intention of his philosophical treatise is to show that thought and extension, which for Descartes were discrete substances, are in fact two ways of perceiving one and the same thing. But more importantly, Marx's conception of the capitalist totality as an organic whole – a 'real subject' encompassing a complex interconnection of political institutions, social relations and economic transactions – has nothing to do with what Spinoza intends by the attribute of 'extension'. Althusser's forced connection is like someone trying to explain climate change by arguing that the earth revolves around the sun.[21]

Marx's other intention in this methodological section of the *Grundrisse* is to explain the counterintuitive relationship between the historical development of economic categories and the order of their logical priority in modern, bourgeois society. Marx notes, for example, that landed property is a feature of many different modes of production, and that this therefore seems like a reasonable starting point in elucidating the economic complexity of bourgeois society. However, the progression of modes of production do not follow in an accretive manner, such that a category like landed property would remain a bedrock of later modes, but rather the structure of the contemporary mode of production exercises logical priority over the economic categories handed down from earlier stages. This is what Marx means when he writes that the logical sequence of economic categories is 'precisely the opposite' of their historical emergence.[22] Marx concludes this point by stating, 'in all forms of society there is one specific kind of production which predominates over the rest, whose relations thus assign rank and influence to the others. It is a general illumination which bathes all the other colours and modifies their particularity. It is a particular ether which determines the specific gravity of every being which has materialised within it.'[23]

Althusser cites the first of these three sentences, with its reference to 'rank and influence', to justify his fanciful theory of a non-Hegelian whole: a 'decentred' structure with 'levels' or 'regions', each with its own 'peculiar time'. Each of these levels, among which one finds 'the political superstructure', 'philosophy', 'aesthetic productions' and 'scientific formations', is 'relatively autonomous' and each thus contains its own 'historical existence' which is 'punctuated with peculiar rhythms'. These different levels are related to each other according to 'a certain type of articulation of the whole' in its 'articulated decentricity'.[24] These are the passages to which Haider refers when he endorses Althusser's 'theory of dislocations between temporalities'. It is hard to know how to evaluate what is essentially a creative writing exercise. Nothing in Marx's text lends credence to this vision of intertwined spheres of cultural production with polyrhythmic temporalities, and Haider follows Althusser's lead by enthusiastically repackaging these ideas without providing any evidentiary textual sources that would lend to support to this interpretation.

Marx's simple but profound point suggests the opposite: 'capital is the all-dominating economic power of bourgeois society', and therefore all other economic categories in modern society must be subsumed under its logic.[25] Indeed, how does Althusser account for Marx's evocative description of the capitalist mode of production as an 'ether' which 'determines the specific gravity of every being which has materialised within it'? This would seem to deprive 'scientific formations', 'aesthetic productions' and whatever else might be considered of their relatively autonomous rhythm; it would seem to suggest nothing other than an 'expressive totality'. Althusser responds by lamenting that Marx was not able to complete his scientific achievement 'without completely avoiding a relapse into earlier schemata'.[26] Althusser's reading of Marx proudly endorses one sentence for every two sentences that are deemed anachronistic because they do not conform to the Parisian scientific paradigm of the 1960s.

A necessary consequence of this rejection of 'expressive causality' is Althusser's inability to relate the dramatic texture of modern life to the economic structure of the whole. Adorno was attracted to the concept of the 'character mask' because it grounds the universality of being-for-another – the performative character of modern life – in the universality of commodity exchange.[27] Althusser and his collaborators, in their attempt to extract a general scientific theory from *Capital*, sacrifice this historically contingent nature of Marx's critical concepts in order to make transhistorical claims about existence and appearance. What then is the point of reading Marx? Haider aspires to something like a Marxian cultural criticism when he writes: 'As an already existing person, I put a mask endowed with its own autonomous existence on my already existing face, to work, purchase commodities, or perform in a play.' But this still lags considerably behind the calibre of analysis that is possible when one seriously examines Marx's development of capitalist forms of appearance.

When I go to 'purchase commodities', for example, at a grocery store, I appear to the personification of capital – the hierarchy of managers employed in the capitalist's stead – as the bearer of money. This causes all of the higher-level employees at the store to eye me with an artificially obsequious gaze, which reciprocally colours my self-understanding with entitlement. I do not appear as the bearer of money to the checkout operator – it is her boss to whom she sells her services – but in the mask of surveillance, indirectly connected to her employer through the feedback channels available to me if I choose to vent my dissatisfaction with her performance. The mediation of our social interaction by the logic of the modern capitalist enterprise is legible in her tone; it is why she says 'hello' with an adept synthesis of fear and gracious servility. It is also why, when I show up in her lane towards the end of her shift, she masks her frustration with a grimace of hospitality in the form of a cryptic and tight-lipped 'find everything okay?' to which I respond with a terse and apologetic 'yes, thanks', pained by her dissimulated expression and wondering whether I still have time to choose another lane without arousing her supervisor's suspicion.

Society is nearly at the point of collapsing under the weight of anxiety concentrated in such moments of our lives. The aim of Critical Theory is to give society a push, or in the words of Marx, to 'shorten and lessen the birth-pangs', to assist this ailing mode of production in its ever-miscarried generation of a new form of life. When Haider claims that 'an unsettling aspect of our "lived experience" is shock or disgust at the sight of a human face', he pulls from the playbook of mid-century existentialist kitsch in order to transfigure these birth-pangs into a transhistorical feature of the *conditio humana*.

It is time to give *Capital* another chance. This does not require that one harbour illusions about the capacity for individuals to spontaneously act; individuals who appear on the stage of modern history should still be treated as personifications of economic categories. But there is no reason that this treatment should fall short of the dynamic complexity that one finds in the description of characters who appear on the pages of a Virginia Woolf novel. Critical Theory begins in the checkout lane.

Kyle Baasch is a PhD student at the University of Minnesota.

Notes

1. Asad Haider, 'The Human Mask', *Radical Philosophy* 2.10 (Summer 2021); Kyle Baasch, 'The Theatre Of Economic Categories: Rediscovering *Capital* in the Late 1960s', *Radical Philosophy* 2.08 (Autumn 2020), 18–32. Subsequent references to the latter given as page numbers in the text.

2. Incidentally, this obscure letter from Marx to Feuerbach cited by Haider teems with 'historicist' distinctions between German and French intellectual culture.

3. Karl Marx, 'Marx to Ferdinand Lasalle. 12 November 1858', in *Marx and Engels Collected Works: Volume 40* (London: Lawrence and Wishart, 1983), 355. Compare Marx's comment with a remark on Althusser by Iring Fetscher, the organiser of the Frankfurt colloquium attended by Nicos Poulantzas in 1967. 'I think [Althusser] wished to make Marx into a real scientific theory, in the sense of traditional French concepts of science. That seemed to me to make no sense because Marx's theory is something different, and that of course had something to do with his German background', quoted in Kevin Anderson, 'On Marx, Hegel, and Critical Theory in Postwar Germany: A Conversation with Iring Fetscher', *Studies in Eastern European Thought* 50 (1998), 8. I recognise that these kinds of generalisations, which Haider calls 'national stereotypes', assault the radical nominalism that grounds contemporary standards of political correctness.

4. Louis Althusser and Etienne Balibar, *Reading Capital*, trans. Ben Brewster (London: New Left Books, 1970), 300. Italics in original.

5. Karl Marx, *Capital: A Critique of Political Economy, Volume 1*, trans. Ben Fowkes (New York: Penguin, 1976), 170, 711, 757. Translations amended. Incidentally, Michael Heinrich notes that 'not only does Marx see concrete humans behind the character mask, he also emphasises their capacity for reflection on their own action, the possibility of subjectively "lifting" themselves above social relations.' Michael Heinrich, 'Individuum, Personifikation und unpersönliche Herrschaft in Marx' Kritik der politischen Ökonomie', in *Anonyme Herrschaft: Zur Struktur moderner Machtverhältnisse* (Münster: Westphalisches Dampfboot, 2012), 19.

6. Marx, *Capital*, 757.

7. Karl Marx, *Grundrisse: Foundations of the Critique of Political Economy*, trans. Martin Nicolaus (London: Penguin, 1993), 197. Italics in original.

8. Marx, *Capital*, 175.

9. Marx, *Grundrisse*, 162.

10. Marx, *Grundrisse*, 197.

11. Marx, *Capital*, 172–173. Translation amended.

12. Rahel Jaeggi, *Critique of Forms of Life*, trans. Ciaran Cronin (Cambridge: Harvard University Press, 2018), 174.

13. Marx, *Grundrisse*, 101.

14. G.W.F. Hegel, *Elements of the Philosophy of Right*, ed. Allen Wood, trans. H.B. Nisbet (Cambridge: Cambridge University Press, 1991), 62.

15. Marx, *Capital*, 102.

16. Marx, *Grundrisse*, 102.

17. Max Weber, 'The "Objectivity" of Knowledge in Social Science and Social Policy', in *Max Weber: Collected Methodological Writings*, eds. Hans Henrik Bruun and Sam Whimster, trans. Hans Henrik Bruun (London: Routledge, 2012), 125. For a comprehensive account of attempts to solve this particular problem of historical knowledge in German theories of historiography, see Frederick C. Beiser, *The German Historicist Tradition* (Oxford: Oxford UP, 2011), especially the chapters on Heinrich Rickert, Emil Lask, Georg Simmel and Weber.

18. Althusser repeats this erroneous use of 'the real object' in over 60 instances in this opening section of *Reading Capital*. It is perhaps his most famous term that masquerades as Marxist when it is not.

19. *Reading Capital*, 43.

20. This is presumably what Haider has in mind when he stresses the importance of Spinoza's 'conception of a substance which exists only in its attributes.' It would be more precise to say that the attributes are 'that which the intellect *perceives* of substance as constituting its essence', for substance, the inspiration for the German Idealist conception of the 'absolute', does not rely on anything for its existence. Baruch Spinoza, *Ethics*, in *The Essential Spinoza*, ed. Michael L. Morgan, trans. Samuel Shirley (Indianapolis: Hackett, 2006), 4. Italics added. Furthermore, this eminently metaphysical concept has nothing to do with the 'substantialist theory of value', a bogus economic doctrine which asserts that the value of a commodity is equivalent to a definite expenditure of human muscles and nerves stored up in the object.

21. Spinoza functions as a *deus ex machina* for Haider as much as for Althusser. Haider notes that 'Spinoza's entire exposition is directed towards human freedom'; this much is true, and this is why Spinoza is the single most important philosophical figure in any account of the development of German Idealism. Haider then elaborates a homeopathic version of Spinoza's conception of freedom as the ability to 'organise our relations to increase our powers of acting.' Actually, Spinoza's conception of human freedom entails the consciousness of the divine as the cause of our actions, which Spinoza describes as an 'intellectual love of God', or 'blessedness'. Spinoza does not believe that humans can voluntarily decide how to organise their social relations; that would be castigated as an anthropocentric delusion. It is this attempt to supplement Spinoza's compatibilism with a transformative politics without having recourse to Hegel's humanistic teleology that embroils Haider in a performative contradiction.

22. Marx, *Grundrisse*, 107. Haider notes that Althusser 'rejects this view', without noting that 'this view' is a quotation from the *Grundrisse*.

23. Marx, *Grundrisse*, 106–7.

24. *Reading Capital*, 109–111.

25. Marx, *Grundrisse*, 107.

26. *Reading Capital*, 207.

27. Theodor W. Adorno, 'Society', trans. Fredric Jameson, in *Can One Live After Auschwitz? A Philosophical Reader*, ed. Rolf Tiedemann (Stanford: Stanford University Press, 2003), 147–8.